# The Highland Railway System

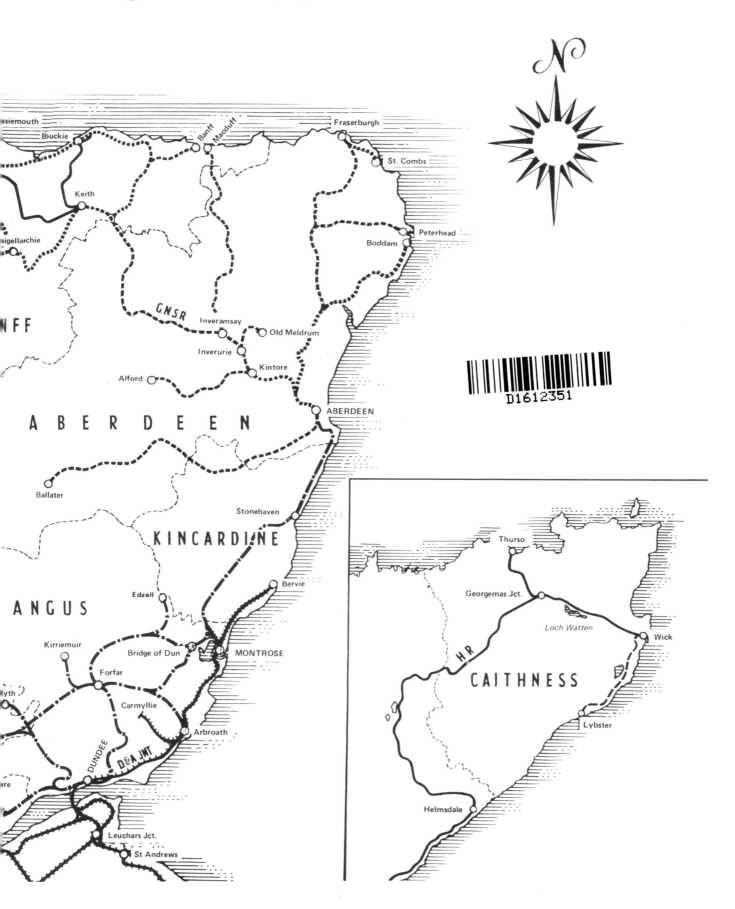

# Highland Railway
# Carriages and Wagons

## Peter Tatlow

Noodle Books in association with the Highland Railway Society

© Peter Tatlow & Noodle Books (Kevin Robertson) 2014

ISBN 978-1-909328-13-6

First published in 2014 by Kevin Robertson under the Noodle Books imprint
and in conjunction with the Highland Railway Society

**NOODLE BOOKS**, PO Box 279,  Corhampton,  SOUTHAMPTON.  SO32 3ZX

www.noodlebooks.co.uk

Printed in England by Berforts Information Press
.

**Front cover, top** - *Typical early Highland Railway 4-wheel rib-sided Third-class coach, No. 139 to which vacuum brake has been added from 1890, but nonetheless still fitted with wooden buffer faces and side chains.*
*(HRS collection)*

**Front cover, bottom -** *HR 11-ton 17ft 6in long meat van built in 1911 with an 11 foot wheel base, piped for both vacuum and Westinghouse brake, fitted with safety chains and with a single hand brake lever.  (Author's collection)*

**Rear cover** - *Stopped by the signal near the summit of the line at Drumochter Highland Railway 4-6-0 No. 149* Duncraig Castle *one morning early in the 20th century heads what purports to be the Down Mail train, but more likely a mid-morning train from Perth to Inverness.  This is made up of First-class saloon No. 56 to diagram 6, two Lavatory Composites to diagram 17, a Lavatory Third to diagram 28, 6-wheel Lavatory First, a 6-wheel Third to diagram 22, a 4-wheel luggage van and 6-wheel Passenger Brake Van. (Knight series No. 987)*

# Contents

**Foreword**     4

**Preface**     5

**Introduction**
Locomotive Superintendents     6
Lochgorm & Needlefield works     9
Carriage & Wagon builders     14
Drawings     14

**Carriages & Non-passenger coaching stock**     15
General Review
Building styles     15
Carriage diagrams     16
Numbering     16
Wheels & axle-boxes     17
Bogies     19
Brakes     19
Passenger alarm apparatus     22
Lighting     22
Heating     24
Passenger comfort     24
Livery     25

**Pre-Jones Coaches**     27
**Jones Coaches**     33
4-wheel     33
Sleeping cars     35
6-wheel Cleminson     38
6-wheel     41
Bogie     48
Pullman cars on HR     51
Duke of Sutherland's saloons     54

**Drummond coaches**     59
Low-arc roof 6-wheel     59
Cove roof 6-wheel     59
Low-arc roof bogie     65
Directors' saloon     72
Sleeping cars     73
Later non-corridor bogie stock     77
Corridor stock     82

**Non-Passenger coaching stock**     98
Rib-sided Passenger Brake Vans     98
Jones 6-wheel Passenger Brake Vans     101
Drummond 6-wheel Passenger Brake Vans     106
Drummond bogie Passenger Brake Vans     108
Passenger brake vans converted from
Post Office mail vans     113
Early Mail Vans     113
Jones 37ft 9in Mail Vans     116
Later bogie Mail Vans     118
Luggage vans     125
Horse boxes     126
Valuable cattle van     127
Carriage trucks     129
11-ton meat vans     133
Open fish trucks     136

**Goods Wagons**     141
General review     141
Building styles     141
Drawings and diagrams     143
Buffers     143
Miscellaneous     143
Common User     143
Brakes     143
Numbering     144
Livery     144
Wagon sheets     144

Wagons
8-ton Open wagons     144
Covered goods vans     148
Road vans     151
Mineral wagons     151
Timber & bolster wagons     157
Specially constructed vehicles     162
Cattle wagons     163
Sheep vans     165
Non-revenue earning     170
Goods brake vans     178
Passengers travelling in a
      Goods brake van     189

**Appendices**
1. List of carriage & non-passenger coaching
    stock diagrams     193
2. List of wagon diagrams     195

The Highland Railway Society     197
Bibliography and References     197
Acknowledgements     198
Index     198

# Foreword

The Highland Railway was unique in many ways, and has had a significant and enthusiastic following ever since its demise as an independent company in 1923, and which continues to this day nearly a hundred years later. However, the subject of the Company's rolling stock has historically been poorly covered: in no small way due to the dearth of contemporary photographs from both official and private sources when compared to many of the other Pre-Grouping companies. Added to this, much of the stock did not last long after the Grouping, as the LMS replaced a significant proportion of the often elderly and non-standard Highland designs with more modern equipment.

Although we are indebted to the past work of the likes of Sir Eric Hutchinson, Kenneth Werrett and in particular David Hunter, the information on the subject available to the enthusiast of the Highland has up to now been incomplete and in some cases, downright erroneous. It is with great pleasure therefore, that the Highland Railway Society has been able to assist with the production of this new publication, which at last presents to the reader the full scope of the known information on the carriages and wagons of the Highland Railway. Peter Tatlow has long been recognised as the leading authority on the subject, and we owe him a considerable debt of gratitude for his efforts in compiling this volume.

Ray Nolton MBE
Hon Chairman, Highland Railway Society

*Late in the Highland Railway's independent existence, Loch class locomotive No. 121* Loch Ericht *stands in Blair Atholl station on 29 June 1915 at the head of a stopping train for Perth. All the vehicles are to David Jones' design, except the third by Peter Drummond. Immediately behind the tender is the only bogie coach in the train, a Brake Third, the rest being 6-wheel. The second is a Locker Composite followed by a Drummond Third; a Jones coupé ended Lavatory First; a Third; and a Brake Van. (Ken Nunn, courtesy LCGB)*

It has long been my ambition to set out the history of the Highland Railway's carriages and wagons and indeed in my *Highland Miscellany* published by the Oxford Publishing Co as long ago as 1979 I deliberately held back on the topic in the hope that sometime soon a more detailed publication might appear. Well, it has been over thirty years, for which apologies, but at least it means more material has been unearthed in the interval.

It is now over forty years since David LG Hunter's limp covered book *Carriages & wagons of the Highland Railway* was published by Turntable Enterprises and in the meantime readers' expectations have grown considerably. It will, nonetheless, be necessary to refer to Hunter's work so that the owners of this previous work can relate information contained there and herein, not least in the matter of the development of the diagram numbers he adopted.

Few pre-Drummond general arrangement drawings have survived and the diagrams were so small as to not mean too much other than giving the overall dimensions, seating capacity or load, type of lighting, brake and tare weight of a class of vehicle. Therefore, without contemporary photographs, of which, in the case of goods vehicles of any age, there are equally few apart from goods brake vans, it is difficult to be too certain what a vehicle was actually like. One has to remember too, that the Highland was for much of its time an impecunious railway. This meant that new construction was only authorised by the Board when a sound financial case was presented, which resulted in existing rolling stock remaining in use for extended periods. The railway therefore had to rely on old fashioned 4-wheeled rib-sided carriages long after most other companies had withdrawn such stock and was forced to carry out much 'make do and mend', even converting redundant vehicles for new uses.

There has long been an interest in the Highland Railway greater in proportion than its size might appear to warrant. This was fostered by early enthusiasts, such as Cuthbert Hamilton Ellis, Sir Eric Hutchinson and Gavin Wilson. In particular Hutchinson had numerous drawings of a wide range of prototypes published in the model press, including of course plenty of Highland examples, often with little by way of running gear shown. In the case of the Highland vehicles, I have no doubt Sir Eric recorded what he saw, but what did he see? By that period of the early 20th century, I suspect it was a random collection of old wagons that had been through Lochgorm / Needlefield Works on numerous occasions, where they will have been patched up and repaired as best that could be done, so as to get the wagons back on the road to meet the burgeoning demand, especially during World War 1. For instance, all three of Sir Eric's examples of timber wagons are different, yet there is a particular style of cast iron socket bolted at the centre and on the outside of all three, which I suspect came from the pairs originally attached to the outside of the 7-ton 2-plank timber wagons to diagram 7, see pages 157-160.

Peter Tatlow, 2013.

## Note on the Author

Peter Tatlow is well known for his contribution to railway research over 50 years. An interest in railways and railway modelling has been his main pastime since he can remember. Born during the age of the 'Big Four', some of his earliest memories are of journeys undertaken during World War 2. Following military service in the Royal Engineers, he joined the Chief Civil Engineer's Department of the Southern Region of British Railways. He left BR over ten years later having qualified as a chartered civil engineer and then worked on the design and construction of bridges, in both United Kingdom and overseas. He is now retired from full-time employment.

His interest in railways and modelling has led to his writing numerous articles in the prototype and model railway press and in specialist journals on a wide range of subjects including locomotives, coaches, wagons, travelling cranes, bridges, train ferries and civil engineering activities.

His books include:

*A Pictorial Record of LNER wagons*, OPC, 1976, reprinted twice.
*A History of Highland locomotives*, OPC 1979, reprinted 1989.
*Highland Railway Miscellany*, OPC 1985.
*Historic Carriage Drawings, Volume 3 – Non-passenger coaching stock*, Pendragon 2000.
*Harrow & Wealdstone Accident, 50 years on, clearing up the aftermath*, The Oakwood Press, 2002, reprinted 2008.
*St John's Lewisham, 50 years on, restoring traffic*, The Oakwood Press, 2007.
*Return from Dunkirk, Railways to the rescue, Operation Dynamo (1940)*, Oakwood 2010.
*Railway Breakdown Cranes, Volumes 1 and 2*, Noodle Books, 2012 and 2013.
He has recently revisited the subject of his first work with *An illustrated history of LNER wagons* in five volumes, four of which have been published by Wild Swan in 2005, 2007, 2009 and 2012

# INTRODUCTION

## Locomotive Superintendents

**A Allan and W Barclay**

By the time the first of the Highland Railway's constituents, the Inverness & Nairn Railway was in 1855 setting about acquiring its first rolling stock with which to operate both passenger and goods trains on their 15 miles of track, the design and manufacture of such had reached a fair degree of consistency nation wide, albeit by later standards seemingly crude. Engineering plans for the line had been schemed, steered through the parliamentary process, contracts placed and construction supervised by their Engineer, Joseph Mitchell. It was natural, therefore for the Board of Directors of our nascent railway company to seek his advice on the matter of procuring suitable rolling stock. His response was to recommend the appointment of Alexander Allan, by that time Locomotive Superintendent of the Scottish Central Railway, as a consultant to advise and to arrange for the supply of appropriate plant. On 23 December 1854 this was approved by the Board for a fee of £150.

By April 1855 Mitchell was able to report that, as well as engines, arrangements were in hand for the making of carriages and by July he with Allan were authorised to take the necessary measures for their transportation to Inverness. As at that time of course it had yet to be connected to the national network, this meant shipping items of rolling stock to Inverness harbour and dragging these through the streets to the rail head.

Alexander Allan had been born in Montrose in 1809, where he served his apprenticeship under a wheelwright, before joining Robert Stephenson & Co at Newcastle and subsequently gaining experience in Liverpool under William Buddicom and Francis Trevithick at Crewe. In September 1853 he was appointed Locomotive Superintendent to the Scottish Central Railway at Perth with whom he remained until this amalgamated with the Caledonian Railway in 1865, during which period he acted as a consultant to the fledging railway companies based in the Highlands at Inverness.

Concurrent with his professional services for the railways of Inverness, his nephew William Barclay administered day-to-day locomotive affairs as superintendent at Lochgorm. Unable to manage his somewhat feeble flock of locomotives and during one of a number of crises in motive power, he was spotted fishing beside the line by Col. Fraser-Tytler, a director, as a consequence of which he left under rather a cloud at the end of May 1865. Before issuing a certificate of employment, the Board asked him to provide an inventory to his successor and postponed issuing the certificate until Mr Stroudley had reported. His uncle was asked to settle his account for superintending the construction of rolling stock and hand over any tracings of drawings to Stroudley, who would from then on fulfil the role.

**W Stroudley**

William Stroudley trained at Swindon before moving to a number of positions, including the Edinburgh and Glasgow Railway's works at Cowlairs where he became the Works Manager from 1861. At the age of 32, he came to Inverness as Locomotive Superintendent on 19 June 1865 on a salary of £500 per annum. Although the newly created Highland Railway Company was trying to consolidate and improve facilities, financial constrains rather limited his field for development and innovation, while new construction of rolling stock was limited. Four and a half years later he moved on to a similar position on the much larger London, Brighton and South Coast Railway, where from 1 February 1870 he was of course to make a name for himself. He died in Paris on 20 December 1889 aged 56.

**D Jones**

David Jones was born in Manchester on 25 October 1834 and served his apprenticeship with the LNWR at Longsight, and Crewe under John Ramsbottom. He moved to Inverness ten days after the opening of the Inverness and Nairn Railway rising to be Assistant Locomotive Superintendent and Running Shed Foreman at Inverness on 17 April 1858. On Barclay's departure he acted as Locomotive Superintendent and applied for the permanent position, but this was taken by Stroudley. However, five years later he was appointed on 1 February 1870 on a salary of £500pa, although his responsibilities included the locomotive affairs of the soon to be opened Dingwall and Skye, and Sutherland lines. He remained in post until accidental scalding of his leg on 7 September 1894, during trials with his famous 4-6-0 Big Goods class of locomotive, led to prolonged absence on sick leave and eventual retirement in September 1896. Nonetheless, he survived until 2 December 1906.

**P Drummond**

Peter Drummond, younger brother of the better known

Dugald, was born on 13 August 1850 in Polmont, near Grangemouth. He undertook his engineering training as an apprentice with Forrest and Barr and later worked for Norman and Co., both in Glasgow, after which he followed his brother to the railway works of the LBSC at Brighton and on to the North British at Cowlairs, Glasgow in 1875. In due course he moved within the city to the Caledonian at St Rollox where in January 1895 he became the Works Manager.

He was appointed Locomotive Superintendent at Lochgorm, Inverness on 1 November 1896, sixteen years after his brother, as Works Manager had left for Brighton, being re-titled Chief Mechanical Engineer around 1906. He transferred to Kilmarnock as Locomotive Superintendent of the G&SWR on 26 December 1911 and died there in harness on 30 June 1918.

### FG Smith

Fredrick George Smith, born in Newcastle on 29 April 1872, was from 1888 apprenticed to the NER at Gateshead. Subsequent positions around the country in the broader field of the engineering industry as a whole no doubt commended him to the position of Works Manager at Lochgorm to which he was appointed in December 1903 and Assistant Chief Mechanical Engineer from around 1906. In this he was responsible for the locomotive, carriage and wagon works at Inverness. As such he seems to have performed sufficiently well for the Board to award a £25 per annum increase to his salary from April 1911. He was elevated to Chief Mechanical Engineer from 1 February 1912 upon Drummond's departure. Following his perceived failings in the procurement of the River Class 4-6-0s and a serious backlog in maintenance of the existing stock, he was asked by the Board to resign Sept 1915.

He returned to Newcastle, where, under the pressures on the nation during World War 1, he soon found employment. Following the cessation of hostilities he went into business as a steel stockist and importer of structural steel sections from the Continent until 1933. He died 25 February 1956.

### C Cumming

Christopher Cumming commenced his career on the North British Railway with an apprenticeship at Ladybank followed by Cowlairs, after which he steadily rose up through the Locomotive Department, reaching the position of District Locomotive Superintendent for Fife and the Northern Section of the NBR. In an apparent reversion in title, he was appointed Locomotive Carriage and Wagon Superintendent of the Highland Railway on 24 September 1915 on a salary of £550 per annum, raised by £50 six months later. A breakdown in his health led to his forced retirement in early 1922, dying in 1924.

### DC Urie

David Chalmers Urie was born in Glasgow on 6 July 1884, the son of Robert Wallace Urie, the last Chief Mechanical Engineer of the LSWR. David started his railway career in 1901 as an apprentice under Dugald Drummond at Nine Elms, later by 1906 he was in the drawing office rising to senior draughtsman at Eastleigh, before being appointed Assistant Manager there in 1913, his father by then having succeeded D Drummond. Two years later he moved to the Midland Great Western Railway of Ireland as Assistant Locomotive Carriage and Wagon Superintendent in charge of the running department. He came to the Highland in 1922 where for the last eight months of the Highland Railway's independent existence he was Locomotive Carriage and Wagon Superintendent.

Upon grouping of the railways in 1923, he was initially appointed Mechanical Engineer (Inverness). On 1 May 1925 he succeeded William Pickersgill, upon his retirement, as the Mechanical Engineer Scotland based at St Rollox, on a salary of £2,000 pa. Urie reorganised the former Caledonian Railway St Rollox Works using some of the recently acquired machinery from Lochgorm, much to the consternation of the men at the latter. On 23 April 1931 his title was changed to Divisional Mechanical Engineer (Loco and C&W), still at Glasgow, on a salary of £2,250. From there he went on to become Motive Power Superintendent of the LMS from 27 October 1932 at Derby on a salary of £2,500 pa, rising to £2,750 from 19 December 1935. In this position he was responsible to the Chief Mechanical Engineer for the maintenance of engines at sheds, and for the supervision of any other mechanical matters. From the beginning of 1940 he was promoted to be the Superintendent of Motive Power at Euston on a salary of £3,000 and where he remained until his retirement on 1 March 1943.

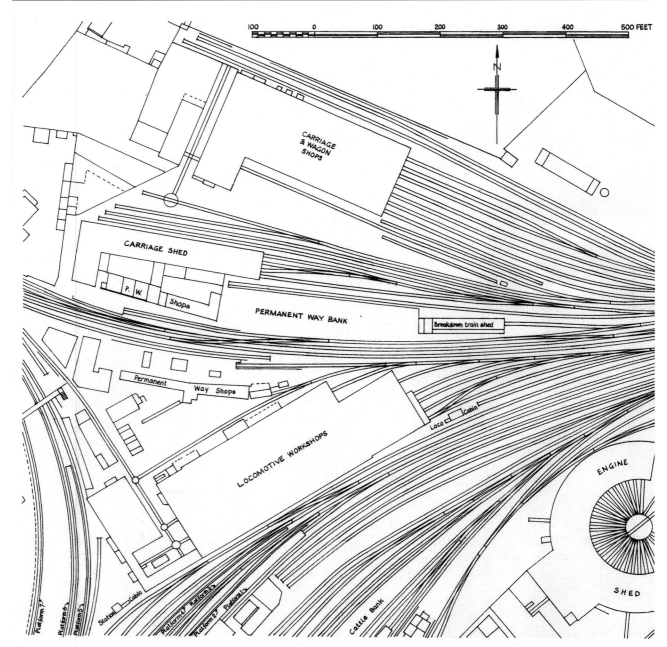

*Figure 1 - Plan of the Highland Railway's Lochgorm Locomotive and Needlefield Carriage & Wagon Works at Inverness. (Author)*

# LOCHGORM & NEEDLEFIELD WORKS

With the opening of the Inverness and Nairn Railway on 6 November 1855 facilities for locomotives were established on a piece of reclaimed land, which had included a small lochan known as Loch Gorm. By early 1857, with the prospect of the line being extended, the need for additional workshops was recognised and by the time the running of the I&NR was taken over by the Inverness and Aberdeen Junction Railway at the end of the year these had yet to be completed.

Lochgorm Works lay just beyond Inverness station platforms and north of the lines heading eastwards to Keith and later south to Perth. It was mainly for the repair and maintenance of locomotives, carriages and wagons, although some new build was undertaken. With the opening of the lines to the north and the construction of the Rose Street curve connecting this with the existing lines to the east a triangle was created which bounded the works premise. In 1863 a new carriage shed was erected north of this curve and the routine servicing of locomotives transferred to the new roundhouse constructed south of the original main line, freeing up the existing facilities for workshop activities.

Soon after William Stroudley's arrival at Inverness the proposals already under consideration by the Board for improvements and additions to the cost of £4,456 were carried out by John Hendrie of Inverness. (His son David A. later served in the Locomotive Department of the HR until 1904, when he moved to the Natal Government Railways, eventually rising to become Chief Mechanical Engineer of the South African Railways.) Stroudley subsequently obtained authority to purchase £2,000 worth of new tools, including a travelling crane, while the steam hammer had to wait a year, although in the meantime five additional forges

*A view inside the machine shop of Lochgorm Works. Note each side of a narrow gauge track way the various items of plant driven by belting from a longitudinal shaft in the roof beams. (WG Chalmers collection)*

*Another view of the machine shop. (WG Chalmers collection)*

were created. As the railway grew gradual improvements were implemented and additional machinery installed to enable the works to meet increasing demand. Room for expansion was made in 1874, when the Company purchased 22 acres north of the line for additional sidings, some of which enabled an extension of the Works in 1877 at a cost of £4,200 and again three years later. Further development took place and later the Needlefield Carriage and Wagon Works created.

The steam heated paint shop adjacent to the erecting shop with four roads was used not only to paint locomotives, but also for finishing off carriages and wagons. Partitioned off within was the carriage trimming department where all such work was undertaken. Equipment within included a hair tearing machine (presumed to be used in the preparation of horse hair for upholstery) and three sewing machines, one of which was adapted for leather work.

Upon his arrival in Inverness, Drummond lost no time in reporting to the Board on the condition of the rolling stock and workshops. He made recommendations for new machines required in the

sawmill and turning shop and in the ensuring years various improvements were carried out and new plant was installed.

By 1902 following Drummond's reorganisation and improvement, the complex extended over 18 acres, employing 700 men. There was a boiler shop in two bays equipped with a Craven Bros 10-ton rope driven over-head crane, pneumatic power to feed portable tools, including tapping and boring machines; in the second bay were five smiths' heaths, a plate furnace, tube brazing and cleaning machines, together with a ferrule making machine, two radial drilling machines and a screw lathe. The smiths' shop contained eighteen hearths, two Rigby 7-cwt steam hammers adjoining a forge containing a Thwaites and Carbut 2-ton double acting steam hammer. In the spring shop were four smiths' hearth and a spring furnace, together with a Marsden's nut and bolt making machine, and a 5-cwt Hulse steam hammer. Outside in the yard were a shearing and punching machine and a hot-saw and tyre furnace.

In 1897 the machine shop had been re-arranged by Drummond in four parallel longitudinal rows, one against each wall and a pair back to back down the middle with access between with rails for small trolleys to and from the erecting shop. A double-cylinder vertical steam engine drove a shaft from which belts led to each machine. Parts of the shop were partitioned off in which to undertake fitting work, whilst another part was dedicated to brass finishing. Further shops existed nearby for patternmaking, brass foundry, copper and tinsmiths' work.

A long erecting shop of one bay, provided with two Cowans Sheldon 25-ton over-head rope driven cranes over two long continuous parallel rows with pits, was capable of accommodating up to 14 engines at a time beyond which were three wheel lathes, a cylinder boring machine and a hydraulic wheel press.

Steam was generated by three locomotive type boilers in conjunction with coke furnaces to provide coke for use in the works. Admittedly much of the above plant and machinery was employed on the construction and maintenance of locomotives; nonetheless these facilities were also available for the heavier work on carriages and wagons.

By the late 1880s, the carriage and wagon works, known as Needlefield, had been established across the Rose Street curve beyond the carriage shed. The building shop was in two bays, one for carriages and the other for wagons, each containing three roads. Also within the shed were three wheel lathes, an axle journal turning lathe, a wheel balancing machine and drilling machine.

In addition there was an electrically lit saw mill of 11,470 sq. ft. floor area equipped with planing, mortising, tenoning, spindle and other tools, the shafting for which was driven by a 12 inch diameter by 24 inch stroke Tangye double-cylinder horizontal steam engine supplied with steam from two locomotive boilers. Adjacent was a large timber yard and drying shed.

Up until the first decade of the 20th century, Lochgorm Works had undertaken the new construction of a measurable proportion of locomotives and an even greater percentage of carriages and wagons. Following a review in 1904, the building of locomotives was halted and that of rolling stock much curtailed. Instead, with the completion of the last Drummond passenger tank in February 1906, the works concentrated on maintenance and from then on locomotives and much rolling stock was bought in from outside makers. Furthermore, had the proposed amalgamation of the Great North of Scotland and the Highland railways gone ahead, as was explored in 1905, undoubtedly all the important work of Lochgorm would have been transferred to the much more up-to-date and larger works at Inverurie.

With its unusual layout with two groups of platforms serving two sides of a triangle, Inverness was, and still is, an awkward station to operate and confusing to unwitting passengers. In 1905, the company, therefore, sought a site upon which to relocate the buildings of Lochgorm Works adjacent to the Rose Street curve so as to enable a through station to be created in its place. But, perhaps with the collapse of negotiations with the GNS for amalgamation, nothing was to come of this scheme.

The use of electricity was expanded so that by 1907 it was being employed to power electric motors driving the two travelling cranes in the erecting shop and boiler shop, together with various plant in the machine shop, including lathes, planing and shearing machines, an air compressor and blowers in the smithy. At that time the HR was in the process of converting the laundry to electric power, installing arc lamps in the station yards and an electric lift in the Station Hotel, so that its power demand was enough to consume two thirds of the Inverness Electric Supply Company's total output.

At the end of 1869 it had been concluded that considerable savings would be achieved by manufacturing their own grease, rather than buying it in from the trade, with the result that the necessary plant was acquired for £50 and a wooden shed erected for £105. By 1902 the plant was in need of renewal, so the matter was reviewed and a three month trial undertaken with grease supplied by Kennedy and Reid of Parkhead, Glasgow. The results, however, were considered unsatisfactory, so the railway reverted to manufacturing its own grease again.

In late 1911 a 153 foot long by 18 foot wide carriage washing shed was erected by the Clyde Structural Iron Co Ltd of Glasgow. In June 1918 the Company acquired a hydraulic wheel press from Fairburns of Leeds at a cost of £67.

With the grouping of the railways from the beginning of 1923 and the incorporation of the Highland Railway into the London, Midland and Scottish Railway, the work undertaken by the works as a whole was scaled back and consolidated. Closure was even considered but, in the event heavy repairs were transferred away to the south, St Rollox and Kilmarnock for locomotives, leaving the workshops to undertake light and service repairs only, plus some light wagon repairs in two bays in main works. As a consequence by 1930 staff numbers had been reduced to 163. Closure for steam locomotives occurred on 4 July 1959. From 1929 Needlefield works ceased to deal with carriage and wagon work and instead became a carriage cleaning shed, while with the rundown of steam traction and impending closure of the roundhouse shed, Lochgorm Works was in 1959 converted into maintenance facilities for diesel locomotives and diesel multiple units, while the carriage shed across the Rose Street curve has been used to service ScotRail's Caledonian sleeping cars.

*Above -* At ground level the approach lines into Inverness from the east are depicted during perhaps the first decade of the 20th century showing the tracks into the station on the extreme left. Behind the three and six doll bracket signals are the main buildings of Lochgorm Works with a 4-4-0 Skye Bogie class locomotive standing outside, while to its right runs the Rose Street curve towards the north, followed by a four doll bracket signal, beneath the right tip of which is the corrugated iron shed for the steam breakdown crane. To the right of that is a series of sidings, the first of which contains the empty stock of the overnight ECJS train from Kings Cross, leading towards the carriage shed with Needlefield Carriage & Wagon Works on the right hand edge. Outside the Works is a pair of shear legs with one end of a coach raised up. (Author's collection)

*Opposite -* Needlefield Carriage and Wagon Works at Inverness on the left-hand with wagons in front awaiting repair and part of the marshalling yards photographed on 17 July 1927. Compared with Figure 1, almost all of the development of buildings and sidings in the middle distance has occurred in the previous 25 years. Directly below the chimney in front of the building is the circular gas holder. Moving to the right of the carriage shed is the end of an ex-HR 0-6-0 Lochgorm Tank locomotive, probably No. 16118. The rest of the middle ground is occupied by the extremities of several sidings. The first contains two HR coaches designed by David Jones, a bogie Brake Third to diagram 30 and a 6-wheel Passenger Brake Van; then four HR 20 foot long goods brake vans; two 6-wheel, one with ramped lookout the other without, and two 4-wheel. These are followed by mainly 4 plank open wagons, at least three lettered HR, interspersed by a medium cattle van and a mineral wagon of unknown origin. On the siding behind is a similar line of vehicles, including three more Jones brake vans; a number of timber wagons, four at least of Highland ancestry; a NB end door mineral wagon; and a number of medium high open wagons, together with a North Staffordshire 3-plank dropside wagon and GC low-sided wagon. Beyond on the right hand side various open wagons are visible and behind these are a line of cattle vans. Closer to the photographer, ex-HR 0-6-0 Scrap Tank No. 16381 shunts an ex-MR 16ft 6in covered goods van. At the very foot of the photograph, behind the stone wall separa-ting Millburn Road from the railway's property, can be seen the tops of a line of locomotive coal wagons, together with some spare HR locomotive tenders. (HC Casserley)

## Carriage & Wagon Builders

Throughout the remainder of the book, particularly in the tables, carriage and wagon builders are referred to in an abbreviated form. Their full titles are as follows:

Birmingham Railway Carriage & Wagon Co, Smethwick, Birmingham
Bray Waddington, Leeds
Brown & Marshall, Birmingham
Brown Marshalls & Co (from 1870), Birmingham
Brush Electrical Engineering Co Ltd., Loughborough
Buchanan & Co, Motherwell
Robert Faulds & Co, Glasgow
Hamilton Wagon Co, Hamilton
Harrison & Camm, Rotherham
Hurst Nelson & Co Ltd, Motherwell
John Ashbury (Ashbury Carriage & Iron Co Ltd. from 1862), Manchester
Leeds Forge Co Ltd, Leeds
Metropolitan Railway Carriage, Wagon & Finance Co Ltd, Birmingham
Metropolitan-Cammell Carriage, Wagon & Finance Co Ltd, Birmingham
Metropolitan-Cammell Carriage & Wagon Co Ltd, Birmingham
Midland Railway Carriage & Wagon Co, Saltley, Birmingham
Railway Carriage & Wagon Co, Oldbury
RY Pickering & Co, Wishaw
Watson, Errol
Joseph Wright & Sons, Birmingham

## Drawings

The availability of official works drawings of pre-Drummond stock is extremely limited, whilst those of Drummond and his successors are relatively prolific, although caution needs to be exercised as to whether all the vehicles were actually constructed according to the drawing, or indeed built at all. The numbers of those known to be associated with diagrams are listed in Appendices 1 and 2, although copies have not always been available.

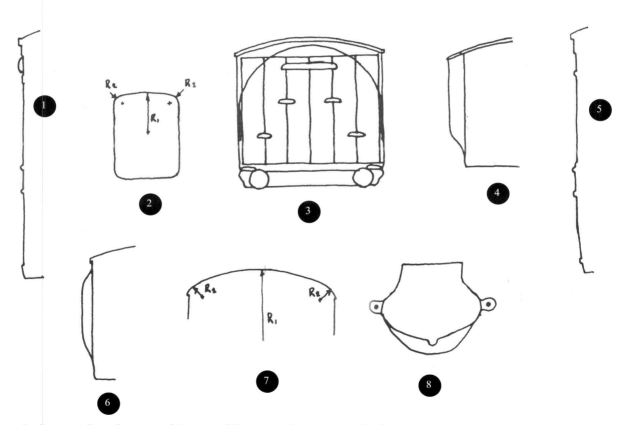

*Figure 2, distinguishing features of Jones and Drummond carriages. (Author)*

# Part 1 - Coaches

## General Review

### Building styles

The building styles of coaches to be seen on the Highland and its constituents can be briefly summarised as follows, and will be discussed in greater detail hereafter.

Most of the 4-wheel coaches of the constituents of the Highland Railway and those built during its early days had vertically ribbed sides with horizontal match boarding behind. Vehicles supplied prior to the great stock deliveries for the opening of the main line in 1863 had outside axle-guard irons and luggage rails on the roofs. All early coaches up to including those produced throughout Jones' tenure in office had individual steps outside each door and continuous lower running boards, although the steps on later vehicles were subsequently made continuous.

By the time Jones came to give consideration to the renewal of the original rib-sided stock on main line duties, he was in the process of progressing from 4 to 6-wheeled and bogie coaches, and ultimately changed to the automatic vacuum brake system. For bodywork construction he adopted a straight vertical sided panelled design with slightly turned in bottom edge (Fig 2/1). The upper panels and windows had distinctive three centre curve at the top (Fig 2/2), while the commode handles beside each compartment door were curved in shape. Ventilators of three centre cross section and round ends were fitted in the eaves panels of doors and

*The headstock features of Jones' designs, as applied to preserved passenger brake van No. 5, including wooden buffer-heads, four bolt fixings to circular buffer housing, the fixing eyes for now discarded safety chains and the oval base to the draw hook. (Author)*

15

lavatories. The ends of coaches were vertically boarded with half-round capping strips, the whole forming a rectangular shape (Fig 2/3). Steps from both sides, but at one end only, met at a broad top step. A semi-circular hand rail was provided at this end and simple vertical grab irons at the other end. From the mid-1880s the 6-wheel and bogie panelled coupé ended First-class stock had swept boot ends beneath the windows in the ends, described by Hamilton Ellis as 'chariot ends'. 4 and 6-wheeled Passenger Brake Vans had the guard's lookout at one end with the low arc roof continuing over the lookout (Fig 2/4).

Drummond brought with him Caledonian practices of panelled coaches in three layers and tumblehome to the lower sides and ends, continuous upper and lower running boards and at first low arc roofs (Fig 2/5). The commode handles were made straight and vertical. Economies were introduced from 1906 with the lower panels and end panelling replaced by vertical match boarding, initially with half-round beading over the edges of the boarding and the frames. It was found with time, however, that the lower horizontal joint admitted rain water which rotted the framing and by Smith's time the vertical match boarding was carried down to the bottom edge of the body, thereby allowing the water to drain out freely. Repairs to lower side panels were often carried out in match boarding, but the earlier style is often evidenced by the presence of panelled ends. Passenger Brake Van lookouts were of double ogee section (Fig 2/6).

With the introduction of sleeping cars and corridor stock capable of being fitted with gangway connections, the roof profile was altered to a three centre curve 'cove roof', which was also applied to some late construction of 6-wheeled stock (Fig 2/7). 'Iracier' pattern axle-boxes were fitted to the bogies of coaches supplied from Smith's tenure of office (Fig 2/8).

### Carriage Diagrams

In 1901 Peter Drummond instituted what appears to have been the first issue of diagrams for the then existing locomotives, carriages and wagons: hence some early examples have escaped having already been withdrawn. These diagrams were finger-nail outlines in blue-print drawn to a scale of $^{1}/_{16}$th inch to one foot inserted in a small pocket book measuring 4¾ by 2 inches (120 x 50mm). At such a small scale, they merely contained an outline side elevation showing windows and wheels, together with a plan view, and are therefore of limited value. As far as coaches are concerned, Hunter's papers indicate that revised versions were prepared in 1908 and 1922, although copies have not come to the author's attention. He does, however, have a book with 'LMS&R Highland Section' inscribed on the cover in which the blue-print diagrams still refer to Highland vehicle numbers and the LMS (first series) numbers have been written in hand on the opposite page in many, but not in all cases. In due course the Northern Division of the LMS went on to prepare a fresh diagram book 'LMS carriages, vans and trucks' in which the format was increased to 8¼ by 6 inches (210 x 152mm), but by then much of the older stock had been scrapped. In this some of the diagram numbers are in two parts, first the Highland Section's number, followed underneath by a sequence number for the Northern Division in which the Highland types are interspersed by those of the former Caledonian and G&SW railways.

Although the 1901 diagram indicates the type letter allocated within each class of vehicle, i.e. First, Third, etc., to each diagram, it is not known whether these were repeated in subsequent HR editions, but they do not appear in the LMS books. The contents of the various books are listed in Appendix 1.

### Numbering

As was the custom at the time, the Highland and its constituents numbered their stock, including carriages and wagons, as a means for the accountant to be able to identify the shareholders' property and to be able to trace vehicles for both traffic and maintenance purposes. Once an item became life expired, its replacement was charged to the Revenue Account and the number of the withdrawn item allocated to its replacement, writing off the displaced vehicle and either breaking it up or, from 1907, relegating it to the duplicate list by adding the suffix D until ultimately scrapped. Additions to stock on the other hand would have been paid for from the Capital Account and given new numbers, usually the next in sequence.

As far as carriages were concerned, fresh number series were created for each class of vehicle starting with 1 in each case. Trying to balance the books by reusing numbers and maintaining the value of the capital account was all very well in the days before rampant inflation and ignored the possible increased value of the much improved and/or larger replacement; but with rapidly increasing prices towards end of and immediately following World War 1, matters got seriously out of hand. By then five or six 4 and 6-wheeled coaches were having to be written off to pay for each modern corridor carriage.

When the LMS renumbered the Highland's carriage stock, it simply applied a sequential number to each group of passenger vehicles in the following order:

1st LMS Number Series - Carriages

| | |
|---|---|
| 18591-18615 | First-class, including First saloons |
| 18616-18693 | Composite, including Brake Composite |

|          |                          |
|----------|--------------------------|
| 18694-18847 | Third-class, including Third saloons |
| 18848-18864 | Brake Third, including converted sleeping cars |

On the other hand, LMS non-passenger coaching stock had its own list, those for the Highland being as follows:

1st LMS Number Series - Non-passenger coaching stock: 7361 to 7848

|           |                          |
|-----------|--------------------------|
| 7361-7375 | Post Office Vans         |
| 7384-7446 | Passenger Brake Vans     |
| 7457-7464 | Passenger luggage vans   |
| 7472-7503 | Covered carriage trucks  |
| 7504-7520 | Open carriage trucks     |
| 7521-7545 | Horse boxes              |
| 7547-7845 | Open fish trucks         |
| 7847-7848 | Valuable cattle wagon    |

It will be observed that, while the number sequences for carriage stock are continuous, those for non-passenger coaching stock are not entirely so. Furthermore, it is possible that numbers up to 7880 were former Highland vehicles. This means that it is more than probable that other vehicles were allocated the intervening numbers, which have yet to be identified. Numbers in (parentheses) were allocated, but not carried.

Following nationalisation in 1948, British Railway's initial practice was to apply a prefix letter to the number to indicate the grouping company of origin, in this case M for LMS. Later, however, BR moved this to be a suffix and prefix the number with the region to which the carriage was allocated, i.e. SC, to the few coaches remaining in service. Expediency, however, sometimes resulted in the new prefix merely being temporarily placed ahead of the existing one which remained in place, rather than being removed and repositioned as a suffix, until such time as the vehicle was either repainted, or more likely scrapped.

### Wheels & Axle-boxes

The usual form of wheel for passenger carrying vehicles was the Mansell wheel, consisting of a steel tyre supported on the steel axle by solid teak segments to deaden the sound and cushion the ride. Passenger Brake Vans on the other hand adopted a spoked wheel, usually of the split, or open spoke type, but occasionally of solid cast form. With the adoption of electrical track circuiting on other railways as part of advancing signalling methods it became necessary to bond each tyre of Mansell wheels to the axle.

In 1910, however, Drummond was instructed by the Locomotive Committee to make comparative estimates of costs of steel disc wheels currently being adopted by the Caledonian and other railways. As a

*Spring, axle-guard and grease lubricated axle-box of Passenger Brake Van No. 5 during restoration. The lower footboard has temporarily been removed. (Author)*

***Left -*** *Oil lubricated 9 by 4 inch axle-box fitted to HR 6-wheel Composite coach when in departmental service as No. 2972447. Note also the Lochgorm works plate, dated 1908, attached to the solebar. (JL Stephenson)*

***Right -*** *Iracier 9 by 4 inch patent axle-box on a coach bogie. (Ian Peddie)*

consequence a change was made to steel wheels, after using up 4 tons of teak already on hand and selling off the surplus to the North British Railway.

Initially both carriages and wagons were grease lubricated, but from 1880s onwards oil was substituted for carriages and non-passenger rolling stock expected to run in passenger trains. From about 1912 Iracier axle-boxes were adopted for these classes of vehicle. This patent design was thought up by a Hull & Barnsley Railway driver and developed into a workable form at Springhead Works by 1908. The manufacture and marketing of these, however, was undertaken by the Patent Axle Box Foundry Co. Ltd. in Wednesfield, Staffordshire. Each unit consisted of a thin disc attached to the end of the axle within the axle-box, which, as it

rotated with the movement of the vehicle, picked up oil and raised it into a reservoir above the journal from where the oil was distributed trough holes onto the journal and thereafter drained into a sump for recirculation.

As noted, early construction had provided an individual upper step outside each door with only the lower board being continuous. As early as September 1878 the Board of Trade had been drawing attention to the desirability of having continuous foot boards, but at this time the matter was deferred for consideration at some future date and discrete steps were still being provided in the late Jones period. Only later were these replaced.

From the outset side chains had been provided

*Figure 3 - Outline drawing
of a 6-foot wheel base
Jones carriage bogie.
(Author)*

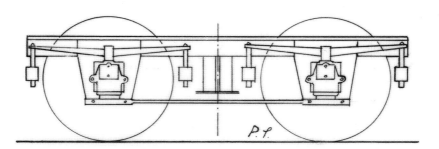

on carriages and wagons, as well as the conventional couplings, as a safeguard against a failed coupling. By 1907 these were generally considered unnecessary and no longer fitted to new vehicles and were gradually removed from existing vehicles.

The more general availability of steel from the late 1880s and its use for wheel springs in particular allowed the substitution of numerous leaves of wrought iron springs by a lesser number of steel springs.

### Bogies

The form of the earlier pivotal bogies fitted under Jones' carriages is difficult to establish due to shadows in most photographs, but they look crude compared with subsequent usual practice, and according to the diagrams had either 9 or 6 foot wheelbases, the latter with a spring length of a little over 4 foot of course being particularly short. On the drawing for his Lavatory Third coach to diagram 17 there are indications of a central pivot and segments of bearing plate, together with possible rubbing supports bearing on the frame at about 7ft 10in each side of the pivot longitudinally and at 6ft 3in lateral centres. This suggests that the arrangement would have permitted the solebars of the bogie frame to rotate in plan, but would have been prevented movement in the vertical direction, i.e. there were no bolster and secondary springing. In general it is apparent that, once the design of bogies had settled down, most subsequent ones were of the swing bolster type of 8 or more feet in wheelbase.

For the benefit of modellers, an outline drawing for the 6-foot bogie is reproduced above, but is naturally devoid of some detail. Regrettably similar information for the 9-foot version has yet to come to hand.

Although usually associated with the arrival of Drummond as Locomotive Superintendent, Fox's bogies seem to have been selected just prior to his arrival at Inverness, being fitted to Jones' Brake Third to diagram 30, while it is possible they were also fitted retrospectively to earlier types. In this type, the carriage is hung by swing links from a transverse bolster the

centre of which was able to rotate relative to the carriage. Those used on the Highland Railway were of pressed steel construction with an 8 foot wheelbase and 3ft 8in diameter wheels mounted on axles with 9 by 4 inch diameter journals. 5 foot laminated springs with the eye bolts were also fitted with auxiliary rubber springs, while there were two 4-coil nests of Timm's unequally loaded springs under the transverse bolster, which was laterally restrained by rubber pads.

### Brakes

A collision occurred at Pitlochry on 31 October 1865, when a train failed to brake and draw to a halt in sufficient time to avoid over-running the length of the loop. Consequently it collided with the incoming train from the opposite direction on the single line and with which it was supposed to cross. According to the BoT's Inspector's report, it appears that, in recognition of the steep gradients to be found on the Highland Line, some at least of the passenger carrying vehicles were equipped with a form of continuous brake. Rule 224 read:

*The Breaks to be used according to circumstances; but Guards are requested not to screw up the continuous Breaks so as to skid the carriage wheels, except in cases of great emergency.*

Nonetheless, this rule did not make it obligatory for the continuous brake to be connected up and it was left to the discretion of the guard on the basis of the load of his train whether to do so or not. Human nature being what it is, one suspects this was not often done, but thereafter at the Inspector's behest the company was persuaded to insist on its use. This was presumably on the Newall system, which was a mechanical continuous brake used by either the enginemen or the guard. Operated initially on the two mail trains, it was subsequently applied to other passenger trains and the next year Stroudley reported it to be working satisfactorily. The method is understood to have been quite effective on the short trains of the time and it remained in use until at least 1888.

*Below - Figure 4, drawing of Fox' Patent pressed steel carriage bogie. (Author)*

*Opposite - Figure 5, Newall's Patent continuous railway brake. (Author)*

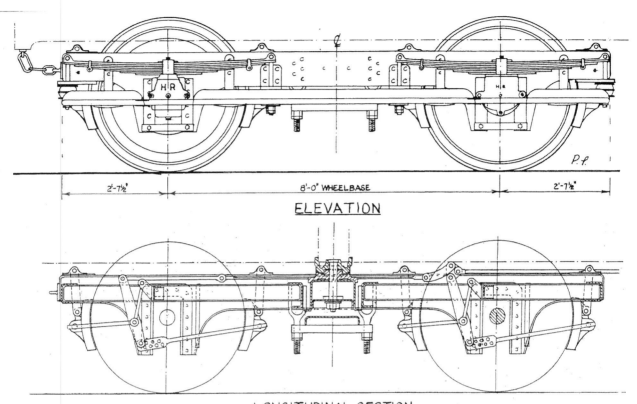

ELEVATION

LONGITUDINAL SECTION

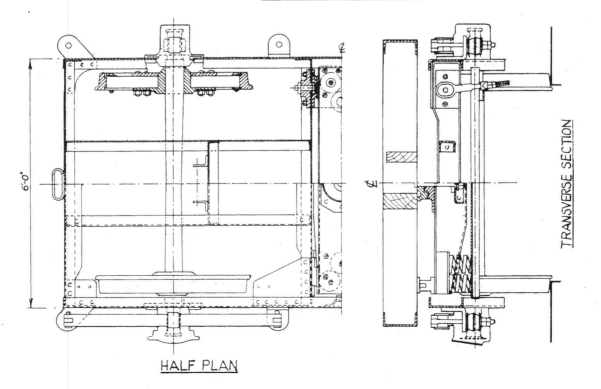

HALF PLAN

# Coaches

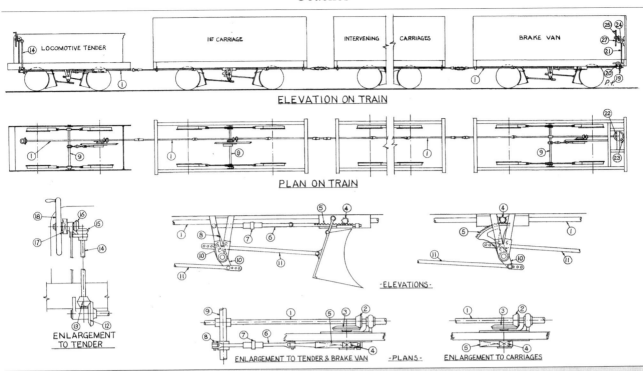

ELEVATION ON TRAIN

PLAN ON TRAIN

ENLARGEMENT TO TENDER

-ELEVATIONS-

ENLARGEMENT TO TENDER & BRAKE VAN   -PLANS-   ENLARGEMENT TO CARRIAGES

| Item | Description | Location |
|---|---|---|
| **Newall's Patent Continuous Railway Brake** | | |
| **On Tender, Carriages & Brake Van** | | |
| 1 | Longitudinal shaft | Beneath under-frame |
| 2 | Bevel pinion | On longitudinal shaft 1 |
| 3 | Bevel wheel | On short transverse shaft |
| 4 | Spur pinion | On short transverse shaft |
| 5 | Rack (flat or segment) | Beneath 4 |
| 6 | Longitudinal rod | Connected to 5 |
| 7 | Adjustable pipe nut | Within lever 6 |
| 8 | Lever | On weigh shaft 9 |
| 9 | Transverse weigh shaft | Between vee hangers |
| 10 | Short levers | Each end of weigh shaft 9 |
| 11 | Push rods | Between 10 & brake block |
| **On Tender** | | |
| 12 | Bevel wheel | On longitudinal shaft 1 |
| 13 | Bevel pinion | At bottom of vertical shaft 14 |
| 14 | Vertical shaft | Between gear wheels 13 & 15 |
| 15 | Mitre wheel | At top of vertical shaft 14 |
| 16 | Mitre wheel | On short longitudinal shaft |
| 17 | Spur wheel | On short longitudinal shaft |
| 18 | Footplatemen's hand wheel | On short longitudinal shaft |
| **On brake van** | | |
| 19 | Bevel wheel | On longitudinal shaft 1 |
| 20 | Bevel pinion | Bottom of short vertical |
| 21 | Spur wheel | Top of short vertical shaft |
| 22 | Spur pinion | At bottom of vertical shaft |
| 23 | Vertical shaft | Between gear wheels 22 & 24 |
| 24 | Mitre wheel | At top of vertical shaft 23 |
| 25 | Mitre wheel | On short longitudinal shaft |
| 26 | Spur wheel | On short longitudinal shaft |
| 27 | Guard's hand wheel | On short longitudinal shaft |

James Newall, the Carriage and Wagon Superintendent of the East Lancashire Railway at Bury since 1848, developed and in 1852 patented one of the first partially self-acting continuous railway brake systems. This was a mechanical arrangement consisting of a series of longitudinal shafts running beneath the under-frames of the locomotive tender and the following carriages, so that connections between them could be made by universal joints and shafts. As conceived this was positioned on the centreline, meaning that individual vehicles could be presented either way round, but thereby necessarily having to incorporate a mechanism for reversing the direction of motion in applying the brake to suit. In each vehicle a set of bevel gears on the shaft acted upon a spur gear, worm and worm wheel, driving onto a rack connected with the brake blocks which were brought to bear on the tread of the wheels by a spiral spring. On the tender and within the brake van, the shafting was redirected vertically upwards by a set of bevel gears to the top of a brake column where a further set of bevel gears was attached to a brake wheel, itself restrained in position while the brake was off by a sprocket and pawl.

Turning of the wheel on either the tender (14), or in the guard's van (23) through a series of bevel gears caused the longitudinal shaft (1) below the vehicles' under-frames to rotate along the length of the train, which in turn activated the brakes simultaneously on each vehicle connected to the system to apply or release the brakes.

The *Circular to Railway Companies with reference to continuous brakes* issued by the Board of Trade in 1877, the source for Figure 5, gives no indication on the diagram of, but refers in the text to, a spring mechanism to assist in applying the braking force, which otherwise presumably would have relied on the vigour with which the enginemen and/or guard turned their hand wheels. Furthermore without such a mechanism there would be no automatic application of the brakes in the event of the train separating. From other sources however, it would appear a spiral spring was compressed by tightening the hand wheel and restrained in its action by a ratchet until released by either of the operatives, or by the train separating.

In 1858 comparative tests of various brake systems, including Newall's, were undertaken by Capt Galton, under the supervision of Lt Col W Yolland of the Railway Inspectorate. From the published results, it is apparent that Newall had continued to develop his brake and, in the absence of any specific details, it remains uncertain exactly the version adopted by the Highland in the 1860s, but presumably it was the latest. It would seem that between taking out the patent and this version being used, some refinements had been incorporated. For instance, it is known that on the

Highland the longitudinal shaft was off-set from the centre line by one foot, so that the connections were handed and would all have to be presented the same way round. Fortunately the Company's lines had no return loops in regular use, so short of placing on a turntable, once correctly placed the carriages at least would remain so, but not so the engines. While Newall's brake clearly was an advance on current practice up to that time, what was really required was a fully automatic continuous 'fail safe' braking system.

By the early 1870s public anxiety at the loss of life due to inadequate brakes elsewhere led to the Newark brake trials taking place in June 1875, when the performance and effectiveness of eight different braking systems were compared. From these it was apparent that only two met the requirements to be fully automatic and fail safe, viz: the automatic version of the vacuum system and the Westinghouse compressed air system. Unfortunately these were not inter-connectable and whilst clearly superior, reluctance to adopt an American patent product in the form of the Westinghouse system, led to a lack of one standard for the country. The tragic accident at Abbots Ripon on the Great Northern Railway in January 1876 led the Board of Trade to chivvy the railway companies by issuing a succession of circulars drawing the railway companies' attention to the importance of continuous brakes for passenger trains.

Whilst wishing to act in concert with the Southern companies, the Highland still had much faith in Newall's system and remained undecided for some time, dithering between the Westinghouse; Clark & Webb's chain, which did not comply with the BoT's regulations; automatic and simple vacuum brake systems; and several trials with borrowed trains and meetings with other companies took place. Finally it appears Jones decided that the automatic vacuum brake should be adopted, for which in October 1884 the Board sought an estimate of cost, including the fitting of through dual pipes to 300 fish trucks. As it turned out, this was the same as adopted by many companies, but incompatible with its neighbours the Caledonian and GNSR, while the North British initially adopted the Westinghouse but later changed to vacuum.

The cost must have frightened the Highland's Board, because it was February 1887 before the tentative response was to instruct Jones to fit up the carriages and vans of the principle trains of the line with the vacuum brake, viz:- the 7.50am from Perth to Inverness and its return at 3.0pm. The problem though was that this train could include fish trucks on most days and all these plus horse boxes had to be equipped with vacuum brake pipe connections as well. Matters were brought a head, however, by the loss of 80 lives in the Armagh accident on 12 June 1889, which resulted from inadequate and non-automatic brakes. This led to the *Regulation of the*

*Railways Act* the same year. Amongst other things, this required the adoption of continuous brakes on trains carrying passengers, which had to be instantaneous in action, self applying in the event of any failure in continuity, capable of being applied to every vehicle of the train and in regular use in daily working. So in December 1889, as well as instructing the Engineer to install signal and point interlocking on the main line, the Board authorised the Locomotive Superintendent to fit up all passenger stock with vacuum brake or with pipes as may be required, while still resisting constraints on the running of mixed trains.

### Passenger Alarm Apparatus

The provision of a means for a passenger to raise the alarm, particularly relevant in the days when all compartment coaches were the norm, was forced on the railways following the enactment of *Regulation of Railways Act* 1868, which required that there be a method to enable passengers to communicate with the guard and/or engine driver. An early means of achieving this was the cord system invented by TE Harrison of the North Eastern Railway and approved by the Board of Trade in 1859. This consisted of a cord threaded through a pair of closely spaced open but overlapping rings attached to the cantrail each side of every door, at the ends and intermediately as required over the length of the vehicle. When assembling a train, the cord of each vehicle would have to be connected to its neighbour, including the guard's van and to the locomotive. During the period in which the apparatus was in use, mounted on the right hand side of the locomotive tender was a circular bell. Should an emergency arise, a passenger would have to open a drop-light window to reach out above his head to be able to tug on the cord, which would sound bells in the brake van and on the locomotive to attract the attention of the train crew who would then take appropriate action.

This had been adopted by the Highland in 1865, but in practice it left a great deal to be desired, and, in complete volte-face, the permission for its use was revoked by the Board of Trade on 1 January 1873 being finally condemned in 1893. Nonetheless, the Highland appears to have continued its use, because the HR Appendix No. 1 dated 1st September 1897 reads:

*All Passenger Trains that run a distance of over 20 miles without stopping, must be fitted with Passengers' Communication Cords. The cord will be attached to a wheel in the rear van, and extend to the tender of the engine, and there be fastened to the bell which is fixed on the tender. At Terminal Stations Stationmasters will, after they are made up, see that all purely Passenger Trains, to which the conditions apply, are fully equipped with Communication Cords and Appliances, and Guards must, before starting, satisfy themselves that communication between the rear van and the engine tender is complete.*

*When any vehicles are attached or detached at roadside Stations, or in the event of the train being re-marshalled, care must be taken that all the cords are properly adjusted, so that communication may be complete throughout before the Train starts again; and in the case of Vehicles which are detached, the cord couplings of these Vehicles must always be secured at both ends on the hooks provided for the purpose, to prevent the cords being lost or damaged.*

Although the vacuum brake system had been in use for some time and the internal cord/chain means communication developed as an accessory to the braking system, it was only in late 1901 that the question of an alternative means of communication between passengers, guards and drivers was reviewed by the Board. The adoption of the automatic vacuum brake system meant that admitting a small quantity of air at any point along the train would result in a partial application of the brakes and more importantly indicate a drop in pressure on the gauges on the engine and in the guard's van. This would alert the driver to the presence of a problem and that he would be expected stop at the soonest opportunity and with the guard investigate. The system adopted used an internal tube passing longitudinally just above the door and windows. Gaps in this in every compartment exposed a small chain running the length of the coach one end of which was attached to a valve. On the chain being pulled by the passenger, the valve opened admitting a small quantity of air into the system and also rotating a red coloured butterfly at the end of the coach. This would direct the guard to the coach within which the cord had been pulled, while the hanging down cord would indicate the compartment. After the problem had been resolved, the guard would reset the butterfly valve and allow the train to continue on its journey. Drummond coaches appear to have been equipped with this system from the outset. The Harrison system ceased to be used around the turn of the century, but the brass rings along the carriage cornice may have remained in position on older carriages for many years.

### Lighting

At first the lighting of carriages was by oil lamps lowered through holes in the roof. In the absence of a lamp, such as during daylight hours, a wooden plug was inserted in its place, while the plug was provided with an adjacent socket in which it was otherwise placed.

In July 1895 a brave experiment was initiated whereby at a cost of £400 a train of eight carriages was fitted out with an electric light system by Stone & Co of

Deptford and entered service in late September 1896. Four years later, however, a number of dynamos, batteries and fittings had become defective and the experiment was terminated. In the meantime, a year earlier, a carriage seems to have been fitted up with Pintsch's gas means of lighting with which to compare the two systems, the necessary gas being provided by the Caledonian Railway at Perth.

By October 1901, the decision was taken to adopt gas for the lighting of carriages in use on the main line. A month later Pintsch's Patent Lighting Co Ltd's offer for the erection of high pressure oil gas works and the fitting of a number of carriages was accepted. The equipping of all carriages was far from instantaneous and some older coaches were still oil lit at grouping in 1923, nonetheless a larger gasholder was acquired in 1911. Two years later incandescent burners were fitted in carriages running on the main line from Perth to Inverness.

By 1913 a reversion to electric lighting was instigated and from then on all new stock was so fitted and existing gradually converted, the sleeping cars being taken in hand in 1915. In 1920 a new wooden shed as a maintenance shop, siding and pit from which to undertake the work on the electrical equipment were authorised at an eventual total cost of £958-16-5.

### Heating

Train travel through the Highlands during the winter cannot have been much fun with no carriage heating. To ameliorate this foot warmers, consisting of metal pans filled with hot water were made available at terminal stations and exchanged for fresh hot ones at selected stations along the route. As early as 1863 these were available to Third-class passengers, as well as the upper classes. From time to time new pans were made at Lochgorm Works. From 1902 as foot warmers required renewal they were replaced by sealed pans containing acetate of soda, which emitted a greater quantity of heat as the solution re-crystallised.

By 1904, however, through coaches from the Caledonian Railway from Glasgow, soon to be followed by the North British Railway, were equipped with steam heating, which depended on a supply of steam at 25 to 40 pounds per square inch, by means of through pipes and connecting hoses from the locomotive. With some reluctance, the minimum number of carriages and six Castle class locomotives were duly fitted out with steam heating apparatus. The GNS then followed with a proposal for the same on the Aberdeen to Inverness service, which initially was declined, but gradually steam heating was accepted and spread to further trains on the system. Nonetheless, it was September 1911 before approval was given to providing such to passengers on the morning train to Kyle of Lochalsh and

the following year on the Further North line. Thereafter, new stock was so fitted from the outset, while an ongoing programme to fit out existing stock continued during 1915 to 1922 and then extended to pipes for non-passenger coaching stock, except initially fish trucks.

For all this, heating pans continued to be used on the Fochabers, Fort George, Strathpeffer and Burghead branches during the winter of 1918, while Perth General Station intimated that coal for heating pans would no longer be available. Steam heating on the Eastern Section of the line and in passenger brake vans was only undertaken in time for the following winter. The vehicles on the Aberfeldy branch were taken in hand in 1922 and the need to pipe fish trucks eventually accepted. The whole process may not have been completed by the grouping the following year.

### Passenger comfort

The standard of comfort provided for passengers in the early days varied widely. Lucky First-class passengers were afforded amply proportioned compartments with no more than three fully upholstered seats in the width of the coach. Although some padding would be provided to Second-class passengers, the size of their compartments were often no greater than Third-class. Those who could afford no more than a Third-class or Parliamentary fare would be forced to sit on hard wooden seats with only half height partitions separating them from the adjacent compartments and at night sharing one miserable oil lamp between two compartments. The only concession was that smoking compartments were divided from their neighbours by a full height partition and had their own lamp. In the early days the narrowness of the compartments for the lower classes meant that interlocking of passengers' knees was unavoidable, which in the case of mixed genders must have given meaning to the desire for 'Ladies only' compartments, not that the Highland ever provided such. On the other hand, in the absence of any form of heating, unless a warming pan was hired, perhaps the close proximity of ones fellow passengers was in winter a welcome blessing.

With the advent of through coaches for the length of the system from Wick to Perth, some improvements were put in hand. In the First-class compartments the elbow rests in six carriages were altered at a cost of £4 each so that they tilted up in the same way as those in the East and West Coast companies. Second-class was granted a coconut mat in each compartment at 10 shillings a mat, while Third-class had the partitions extended up to the roof at a cost of 15 shillings (75p) each and net racks for small parcels were added at another 12 shillings and 6 pence (62.5p), but in 1875 the provision of cushions was deferred. In July 1881 cushions in Third-class compartments were finally conceded for the carriages which ran in the through trains between Perth and Inverness and Inverness and Wick, at a cost of £2-5-0 (£2.25) per cushion in the carriages provided with divisions carried to the top and fitted with racks. In 1897 an arrangement was introduced whereby rugs and pillows were made available for hire to passengers of the two overnight trains, viz: the 10.30pm form Inverness and 12.40am from Perth.

As early as 1858 First-class smoking saloon carriages were on order from Brown Marshall and by September that year the Manager was instructed to have the words 'First-class smoking saloon' covered with a board for the present, in order that the carriage might be used during the 'meeting days', presumed to be Board meetings. Ten years later the Regulation of the Railways Act of 1868 with regard to smoking led to the adoption of the Midland Company's regulations on the subject. Mr Stroudley was authorised to fix four slots on each carriage and provide 150 boards labelled "Smoking Compartment" and instructed to board up to full height one compartment in each Third-class carriage and provide one lamp holder therein.

Soon after his appointment Jones invented and patented a carriage door handle, which the Board authorised him to fit in place of old handles on carriages on the Highland line as they became worn out at a cost of 1s 6d (7.5p), but with no royalty fee being paid. Nonetheless, five years later they rescinded the order. In 1902, it was decided to remove the handles from inside the compartments relying solely on the single handle outside.

The GNS, with which the I&AJR at first connected, only offered First and Third-class accommodation, so there was initially only the need to match these. Elsewhere in the country, however, in the early days of the railways it was customary to offer First, Second and Third-class accommodation on passenger trains and once the I&PJR connected with the SCR at Perth, Second-class was required as well. Typically from 1871 to 1882 the Highland was regularly providing for all three classes on all lines except the Burghead branch which offered only First and Third. It was, therefore, necessary for the Company to have a stock of vehicles with Second-class accommodation. This was achieved exclusively in the form of Composite carriages of First/Second, Second/Third or all three classes.

In January 1878 the Midland Railway abolished Second-class and upgraded Third-class accommodation to a similar standard prior to the opening of Settle & Carlisle route and the starting of its Anglo-Scottish services. In April 1886 the Caledonian Railway intimated its wish to dispense with through booking of Second-class passengers from their stations to the Highland, to the displeasure of the Highland's Board. By 1893, however, both the West and East Coast route companies decided to discontinue booking through Second-class fares and the Highland relented and followed suit from 1 May, reclassifying Second-class compartments as Thirds.

For passengers holding First-class tickets, the facility of on board lavatories became available with the introduction of the 6-wheel First-class carriages to diagram 1 in 1887 and was continued with bogie coaches. It was extended to Third-class passengers with the Composites to diagram 15 in 1889 and the all Third-class of 1893 to diagram 26. Access to these, however, was restricted to those who travelled in the adjacent compartments, which usually averaged about two thirds of the total capacity of the carriage. This limitation was only really overcome with the introduction of corridor coaches during the first decade of the 20th century.

With the advent of lavatories water bottles and glasses had been provided, but by March 1909 these were clearly being broken or stolen, so it was agreed to withdraw all water bottles and glasses from lavatory compartments of Highland Railway carriages, other than sleeping cars, with the fittings removed as the carriages came into the workshops.

## Livery

The livery of all aspects of the Highland Railway, including that applied following take over by the LMS in 1923 and nationalisation in 1948, have been very adequately explored in *Highland Railway liveries* by H Geddes and E Bellass, published by The Pendragon Partnership in association with the Highland Railway Society in 1995 and to which the reader is referred.

Although the dark green and white livery is associated with Drummond's early years in office, it was actually devised and approved on 10 October 1896, very shortly before he took up his post. Lace trimmings in First-class compartments were dispensed with as unnecessary from 1910. By 1920 green cloth linings to upholstery was adopted in place of moquette in First-class compartments. By the beginning of the twentieth century photographs of the Highland line in the compartments of Third-class carriages had been suggested, but rejected. By 1908, however, the small income to be generated by allowing advertisements instead appealed.

*A fascinating collection of 4-wheel carriages at Aberfeldy showing a range of early 4-wheel types available for use on the branch from Ballinluig in the late 1870s. From left to right the first, third and fourth are rib-sided 4-compartment Thirds; the second and sixth panelled 3-compartment Firsts; while the fifth is a First/Second Composite of similar design; the seventh is a rib-sided Passenger Brake Van and the last an outside framed covered goods van. All are 19 to 20 feet long, except the last which is about 16 feet. (GW Wilson, courtesy Aberdeen University Library)*

# Pre-Jones Coaches

Prior to Stroudley's arrival on the scene, the responsibility for the design, specification and supervision of locomotives and rolling stock construction was undertaken by Alexander Allan. In this context, therefore, it is perhaps not surprising to find some similarity between the plant supplied to the Inverness & Nairn Railway and Inverness & Aberdeen Junction Railway and that of his employer, the Scottish Central; although mention has also been made of some of the earliest following the precedent set by their intended neighbour the Great North of Scotland Railway.

Orders were placed by the Inverness & Nairn Railway with Brown & Marshall for three First-class carriages for £1,065, two similar to Deeside Railway

and one like GNSR examples; four Third-class carriages for £800 and one brake van £215. Four carriages and the brake van arrived on 5 October 1855 and all but one of the remaining coaches by two weeks later. Faulds supplied two carriage trucks for £150. With the line having opened on 5 November, by the beginning of the next month the Manager, Andrew Dougall, was recommending the purchase of more carriages, as a consequence of which six Third-class and a luggage van from Brown & Marshall were authorised by the end of the year.

With this stock the I&NR carried on operations until, with the development of the line eastwards under the auspices of the I&AJR, further stock was required in anticipation of opening first from Nairn to Dalvey on 22

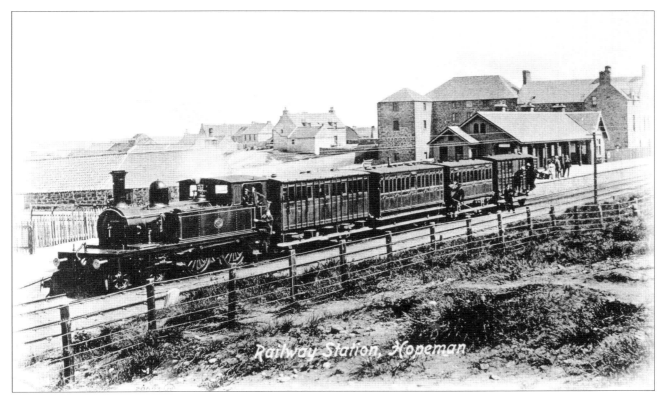

*Yankee Tank No. 101 in Jones livery at Hopemen following the extension of the branch from Burghead in 1892 and before repainting in Drummond livery sometime after his arrival in 1896. An interesting collection of old 4-wheel coaches make up the branch train, consisting of a 5-compartment rib-sided Third, a 5-compartment flush sided Composite, a shorter flush-sided Saloon and a Passenger Brake Van. The first may be to diagram 23 and the last to diagram 32, while the second and third coaches may have originally been of that form or have possibly been heavily altered during their lives. They seem to have escaped the preparation of the diagram book in 1901. Nonetheless, they are typical of the heterogeneous collection of old vehicles that were employed to operate on the HR's shorter branches up to World War 1. (Author's collection)*

| I&NR 4-wheel Passenger Coaches | | | | | | |
|---|---|---|---|---|---|---|
| _Descr-iption_ | _Built_ | | _Intr'd_ | _Cost_ | _Body l x w_ | _Tare wt_ |
| | _By_ | _No. off_ | | _(£)_ | _(ft-in)_ | _(T-c)_ |
| 1st | Brown | 3 | 1855 | 355 | 20-6 x 7-4 | 9-0 |
| 3rd | Brown | 4 + 6 | 1855 | 200 | 20-6 x 7-4 | 9-0 |
| Brake | Brown | 1 + 1 | 1855 | 215 | 20-6 x 7-4 | 10-0 |
| OCT | Faulds | 2 | 1855 | 150 | | |

| I&AJR 4-wheel Passenger Coaches pre-1863 | | | | | | | |
|---|---|---|---|---|---|---|---|
| _1901 diagram_ | _Description_ | _Type_ | _Built by_ | _Intr'd_ | _Body l x w (ft-in)_ | _Nos. HR_ | _Tare wt (T-c)_ |
| | Brake | | Brown | | 20-10 x 7-9½ | | |
| | Mail | | Brown | | 20-10 x 7-9½ | | |
| 24? | 3rd | F? | | c'60 | | | |
| | Bke/3rd | | | c'60 | 20-1 x 7-4 | 75-78 | 8-0 |

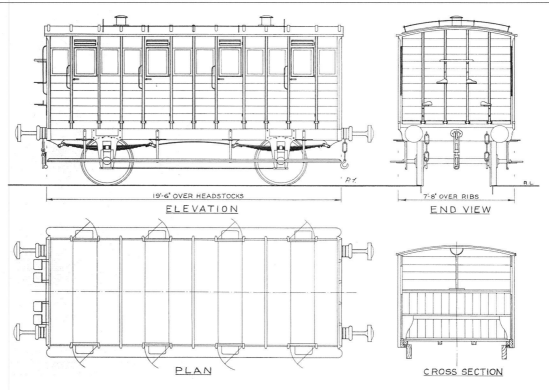

_Figure 6 - Inverness & Aberdeen Junction Railway 4-wheel 4-compartment un-diagrammed Third-class rib-sided coach.  (Author)_

December 1857, beyond to Elgin on 25 March 1858 and finally to Keith by 18 August the same year.  Here it met up with the Great North of Scotland thereby opening up a through route to Aberdeen and the rest of the country further south.  In the process the I&AJR took over the engines, carriages, trucks and wagons and also the plant in the workshops and warehouses of the I&NR on 30 June 1858.

Ongoing increases in traffic led in August 1861 to the ordering from Joseph Wright & Sons, Birmingham of ten Third-class carriages and two

Passenger Vans all at £216 each, while a month later three First-class carriages at £408 each were added to the former's order.

The requirement for rolling stock of all kinds took an even greater leap with preparations for the opening of the Inverness and Perth Junction Railway in phases during 1863.  The purchase of locomotives and rolling stock was entrusted to the I&AJR.  To this end in September 1862 the contract to supply the following was placed with the Metropolitan Carriage & Wagon Co, Saltley Works, Birmingham (late J Wright & Sons):

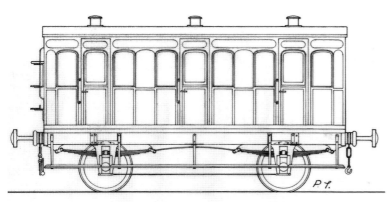

**Left,** *Figure 7 - I&AJR 4-wheel 3-compartment un-diagrammed First-class coach. (Author)*
**Bottom -** *The great and the good stand proudly in front of a 4-wheeled rib-sided coach at Helmsdale on the occasion of the visit of the Prince and Princess Christian (she was a daughter of Queen Victoria) in September 1870, when they were taken there by the Duke of Sutherland on Saturday 17th. This was well in advance of the inauguration of a passenger service on the Duke's Railway which appears to have started on 1 November. This coach had been converted into a Brake Third. (Ballast Trust/HRS collection).*

| 20 | 1st class carriages | @£390 each |
|---|---|---|
| 4 | Composite carriages | @ £322-10 |
| 31 | 3rd class carriages | @ £216 |
| 17 | Vans | @ £215 |
| 8 | Guards brake vans | @ £144 |
| 3 | Horse boxes | @ £158 |
| 3 | Carriage trucks | @ £104-10 |

One First-class saloon was envisaged as early as 1862.

To date all passenger stock was mounted on 4-wheel under-frames with outside guard irons and luggage rails on the roof. The First-class coaches had three compartments, while the Composites consisted of one First and two Second-class, and 19ft 6in long four Third-class passengers carriages with a 11ft 6in wheel base. Limited contemporary illustrative material suggests that the bodywork was frequently with the vertical rib-sided construction to the body sides and ends, indicating single skin sheeting and therefore not offering much insulation in the cold weather in those northern climes. The window frames to the superior class exhibited three-centre radius curved moulding to

*The grounded body of a Second/Third Composite rib-sided coach with curved tops to the windows of the Second-class compartments. It was by then in use as a bothy at an unknown location. Note the stove pipe protruding from the end and the ladder hung on the side. (AG Ellis collection)*

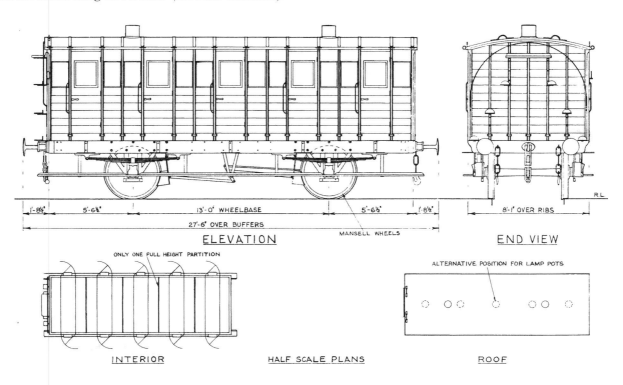

*Figure 8 - I&AJR 4-wheel 5-compartment Third-class rib-sided coach to diagram 23. (Author)*

the tops of the door and quarter lights, whilst Third-class windows had square corned frames. The original Brake Vans are thought to have had side lookouts. At least one included Third-class compartments and is possibly that shown in the photograph of the opening of the Duke of Sutherland's Railway on 1 November 1870.

Comparison between the three-compartment First-class coaches, however, shows that while those built by the Metropolitan Carriage & Wagon in 1864 for the SCR were rib-sided, the Highland's version photographed at Aberfeldy show panelled upper panels and flush external sheeting below with the joints merely covered with moulding strips. This arrangement and the form of construction have some, but not total, similarities to contemporary GNS coaches Type A1. It appears that the racks and transverse strips to the covering have been removed from the roofs of the Third-class carriages and Brake Vans. The Third-class carriages on the other hand remained at that period with exposed vertical ribs adequate for that class of passenger, although with time a few may also have been sheeted over, witness the branch train at Hopeman. One of the flush sided coaches at Aberfeldy appears to be externally similar to other First-class vehicles, but is marked up as Second-class on the doors of the two outer

| I&AJR 4-wheel Passenger Coaches post-1862 | | | |
|---|---|---|---|
| Description | | Built | |
| Type | Comp'ts | By | No. off |
| 1st | ? | Metro | 21 |
| 2nd | 5 | Metro | 4 |
| 3rd | 5 | Metro | 31 |
| 1st/2nd | ? | Metro | 9 |
| 2nd/3rd | 5 | Metro | 12 |
| Saloon | 1 | | 3 |
| Brake | - | | 23 |

compartments. Presumably the standard of internal fitting out reflected the intermediate status of Second-class passengers. Whereas the First and Second-class was provided with a lamp to each compartment, in the Third-class one was shared between two compartments. One Third-class carriage was replaced in 1868, while three First/Second Composites carriages were converted to First/Third Composites in the period ended 28 February 1869.

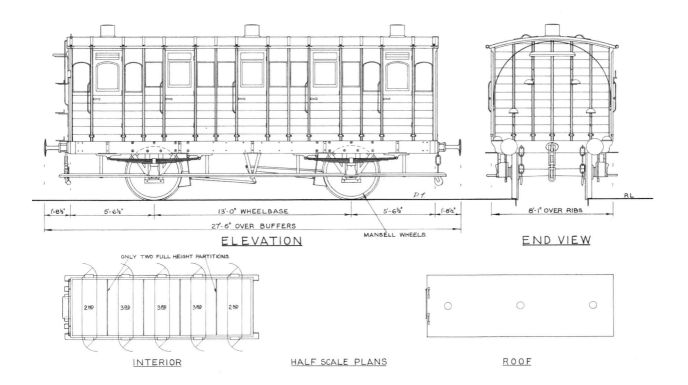

*Figure 9 - I&AJR 4-wheel 5-compartment Second/Third rib-sided Composite coach, later down-graded to all Third*

*The impending extension of the northern lines, which eventually reached Wick and Thurso in 1874, led to the need for significant additions to the stock. Here a south-bound passenger train is drawn up at Invershin station in Sutherland soon after the opening of the line throughout. Behind the locomotive tender is an outside framed covered goods van; a 4-wheel rib-sided First/Second Composite to diagram 10 and a Third-class to diagram 23, which carries a name-board labelled Inverness; and a 6-wheel Passenger Brake to diagram 35, all the coaches having been supplied in 1873. (GW Wilson, courtesy Aberdeen University Library)*

# JONES COACHES

By the time Jones took up the reins at Inverness, the bulk of the rolling stock had been acquired and was in service following the opening of the main line to Perth and a start made on the lines to the north. Leaving aside the opening of the extension from Bonar Bridge to Golspie and the Skye line to Strome Ferry, for which no special purchase of passenger vehicles appears to have been made; the next challenge was to provide for the working of the extension of the Sutherland and Caithness line to Wick and Thurso on 28 July 1874. For this he continued to employ improved versions of the 4-wheeled stock acquired a decade earlier, except that 6 wheels were considered necessary for the Passenger Brake Vans.

Finally, by the time the renewal of the older stock was becoming necessary, the rib sides were replaced by the straight vertical sided panelled design with radiused corners, as described above. So far all carriages are thought to have been rib-sided, but the four carriages to diagram 20 were definitely panelled, while the increase in width from 7ft 4in to 7ft 11in might suggest that those to diagram 25 were also, as Hunter asserts, but this author has found no confirmatory evidence.

The unusual style of coupé ended four compartment First-class rib-sided 4-wheel coach had appeared on the SCR in 1862, so, as Allan arranged for

*An end view of a First-class coach showing the windows in the coupé end. Note the spoked wheel to the left of the coupling part of the Newall braking system. (N Sinclair collection)*

*A 24ft 1in long 4-wheel rib-sided First-class carriage No. 36 to diagram 4 at Aberfeldy in 1912. Adjacent is Passenger Brake Van No. 9. (LGRP, HRS collection)*

# Highland Railway Carriages and Wagons

| Diagrams 1901 | Diagrams 1923 | Description | Type | Built by & no. | Date | Cost (£) | Body l x w (ft-in) | Nos HR | Tare wt (T-c) |
|---|---|---|---|---|---|---|---|---|---|
| **HR Jones 4-wheel Passenger Coaches** | | | | | | | | | |
| 4 | - | 1st | D | Metro 15 ? | 1873 ? | 517.5? | 24-1 x 7-4 | 24-40 41-55 | 9-10 |
| 5 | - | 1st saloon | E | Conversion | | | 24-1 x 7-4 | 40 | 9-10 |
| 10 | 10 | 1st/2nd (1) | B | Metro 10 + HR? | 1873 | 466.7 | 24-1 x 7-4 | 7-19, 81-2 | 9-10 |
| 23 | 30 | 3rd | E | Metro 20 + ? | 1873 | 290 | 24-1 x 7-4 | 74, 79-97, (136-55, 176-84?) | 9-10 |
| 25 | 31 | 3rd | G | Midland 20 | 1878 | 260.6 | 25-1 x 7-11 | 98-117(2) | 9-10 |
| 20 | 27 | 3rd | B | | | | 27-3 x 7-11 | 23-28(3) | 10-10 |

Notes:

(1)    Later all Second-class compartments were down-graded to Third-class, while following withdrawal of Compo No. 19 was converted into Brake 3rd for Engineer's Dept.

(2)    Nos. 103/6/8-10 sold to North Sunderland Rly in 1898.

(3)    Only two diagram 20 carriages were accorded LMS Nos., viz: 18716-7.

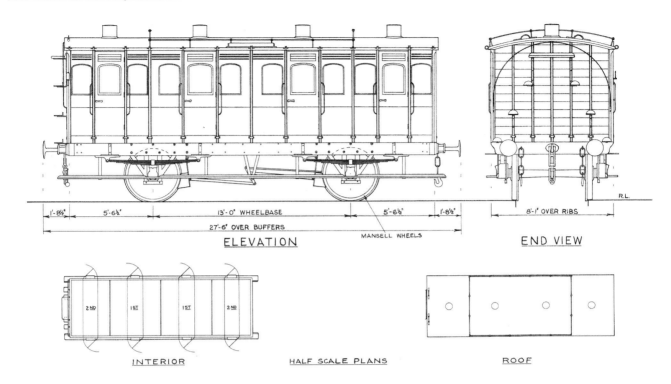

*Figure 10 - Highland Railway 4-wheel 4-compartment First/Second Composite rib-sided coach; later the Second-class was down-graded to Third to diagram 10. (Author)*

the provision of rolling stock to both the SCR and the I&AJR, it may be presumed that these had been provided to the latter from the early 1860s.

In 1898 Nos. 103/6/8-10 were sold to the North Sunderland Railway and scrapped or relegated to other uses by 1913. They were stated, however, to be 27ft 4in long with five 5 foot compartments and to have been built by Metropolitan, which better suits diagram 20! In 1900 the Locomotive Superintendent informed the Locomotive Committee that he had an enquiry from a firm in Newcastle-upon-Tyne for four old Third-class carriages suitable for use on a colliery branch line. Having four old 3rd duplicates to dispose of, the Committee recommended that they be sold for £60 each, while three years later it was agreed to break up twenty 4-wheel carriages Nos. 83 to 102. With 4-wheeled First-

class coaches still on hand the Committee recommended that Nos. 42, 45 and 49 and 4-wheel Composite No. 33 be made Third-class carriages. By 1909 4-wheelers were becoming an anachronism and it was recommended that they be replaced. A year later an edict was issued by the Board to the effect that rib-sided coaches were not to be used on coupled trains and banished to branch lines. Few, if any, remained to be taken over by the LMS in 1923.

**Jones Sleeping Cars**

Towards the end of 1875, the Highland explored with the Pullman Car Co the possibility of them running a sleeping car service on the line. However, the dead weight of the car for so few passengers on such steep gradients and the proposed 15 year contract were

***Opposite, middle*** - *24ft 1in long rib-sided Third-class coach No. 145 to diagram 23, typical of the twenty built by the Midland Wagon Co in 1873. (WG Chalmer's collection).*

***Opposite, bottom*** - *Another Third-class coach to diagram 23, No. 139 probably later in life, as it is equipped with vacuum brake introduced from 1890. It is nonetheless still fitted with wooden buffer faces and side chains. Along the cantrail can be discerned the loops through which the cords to the Harrison alarm system would be threaded. (HRS collection)*

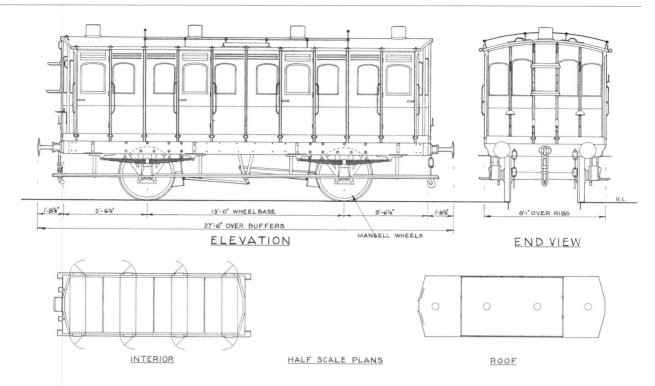

*Figure 11 - HR 4-wheel 4-compartment First-class rib-sided coach to diagram 1. (Author)*

*One of the panelled Third-class carriages passed into departmental service and was photographed on 16 June 1935 as LMS No. 297247 in use by the Telegraph and Electric Department at Inverness, with several doors sealed up, windows blanked off and external hand brake lever added. This survived until at least July 1939. (DLG Hunter, HRS collection)*

*Perhaps a more remarkable survival story still is the body of No. 23D, which had been partially incorporated into a building, before finally being rescued and sent to the Strathspey Railway at Boat of Garten, where it was photographed on 24 June 1983 awaiting restoration. (Author)*

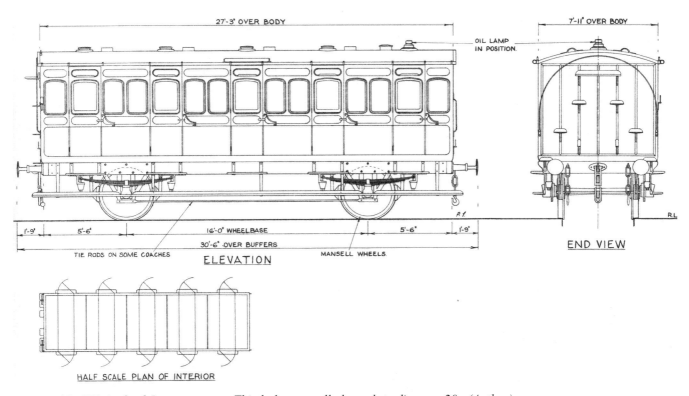

*Figure 12 - HR 4-wheel 5-compartment Third-class panelled coach to diagram 20. (Author)*

thought to be too onerous. Instead the Board had Jones draw up plans for their own car of 46 feet in length and 8 foot wide. Cleminson's Patent radiating wheels and axles (see below) were considered, but in the event bogies were chosen. Three cars were built by Brown Marshalls & Co at a cost reportedly not much less than £1,000 each and put into service from 1 May 1878. These were the first British side corridor coaches, although with no gangway connection, not least because each end of the coach was taken up by single coupé berths. As well as these berths, each car was divided into two larger sleeping saloons and two water-flushed lavatories. The sleeping saloons, one each for ladies and gentlemen, were in the centre elegantly furnished with comfortable rich scarlet coloured cushions, carpets and curtains. The women's three berth compartment, when not in use for sleeping, could be converted into a day compartment. The upper berths of the men's four-berth two-tier compartment, similar to the cabin of a steamship, could also be folded up into the roof when not in use to likewise create a travelling saloon.

Two cars ran on the 10.0pm Up and 12.15am Down (Nov 1881-Jan 1882 timetable) over-night services between Perth and Inverness, except on Saturday night and Sunday morning, with onward connections south to Edinburgh, Glasgow and London. On alternate nights the third carriage was put to use between Inverness and Wick, returning the next day. The charge for a berth was 5s (25p) irrespective of distance travelled in addition to the ordinary First-class fare. These cars were marshalled in mixed trains, with shunting to be expected at intermediate stations on the way. The Company was, therefore, at pains to point out that only passengers who were prepared tolerate the inconvenience and accept no guarantee of timing or achieving onward connections should travel. 97 berths were taken up during the first month of operation, netting £24-5-0, and 307 in the first four months on the main line. On the Further North line, however, only 22 berths were taken up during three weeks, and occupancy the following year amounted to one per day, so it was taken off. Nonetheless, the sleeping cars remained in use between Perth and Inverness until displaced by Pullman car service in 1885.

Hamilton Ellis suggests that thereafter they were converted into First-class corridor coaches. Whilst the half-yearly stock returns last show three sleeping cars in 28 February 1887, by 31 August 1887 the increase in Firsts was from 50 to 54, which does not fully confirm the suggestion!

### Jones 6-wheel Cleminson Coaches

As the length of carriages increased, four wheels gave way to six, but there was a limit to the total wheel base if the vehicle was to negotiate the curves in the track, not least those to be encountered on such sinuous routes as the Skye Line. The simple solution was to permit a small amount of transverse movement between the horn-guides and axle-guards of the centre axle, thereby allowing a maximum wheel base of 21 to 23 feet and hence limiting the body length to say 33 to 36 feet.

On 27 July 1876 Mr Cleminson, however, patented his self-adjusting radial articulated under-frames which permitted the wheel base to be increased to 29 to 30 feet and the body to about 38 feet. To achieve this, the three axles, with their axle-boxes, springs, and guard irons, were mounted on independent sub-frames, one to each axle, separate from and under the main under-frame of the carriage. The two end sub-frames were fitted with central vertical pivots, about which they were free to rotate in plan, whilst the middle sub-frame was vertically supported but able to slide transversely, while longitudinally constrained. Beneath the main-frames, the three sub-frames were interconnected by radial arms projecting longitudinally from the sub-frames and adjacent arms pinned together at mid-point by a short coupling link. As the vehicle entered a curve, the lateral displacement of the centre sub-frame relative the main-frame caused a small lateral movement to be transmitted through the linked arms to the end sub-frames resulting in their slight rotation in plan to follow the alignment of the curve; the reverse action taking place as it left the curve. It was claimed that by means of such self-acting adjustment, the vehicle freely traversed the curve with each axle in theory radial to the curve at each point of contact; not a true bogie but achieving much the same purpose.

| HR Jones 6-Wheel Cleminson Coaches | | | | | | | | | | |
|---|---|---|---|---|---|---|---|---|---|---|
| Diagrams | | Class | Type | Nos. | | Size l x w | Built | | Tare wt | Cost (£) |
| HR 1901 | LMS 1923 | | | HR | 1st LMS | (ft-in) | Date | By | (T-c) | |
| 13 | 15 | 321123 | E | 25-30 | - | 35-1 x 7-11 | 1879 | Ashbury | 14-10 | 499 |
| 6 | ? | Saloon | F | 56 | - | 35-1 x 7-11 | 1879 | Ashbury | 13-0 | 580 |
| 26 | 32 | 6 x 3 | H | 118 | | 37-9 x 7-11 | | | 18-5 | |
| 27 | 33 | 6 x 3 | J | 119-125 | - | 37-9 x 7-11 | | | 18-5 | |
| 14 | 16 | 133331 | F | 31/2 | (18638) 18639 | 37-9 x 7-11 | | | 18-5 | |
| | 21 | 331113 | | 83-5/90/1 | - | 38-0 x 7-11 | | | 18-5 | |

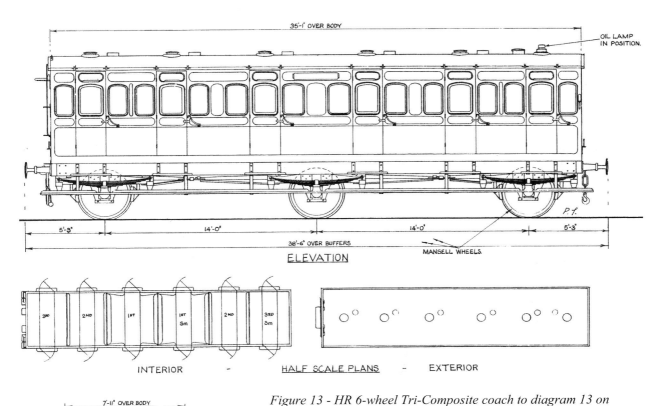

35'-1" OVER BODY

OIL LAMP
IN POSITION.

5'-3"  14'-0"  14'-0"  5'-3"

38'-6" OVER BUFFERS

MANSELL WHEELS

ELEVATION

3RD  2ND  1ST  1ST Sm  2ND  3RD Sm

INTERIOR  -  HALF SCALE PLANS  -  EXTERIOR

7'-11" OVER BODY

END VIEW

*Figure 13 - HR 6-wheel Tri-Composite coach to diagram 13 on Cleminson under-frame. (Author)*

### Tri-Composite

Diagram 13 was definitely tri-Composite, as a photograph of No. 29 following the accident at Dunachton, between Kingussie and Kincraig, on 2 August 1888, shows the inscriptions First, Second and Third applied to the door panels. When Second-class was dispensed with in 1893, the Second-class compartments were downgraded to Thirds. Thereafter one end Third-class and one First-class compartment were allocated for smokers, duly being marked as such on one of the quarter lights; whether earlier a Second-class compartment was likewise annotated is unknown. It is unclear whether these vehicles were automatic vacuum brake fitted from the outset, but, if not, it is apparent that they were by 1888.

### Family saloon

To cater for well-to-do families travelling with their personal servants, First-class saloons were made available. No. 56 to diagram 6 was provided with a saloon with tables and chairs. Beside a central passageway were a lavatory one side and a wash room opposite, leading to conventional seating in a compartment with a luggage locker beyond. On 27 October 1914 it was agreed to down-grade this First-class saloon to Third-class.

Like Stroudley on the LBSC, after receiving reports from the LC&D and LSWR, Jones used Cleminson's Patent 6-wheel flexible wheelbase for a number of types of carriage. Good in theory, but bumpy in practice! Nonetheless, some may have remained in use for twenty years, although by September 1906 quotations were being sought for the sale of scrap metal from Cleminson under-frames, suggesting that by then some of this type of carriage had either been withdrawn or remounted on bogies.

*The body of Tri-Composite No. 29 following the derailment at Dunachton on 2 August 1888, an adventure from which it did not recover. The breakdown crane has over-turned trying to lift the coach's separated under-frame, while a panelled 4-wheel Third lies at the top of the embankment. (Author's collection)*

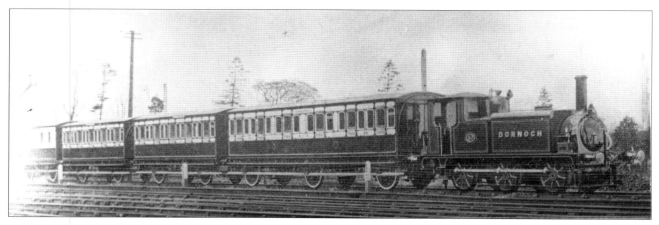

*A former Tri-Composite on a Cleminson under-frame, by then only offering First and Third class heads a train of recently renovated coaches behind Stroudley 0-6-0T No. 56* Dornoch, *probably in 1902, the branch to Dornoch opening on 2 June that year. The rest of the train is made up of two panelled 4-wheel Thirds and a 4-wheel panelled Passenger Brake Van. (HRS collection)*

### Third-Class

The all Third-class carriages to diagram 27 had six compartments. In 1886, Nos. 31 and 32 were taken in hand and the two end compartments converted to First-class coupés and placed in the 7.50am Down train from Perth, and 3.0pm up train from Inverness. Both survived to be allocated LMS numbers, only No. 32 carrying this; it went on to become a departmental vehicle. Again in 1909 Third-class Nos. 122 and 123 were modified to provide three First and three Third-class compartments at a cost of £51-10-0 each. In 1890 a Third-class carriage to diagram 27 was remounted by replacing the Cleminson articulation by bogies with 6 foot wheel base and assigned to Type H No. 118 to diagram 26. It was allocated LMS No. 18802, but this was never carried and it had disappeared by 1926.

| Diagrams 1901 | Diagrams 1923 | Description | Type | Built by & no. | Date/ con- vers'n | Length (ft-in) | Nos HR | Nos 1st LMS | Tare wt (T-c) |
|---|---|---|---|---|---|---|---|---|---|
| | | | | | | | | | |
| 1 | 1 | 1st | A | HR | 1887/8 | 33-3 | 1-6 | 18591-6 (5) | 14-10 |
| 2 | 2 | Lav/1st | B | | 1887/8 | 31-3 | 7-10, 12-23 | 18597-612 (6) | 13-17 |
| 3 | - | 1st saloon | C | | 1894 | 33-3 | 11 | - | 13-17 |
| 19 | 26 | Third | A | HR | 1888-93 | 31-3 | 1-22, 29-52 | 18694-715/ 18718-41(2) | 13-17 |
| 9 | 9 | Lug/tri-compo | N | Oldbury 8 HR 6 | 1889-1891 | 33-3 | 41/5/6 | 18648/52/3 | 14-10 |
| | 8(1) | Compo | - | HR | 1902 1908 | 33-3 | 1-6, 29, 42-4 | 18621 18637/49/50/1 | 14-10 |
| 21 | 28(3) | 3rd saloon | C | HR | 1897 | 31-3 | 53-58 | 18742-7 (4) | 13-0 |

**HR Jones 6-wheel Passenger Coaches**

Notes:
(1) Luggage compartments converted into First compartment.
(2) LMS No. 18704 renumbered 26911 in 2nd series and lasted until June 1938, while Nos. 18708/14/8/21/2/36 were never carried.
(3) Also LMS Northern Division diagram 28/13.
(4) LMS No. 18747 allocated to 972 in 2nd series, but not carried, written off in May 1955 as No. 18747.
(5) Nos. 18591-1 not carried.
(6) Nos. 18602/3/11 not carried.

## Jones 6-wheel Coaches

By 1886 the desirability of employing only 6-wheel coaches on the main line had been recognised. Dissatisfied with the Cleminson arrangement for any further construction, a compromise in length was made by adopting the more conventional layout of 6-wheel under-frame with a 10ft 6in plus 10ft 6in wheelbase, 1½ inch side play on the centre axle being found sufficient on the HR and resulting in a body length of 31ft 3in or 33ft 3in. Utilising these two options, two forms of all First-class; a Luggage Composite; a 5-compartment Third-class; a Third-class saloon; and two versions of Passenger Brake Van were developed. All were fitted with automatic vacuum brake, while the 5-compartment First-class coaches, at least, were also still equipped

*Jones 6-wheel Lavatory First No. 15 to diagram 2 in the sidings beside Perth General station in the two-tone livery current between 1896 and 1902. The destination board in the left-hand eaves panel reads: Inverness & Perth. Unfortunately insufficient of the Jones mail van to the left is showing to determine its type. (HRS collection)*

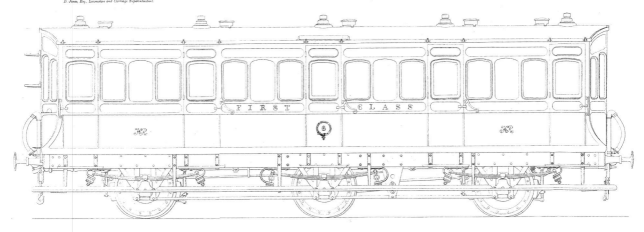

FIRST CLASS CARRIAGE.  HIGHLAND RAILWAY.
D. Jones, Esq., Locomotive and Carriage Superintendent.

THE RAILWAY ENGINEER.

FIRST CLASS

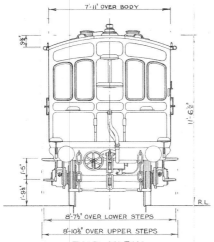

7'-11" OVER BODY

9¾"

11'-6½"

1'-5"

1'-9½"

R.L

8'-7½" OVER LOWER STEPS

8'-10½" OVER UPPER STEPS

END VIEW

**Top and right,** *Figure 14 - HR 6-wheel 5-compartment First-class coach. (Railway Engineer, author's collection)*

**Left and bottom,** *Figure 15 - HR 6-wheel 4-compartment Lavatory First-class coach. (Author)*

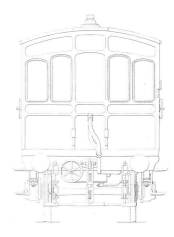

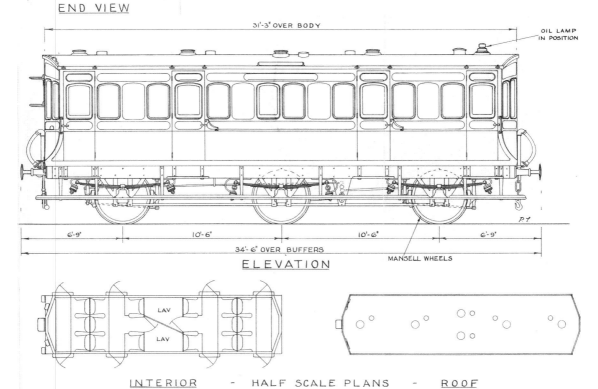

31'-3" OVER BODY

OIL LAMP IN POSITION

6'-9"        10'-6"        10'-6"        6'-9"

34'-6" OVER BUFFERS

ELEVATION

MANSELL WHEELS

P.1

INTERIOR    -    HALF SCALE PLANS    -    ROOF

LAV

LAV

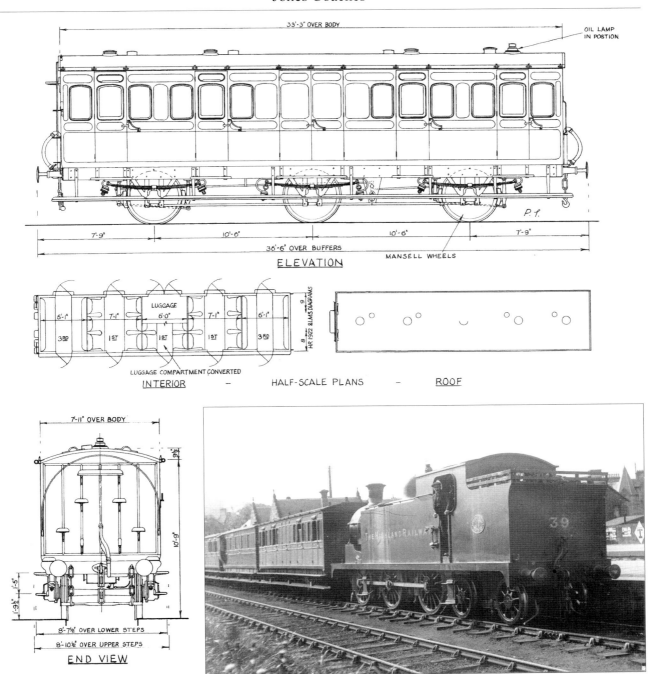

*Figure 16 - HR 6-wheel 4-compartment Luggage First/Third-class Composite coach. (Author)*

**Above -** *Peter Drummond Banking Tank 0-6-4T No. 39 at the head of the branch train of Jones 6-wheel stock at Aberfeldy in 1912. The leading coach is a Locker Composite to diagram 9, followed by a Passenger Brake Van and another Composite. (LGRP, author's collection)*

with the Newall brake. Except where noted, most were withdrawn soon after grouping.

### First-Class Coaches

The six the 5-compartment First-class coaches without

lavatories to diagram 1 were mounted on the longer under-frame, whilst the 4-compartment Lavatory version to HR Diagram 2 required the shorter. Both types had coupé compartments at each end. As before in plan these featured the chamfered ends, but this time the

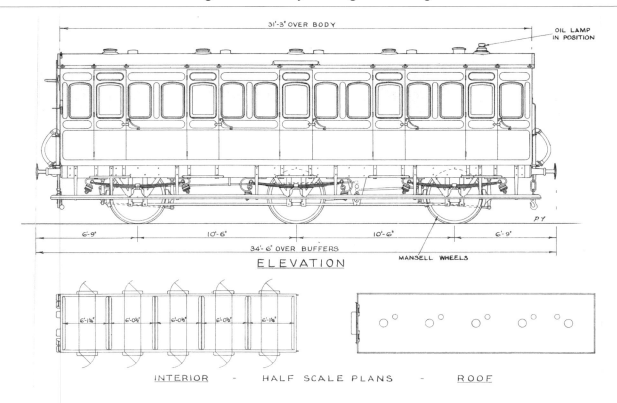

31'-3" OVER BODY

OIL LAMP
IN POSITION

6'-9"    10'-6"    10'-6"    6'-9"

34'-6" OVER BUFFERS

MANSELL WHEELS

ELEVATION

6'-1⅛"   6'-0½"   6'-0½"   6'-0½"   6'-1⅛"

INTERIOR   -   HALF SCALE PLANS   -   ROOF

7'-11" OVER BODY

8'-7½" OVER LOWER STEPS

8'-10½" OVER UPPER STEPS

END VIEW

*Figure 17 - HR 6-wheel 5-compartment Third-class coach to diagram 19. (Author)*

lower edge of the chamfer on each side was swept out in a complex curve to meet the top of the headstock for the full width, described by Hamilton Ellis as 'chariot ends'. This was supposedly to accommodate the long legs of First-class passengers sitting to the outside of the compartment. To the chagrin of railway enthusiasts of the day, these carriages were not supposed to be marshalled immediately behind the engine and, if they were, to be locked out of use. Other than the sleeping cars, those to diagram 2 were the first coaches to have on-board lavatories.

An attempt to rescue the body of No. 21 from a garden in Inverness resulted in its removal on 27 August 1978 to Aviemore on the Strathspey Railway, where it lingered for some years. Remnants of the internal

furnishings indicated leather padding to the doors, droplights held in position by leather straps, deep blue cloth upholstery and its number painted on the inside of the doors. Unfortunately, some time later, when attempting to reposition the body, it fell apart and the components, other than a few fittings and an etched toilet window, subsequently burnt.

### Composite Coaches

For use on the through carriages from Glasgow and Edinburgh, eight locker Composite coaches were ordered from the Oldbury Railway Carriage & Wagon Co at the end of 1888 for a price of £994 each. To HR diagram 9 these also used the longer under-frame. They had two First-class compartments either side of a luggage locker flanked on each side by a Second and a Third-class compartment, one on each side. In 1909, by then displaced from main line services, the lockers of Nos. 29, 42, 43 and 44 were converted into another First-class compartment only 6 feet wide, one inch less than the Third-class compartments!

### Third-Class Carriages

The Third-class coaches of 5-compartments to HR diagram 19 used the shorter under-frame. Internally

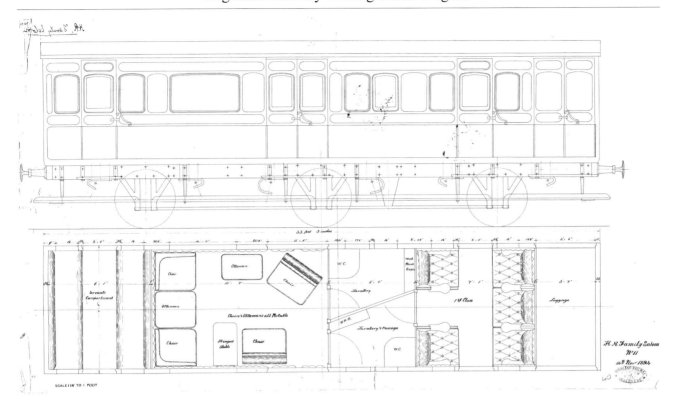

*Figure 18 - HR 6-wheel First-class family coach to diagram 3. (Highland Railway, GNSRA collection)*

**Bottom -** *Adjacent to the First-class coach above is a 5-compartment Third-class coach No. 29 to diagram 19. (HRS collection)*

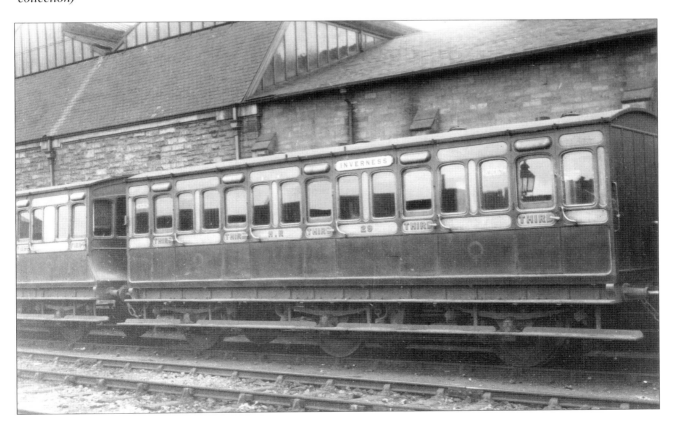

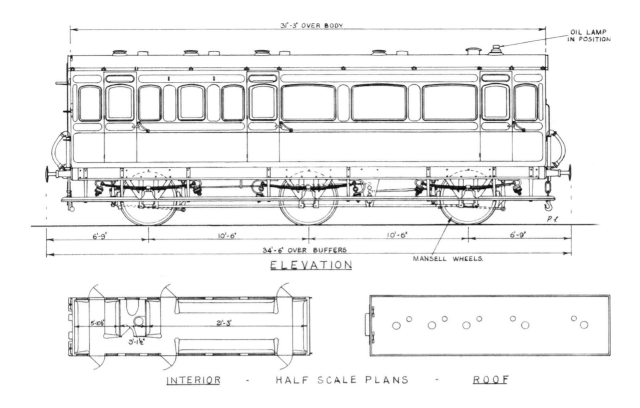

31'-3" OVER BODY

OIL LAMP
IN POSITION

ELEVATION

6'-9"    10'-6"    10'-6"    6'-9"

34'-6" OVER BUFFERS

MANSELL WHEELS.

5'-10½"    21'-3"

3'-1½"

INTERIOR  -  HALF SCALE PLANS  -  ROOF

*Figure 19 - HR 6-wheel Third-class saloon coach to diagram 21.  (Author)*

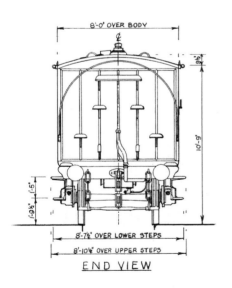

8'-0" OVER BODY

9'-6"

10'-9"

1'-5"

1'-9½"

8'-7½" OVER LOWER STEPS

8'-10⅛" OVER UPPER STEPS

END VIEW

**Opposite top -** *Jones 6-wheel Third saloon No. 53, also in the two-tone livery.  It is dual braked and still has the safety chains each side of the draw hook, but lacks any sign of the Newall brake gear.  Note the loose cord of the Harrison alarm system hanging between the loops below the cantrail. (HRS collection)*

**Opposite bottom -** *A part view of a Jones Third-class saloon in LMS fully lined livery in the sidings beside the ticket platform on the northern outskirts of Perth, as rebuilt Loch class No. 14392* Loch Naver *is about to pass with a local train.  (AG Ellis collection)*

they were provided with luggage racks, cushions and curtains, together with Maxwell patent double-locking doors latches.

access to a First compartment with conventional seating for five persons as well as the saloon.  A separate compartment for the servants and a locker for luggage were provided at each end.  It also was converted into a Third-class saloon in 1914.

### Family saloons

First-class saloon No. 11 to diagram 3 was built in 1894 principally for use by families, although with double doors could equally serve as an invalid saloon.  It had a central saloon with a hinged table, an Ottoman and easy chairs, three of which could have formed a bed; also two lavatories; one of which, by virtue of two doors, gave

### Third-Class Saloons

The five Third-class saloons to HR diagram 21 were 8 foot wide, an extra one inch over most previous designs at 7ft 11in, achieved by a slight tumble-home in the sides.  The sides were a mirror image of each other, except that the doors were still hung on the left hand side.  Obscure glass was fitted in the lavatory window together with that opposite on the corridor side.  Curtains were provided inside the windows and smoking was permitted.   The carriages were originally oil-lit, later converted to gas.

47

## Jones' Bogie Coaches

The Company having found the Cleminson Patent 6-wheel articulation system unsatisfactory, a number of vehicles so fitted were in due course provided instead with a pair of bogies. Despite this not all were converted and examples survived for what might regarded as a normal life span. Whatever, towards the end of his tenure in office Jones embarked on a series of bogie carriages. On the other hand, early bogies were not yet fully developed and were not entirely satisfactory either. It is possible, therefore, that the earlier bogies were replaced during the life of the vehicle by the Fox type.

The bodies to all Jones' bogie carriages were 7ft 11in wide. As built the Composite and Third-class coaches were provided with individual steps outside each compartment. In due course these were replaced by continuous boards, probably by Drummond at their first visit to the workshops for overhaul. The Brake Third was fitted with continuous boards from the outset. All were originally oil lit, but subsequently provided with gas lighting.

### *Lavatory Tri-Composite*

These chariot-ended Composite coaches to diagram 15 were built by Lochgorm Works in 1889 with both vacuum and Westinghouse brake systems for use as through coaches on the 10.10am and 3.0pm to Glasgow and Edinburgh, returning at 9.25am and 4.30pm. The First-class passengers were accommodated at one end in one of the coupés and adjacent compartment each with adjoining lavatory. The Second-class occupied the other coupé without lavatory facilities, whilst the Third-class passengers catered for in two compartments. The introduction of a short corridor to a lavatory carved out of the luggage locker was a possible later alteration, which meant that the doors had to be narrower on that side. These were the only coaches in which initially second-class and later third-class passengers had access to coupé compartments.

As a result of complaints of rough riding at the turn of the century the crude pivotal type bogies of the Composite carriages running to Glasgow and Edinburgh were replaced by the more sophisticated swing link suspension type at a cost of £33 per carriage and in 1908 4 tons 4 cwt of old bogies was sold for scrap at 35 shillings (£1.75) a ton.

With the suppression of Second-class on 1 May 1893, the coupé end was downgraded to Third-class. In 1902, however, No 33 was upgraded to all First-class as

*Photographs of Jones's bogie coaches have proved difficult to find, but in this distant view of 4-4-0 Strath class No. 100* Glenbruar *approaching Achanalt with a train for Kyle of Lochalsh early in the first decade of the 20th century, the fourth vehicle is a chariot end bogie First or Composite in two-tone livery to diagram 15. The remaining vehicles are a Jones 6-wheel 5-compartment Third, a close van and a Drummond 6-wheel 6-compartment Third, while the last is Drummond bogie Lavatory Third. (AG Ellis collection)*

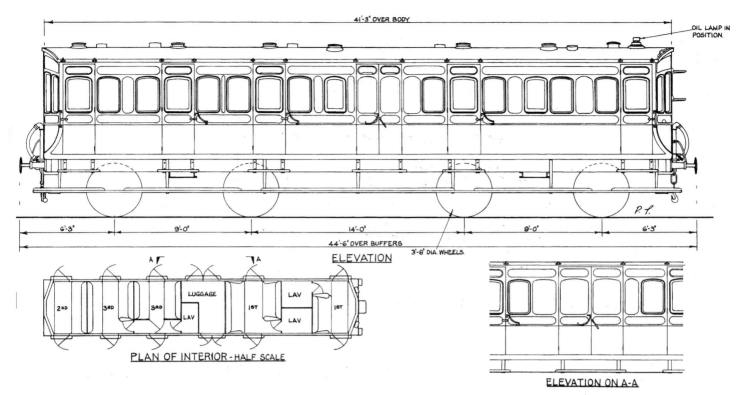

41'-3" OVER BODY

OIL LAMP IN POSITION.

ELEVATION

6'-3"    9'-0"    14'-0"    9'-0"    6'-3"

44'-6" OVER BUFFERS

3'-8" DIA. WHEELS.

PLAN OF INTERIOR - HALF SCALE

LUGGAGE

2ND   3RD   3RD   LAV   IST   LAV   LAV   IST

ELEVATION ON A-A

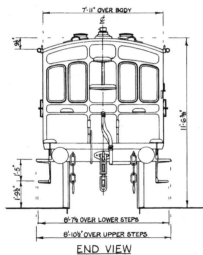

7'-11" OVER BODY

11'-6½"

8'-7½" OVER LOWER STEPS

8'-10½" OVER UPPER STEPS

END VIEW

*Figure 20 - Jones bogie Lavatory First/Third Composite coach to HR diagram 15. (Author)*

No 48 at a cost of £40 for use on the trains to Kyle of Lochalsh and although the Highland appears not to have issued a separate diagram for this conversion the LMS did, as their diagram 4. All vehicles survived to be allocated numbers in the LMS's first series, but the reuse of these suggests that all were withdrawn within three years or so.

### Brake Composites

Three dual braked Brake Lavatory Composite coaches Nos. 20 to 22 Type C to diagram 11 were mounted on 9 foot wheel base bogies with the brake compartment in the middle, and the lavatories accessible to one First and one Third-class compartment.

| HR Jones Bogie Passenger Coaches | | | | | | | | | | | | |
|---|---|---|---|---|---|---|---|---|---|---|---|---|
| Diagrams | | Description | Type | Built by | Date | Length /Bogie (ft-in) | Nos | | Tare wt (T-c) | Drg No. | Withdrawal | |
| 1901 | 1923 | | | | | | HR | 1st LMS | | | First | Last |
| 15 | 17 | CLLg | G | HR | 1889 | 41-3/9-0 | 33-40 | 18641-7 | 21-0 | 2503 | C'25 | C'26 |
| (15) | 4 | FLLg | - | HR | 1889 | 41-3/9-0 | 48(ex33) | 18613 | 21-0 | 2503 | - | C'26 |
| 28 | 34 | TL | K | Brown | 1893 | 46-3/9-0 | 126-135 | 18803-12* | 22-10 | 1232 | C'27 | 4/38+ |
| 11 | 13 | BCLLg | C | | c'95 | 46-1/9-0 | 20-22 | - | 22-10 | 2406 | | C'23 |
| 12 | 14 | CLg | D | | c'95 | 46-1/6-0 | 23-24 | - | 22-10 | | | C'23 |
| 30 | 39 | BT | A | Birm | 1896 | 46-3/8-0 | 1-12 | 18848-58 | 21-10 | | 6/14 | C'30 |

Notes * Renumbered 18965-7 in LMS second series in 1933.
    + These three officially withdrawn in April 1938 may have been written off, having been scrapped somewhat earlier.

## Luggage Composites

Two Luggage Composites on 6 foot wheelbase bogies Nos. 24 and 24 Type D to diagram 12 were also added to stock, with two First and five Third-class compartments and a luggage locker one in from an end. Although listed in the early LMS diagram book, neither the Brake nor Luggage Composites seem to have survived long enough to be numbered by the LMS.

## Lavatory Third-Class

The construction of this batch of coaches to diagram 28 was put out to contract and built by Brown Marshalls & Co at a cost of £690 each in 1893. The first five were equipped with vacuum brake, while the second five were also provided with Westinghouse pipe, with tare weight of 21 tons 10cwt. These were the first coaches to provide lavatories for Third-class passengers, albeit to only four out of the six compartments.

## Brake Third

The construction of these dozen Brake Thirds to diagram 30 was undertaken under contract by the Birmingham Railway Carriage & Wagon Co Ltd in 1896 at a cost of £730 each, six of which were dual brake fitted at an additional cost of £20 each. Surprisingly for a Jones design, a photograph taken on completion of No. 12 clearly shows Fox Patent pressed steel bogies and solid spoked wheels. One has to wonder whether in his final year he chose Fox's bogies otherwise usually associated with Drummond, or whether the later had already taken up office as construction was underway and instructed a change in type of bogie. Spoked wheels were quite usual under brake vans, but these were also passenger carrying vehicles and their adoption in this case was unique.

No. 11 was destroyed as a result of the accident following the washout at Carrbridge on 18 April 1914, otherwise most were withdrawn during the mid-twenties, No. 18858 surviving until at least May 1928, see below.

*The Brake Third-class Jones bogie coach, presumably No 18858 (ex-HR No. 9), is represented by this view taken on 21 May 1928 as 4-4-0 Big Ben class No. 14420 Ben a'Chait stops at Muir of Ord with a double-headed train for the north and 4-4-0 Skye Bogie No. 14277 waits in the bay platform with the branch train for Fortrose. (HC Casserley)*

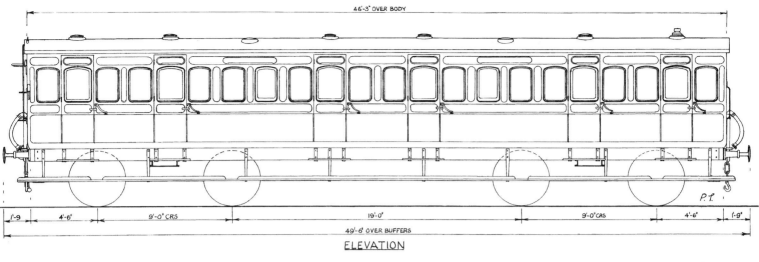

46'-3" OVER BODY

1'-9 | 4'-6" | 9'-0" CRS | 19'-0" | 9'-0" CRS | 4'-6" | 1'-9"

49'-6" OVER BUFFERS

ELEVATION

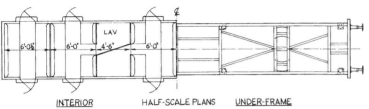

LAV

6'-0½" | 6'-0" | 4'-6" | 6'-0"

INTERIOR HALF-SCALE PLANS UNDER-FRAME

*Figure 21 - Jones bogie Third-class coach to HR diagram 28. (Author)*

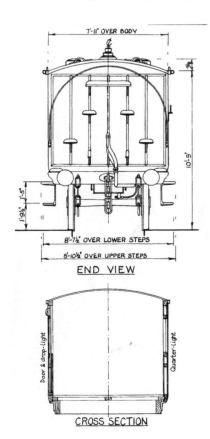

7'-11" OVER BODY

10'-6"

1'-5"
1'-9½"

8'-7½" OVER LOWER STEPS

8'-10½" OVER UPPER STEPS

END VIEW

Door & drop-light          Quarter-light

CROSS SECTION

**Pullman Cars on HR**

By 1885 the Highland Railway's own sleeping cars were becoming too small for the traffic offered and arrangements were made for the Pullman Co to provide two sleeping cars with sixteen berths and attendants to operate the service between Perth and Inverness from 19 April 1885. A fee of 5 shillings (25p), over and above the First-class fare for the journey, was charged and the custom over the summer period seems to have been adequate. By October, however, Pullman were complaining that takings were insufficient to pay the conductors' wages and so, to maintain the service, the Highland agreed to underwrite their wages of 21 shillings (£1.05) per week for the next year.

By August 1887 the cars were marshalled in the 12.40am mixed train departure from Perth arriving in Inverness at 8.5am, returning by the 10.0pm service from Inverness due in Perth at 7.0am, except Saturday nights in both directions. At the turn of the century the Highland tried to extend the service to Glasgow and Edinburgh, and initially the Caledonian and North British railways declined to oblige, but from 7 March 1904 it was run all the way to and from Glasgow (Buchanan Street), with passengers from Edinburgh joining/leaving at Larbert.

The component parts for four 36ft 3in long sleeping cars were manufactured in 1882 at the Pullman works, Detroit in the USA. Unlike previous Pullman cars, they were without end verandas and with entrance doors set in the middle of the sides of the cars rather than the usual end platform. Crated, these were transported to the United Kingdom and assembled at Derby for use on the Midland and Great Northern Railways. Accommodation was for sixteen berths in four compartments accessed from a centre aisle. Internal furnishings were in mahogany and rosewood with satinwood panels, upholstery in rich crimson plush with cream curtains. They were oil lit and heated by a Baker coke stove supplying a central heating system of radiators. The two allocated to the Great Northern Railway from 3 January 1883 to run between King's Cross and Edinburgh were initially

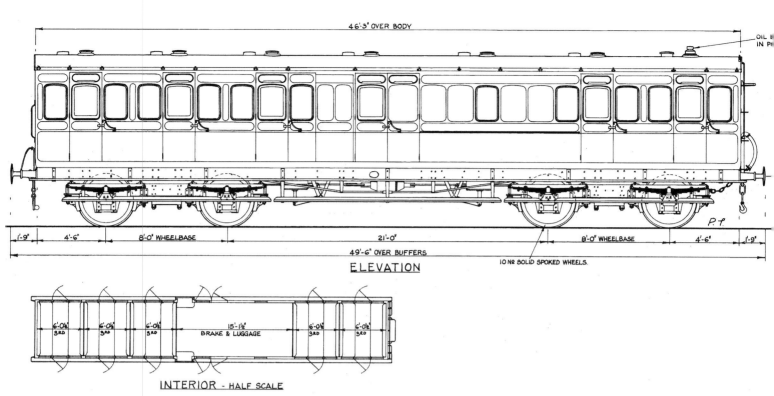

ELEVATION

INTERIOR - HALF SCALE

*Figure 22 - Jones bogie Brake/ Third-class coach to HR diagram 30. (Author)*

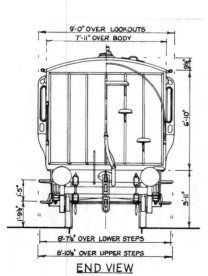

END VIEW

named *Balmoral* and *Culross*. They were not a commercial success, however, and so were available for use on the Highland system, where *Culross* was renamed *Dunrobin*.

Stretton, Radford and Lacey have suggested that these cars were intended to be on 6-wheel under-frames, but no trace of fixing holes for W-irons could be found when the surviving vehicle was examined at Embsay in 2009, see below. So it is believed that, if fitted with a 6-wheel under-frame, they were soon altered to bogies and were definitely running on these by the time they reached the Highland. With transverse secondary leaf springs these bogies resembled those of Clayton design on the Midland Railway.

The two Pullman sleeping cars operated regularly on the Highland from 1885 until 1907, when they were displaced by new Composite sleeping cars owned and operated by the Highland Railway. They were kept on hand as spare cars until August 1911, after which they were returned to their owners. In June 1915 the redundant Pullman cars were offered to the Caledonian Railway as spare cars, but this was rejected. They, nonetheless, remained in store available for use until 1918.

In 1920 both were then sold to Mr F Marks, a Pullman employee about to retire. He had them transported to Seaford in Sussex, the last part of the journey at least towed by traction engine. Placed side by side he created a bungalow in which both he and his two spinster daughters saw out the rest of their lives. Over the years the cars were gradually encased in an outer shell until, according to Hamilton Ellis, only the draw hooks projected through the walls, otherwise unrecognisable from the outside. It was only following the daughters' deaths, well into their nineties, that in 1987 the property fell into the hands of developers, who promptly set about it with a JCB until locals drew attention to the contents and rescue was initiated.

The body of *Balmoral* and remnants of *Dunrobin* were taken by the Brighton Railway Museum to the former Pullman works at Preston Park, where they languished along other historical artefacts for many years, eventually being recovered in 2000 and taken to Embsay, Yorkshire where full restoration of *Balmoral* is currently under way.

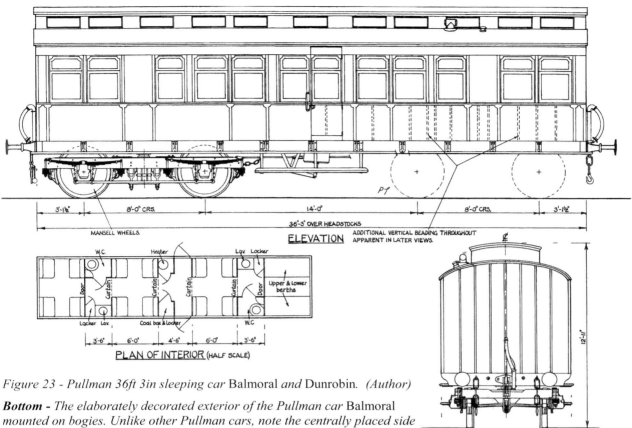

ELEVATION

ADDITIONAL VERTICAL BEADING THROUGHOUT APPARENT IN LATER VIEWS.

PLAN OF INTERIOR (HALF SCALE)

END VIEW

Figure 23 - *Pullman 36ft 3in sleeping car* Balmoral *and* Dunrobin. *(Author)*

**Bottom -** *The elaborately decorated exterior of the Pullman car Balmoral mounted on bogies. Unlike other Pullman cars, note the centrally placed side door and absence of end verandas. The Pullman livery was a dark, almost greenish, brown colour with elaborate lining in gold. The American style elongated serif lettering was in gold leaf, probably outlined in white and shaded below in cream and to the right in black. (HRS collection)*

53

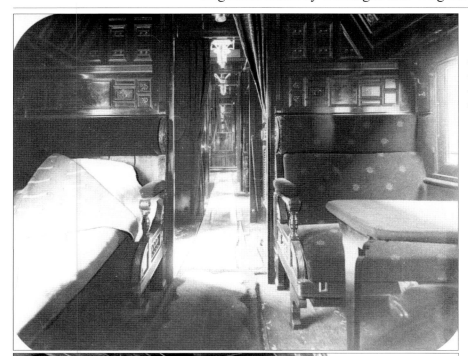

*The interior of a Pullman car showing the bed made up on the left hand side and for use during the day on the right. (HRS collection)*

*The two Pullman car bodies, having been built into a bungalow in Seaford for seventy years; finally saw the light of day following the two Marks' sisters' deaths when a developer commenced demolishing the building. Here the finely carved woodwork and small marquetry panels are exposed, the inclined moulding indicating the position of the upper berth when folded up. (Author's collection).*

## Duke of Sutherland's Saloons

It is a matter of history that in the development of the railway network in the north of Scotland, the third Duke of Sutherland, as well as having large holdings in the HR, personally took on the extension of the line from Golspie to Helmsdale and on completion put into use a steam locomotive and some rolling stock of his own. Once the Highland Railway took over on 28 July 1884, however, he retained ownership of the locomotive and a

coach with the right to run these on the line and this persisted on the LMS following amalgamation in 1923.

### 6-wheel Saloon

Following his father's death in 1892, as well as replacing his locomotive in 1895, the fourth Duke of Sutherland also acquired several saloons for his private use. The first was of was a 33ft 1in long six-wheeler with a 21 foot wheelbase built by David Jones at the Lochgorm

*The Duke of Sutherland's first saloon after it had been acquired by the Cambrian Railways, who made radical alterations to its appearance. As their No. 1 it now has a raised cove-shaped roof, but the detail of the window shapes, side ventilators, the end and its steps reveal its origins. (HRS collection)*

| Duke of Sutherland's 6-wheel Saloon | | | | | | | | | |
|---|---|---|---|---|---|---|---|---|---|
| | Diagram | Built | Date | L x W | | Nos | | | Wdn |
| DLGH | Cambrian | by | | (ft-in) | Cambrian | | GW | | |
| | | | | | | | 1st | 2nd | |
| 67 | S1 | HR | 1894 | 33-1 x 8-0 | 1 | | (9215) | 1211 | 29/8/31 |

Works in 1894. While in the Duke's service the central saloon portion was split into two halves, one with four arm chairs and the other with two couches which could be converted into beds. It was lit by both oil and electricity. A few years later the Duke, having in mind the acquisition of a larger bogie saloon, offered the older one to the Highland, but they seeing no obvious use for it were reluctant to make anything other than a low offer. With the arrival of the new saloon in 1899 it was, instead, acquired by the Cambrian Railways, who numbered it 1.

Once in their ownership various alterations were put in hand. Following grouping the GWR allocated the number 9215, although it is unlikely this was carried as, following removal of the centre axle,

from January 1925 it became No. 1211, a 4-wheel parcel van, being finally withdrawn on 29 August 1931.

### Bogie Saloon

The Duke was also a director of the LNWR and in 1899 had built for himself at their Wolverton Carriage Works a bogie saloon designed by CA Park, the Carriage and Wagon Superintendent of that Company. Internally, the carriage is divided into a 13ft 10in long full width lounge, a 7 foot long smoking room with adjacent toilet, three single berth sleeping compartments (two with adjoined toilets), a pantry, a luggage and attendant's compartments. There were vestibules at each end of the vehicle with end observation windows, but no gangway connections, allowing the Duke to travel in privacy.

It was finished to the very highest standards in

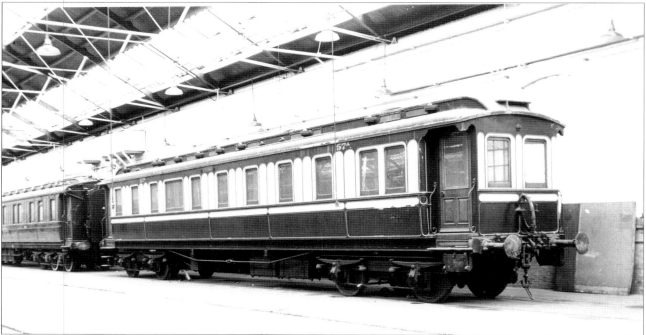

***Top -*** *A side view of the Duke of Sutherland's bogie private clerestory saloon built for him at Wolverton in 1899. Of typical LNWR style, this saloon was the precursor for the Royal train of 1903. (Author's collection)*

***Bottom -*** *A three-quarters view of No. 57$^A$ (below the cantrail) at Wolverton on 11 January 1958 showing the end vestibule and end windows in place of the more usual gangway connection. (HC Casserley)*

*The Duke of Sutherland's 4-wheel clerestory saloon No. 58A built for him at Lochgorm in 1908. It is seen here attached to his locomotive* Dunrobin *and was used for shorter journeys such as from Dunrobin/Golspie to Inverness. (Author's collection)*

dark Sutherland green lower panels, with white upper panels picked out with gold leaf and white roof and wheel tyres. Stone's electric lights, electric bells and electric fans were provided. A self-contained high-pressure hot-water system to warm the vehicle was provided, while conventional steam heating equipment was later fitted. Internally the wood was Spanish mahogany, white enamelled and picked out in gold leaf and the ceilings were figured in lincrusta finished in white and gold leaf. The lounge contained two moveable settees, a round table and four dining chairs; while the smoking room had two folding tables and four fixed chairs, the latter of which could be converted into a pair of beds. There were Turkish pile carpets in the lounge and smoking room, while Wilton was fitted elsewhere. The seating was upholstered in green figured tapestry with loose chintz covers with curtains and pelmets in green silk and chintz to match. The pantry was equipped with oil cooking facilities, a sink and a dresser.

### 4-wheel Saloon

A smaller 4-wheeled 25 foot long by 8ft 6in wide body saloon with 14 foot wheel-base, for more local use, was constructed for the Duke at Lochgorm in 1908. Within this was a 14ft 3in long saloon with side and end windows and a 10 foot brake van. The saloon was furnished with six arm-chairs and a table, while the brake van contained fixed seats. The internal decorations were of mahogany and maple, with the external appearance resembling the bogie saloon.

### The Saloons in Use and Preservation

The smaller of the two saloons was kept with the Duke's locomotive in the shed at Golspie, rather than at Dunrobin where that shed only housed the large saloon. The bogie saloon was used by the Duke on journeys to the south, it being attached to normal passenger services, while journeys north of Inverness were more usually made in the smaller saloon hauled by his own 0-4-4T steam locomotive, *Dunrobin*. The Duke often drove his own locomotive and train between his private station at Dunrobin in Sutherland and Inverness. Within these private saloons were entertained many distinguished guests, including King Edward VII, King George V, King George VI, King Alfonso of Spain, Kaiser Wilhelm II, Neville Chamberlain, and Sir Winston Churchill. It is interesting to note that the Duke's 4-wheel bogie saloon predates the Royal train of 1903 and that the style of the vehicles in the latter was similar. Could it be that King Edward's journey prompted the construction of his new train?

| Built at | Date | Length (ft-in) | HR | Nos LMS | | Disposal |
|---|---|---|---|---|---|---|
| | | | | 1st | 2nd | |
| **Duke of Sutherland's Later Saloons** | | | | | | |
| Wolverton | 1899 | 57-0 x 8-6 | 57A | ? | (45065) | Preserved NRM |
| Lochgorm | 1908 | 25-2 x 8-6 | 58A | ? | ? | Preserved Beamish |

Following nationalisation in 1948, however, the, by then fifth, Duke's arrangement was not acceptable to British Railways. To Britain, the unique arrangement of a rich nobleman's hobby of owning and running his own train on the national network thus came to an end, so in February 1949, the Duke advertised his locomotive and saloons for sale. A Lincolnshire coachbuilder recognised these vehicles from their description, and made enquiries. As a consequence, saloon No. 58A was sold along with his locomotive *Dunrobin* in 1949 to the Lincolnshire Trailer Co of Scunthorpe who made arrangements with Capt. Howey to display the locomotive and saloon at New Romney on the Romney, Hythe & Dymchurch Railway. So in March 1950 the engine and small saloon journeyed south to New Romney in Kent. Following Howey's

death in 1963 and an intermediate owner, in March 1965 both were acquired by Imperial Pageants Ltd of Victoria, British Columbia and shipped out to Canada. By November that year they were transferred to the Provincial Museum at Fort Steel where from September 1966 they were on display for many years. The saloon along with *Dunrobin,* were finally repatriated to Great Britain in May 2011, being taken on by the Museum at Beamish, County Durham and both are currently under restoration.

The bogie saloon, on the other hand, was by 1949 back at Wolverton and, after a spell at Clapham, was transferred in 1990 to the National Railway Museum in York. It is currently on loan to the SRPS Museum, Bo'ness for five years from 2011.

*Saloon No. 58A at Ashford (Kent) on 25 March 1950 at an early stage of its life in retirement. (AG Ellis collection)*

# DRUMMOND COACHES

The appointment of Peter Drummond, as Locomotive Superintendant in late 1896 to a large extent led to the adoption of Caledonian practices in rolling stock design. His arrival was concurrent with the need to provide additional stock in anticipation of the opening of the Direct Line from Aviemore: the scene was set for a change of style. The three-arc shape to the top of quarter lights and doors along the sides, so typical of Jones, was replaced by a straight top with radiused corners. Tumblehome to the sides and ends below the waist panel replaced the straight sides and ends, while continuous upper and lower running boards became the norm. For the first decade panelling continued; but this time the lower panels were raised one layer above the framing, thereby creating three layers. On the coach ends, instead of the rectangular almost square moulding bounding the vertical panels, the vertical moulding was continued to the underside on the low-arc roof.

By 1906 the need for greater economies in construction and maintenance led to the substitution of vertical match-boarding in place of the lower panels and ends. Initially the match-boarding was within the framing with half-round beading to cover the joint. This was found to be a maintenance problem and subsequently the beading was omitted and the boards taken down to the bottom edge of the bodywork to allow the moisture to drain out freely. Repairs to the lower panels were often carried out in match boarding, but the earlier style is usually evidenced by the continued presence of panelled ends.

## Drummond Low-Arc Roof 6-Wheel Carriages

Despite the introduction of bogie coaches on the main line, quite substantial numbers of low-arc roof 6-wheel coaches continued to be built up until 1909, presumably for more local services: although by the summer of 1903, 6-wheeled stock was supposed to be banished from line to Perth. These were 35ft 8in long and had an average tare weight of 14 tons. Most were of panelled construction, but at least the last four Third-class coaches, supplied by Pickering at a cost of £580 each, were match-boarded below the waist.

### Third-Class

With six Third-class compartments, early examples of HR diagram 22 up to No. 75 were initially oil lit and from thereon were gas from the outset, while the earlier ones converted in due course. The first six vehicles built were dual braked, while the rest only had vacuum brake.

### First-Class

The single example, No. 58 to HR diagram 7 built in 1900, had four First-class compartments each served by a lavatory, and was vacuum braked and gas lit from the outset.

## Drummond Cove Roof 6-Wheel Carriages

In 1907 the need for through Composites coaches from Perth to Aberfeldy and Inverness to Strathpeffer led to the construction of four more 6-wheel coaches of a slightly different style. A pair of 36ft 2in long gas lit

| | | | | | | | | | | | | |
|---|---|---|---|---|---|---|---|---|---|---|---|---|
| **HR Drummond 6-wheel Low-Arc Roof Passenger Coaches** | | | | | | | | | | | | |
| | Diagrams | | | Description | Type | Built | Date | | Nos | | | Withdrawal | |
| 1901 | 1923 | LMS | | | | by | | HR | | LMS | | First | Last |
| | | ND | | | | | | | 1st | 2nd | | |
| 22 | 29 | 29 | 3rd | D | HR | 1897 | 59-63 | 18748-52 | 26912-17 (2) | 1/34 | 8/38 |
| | | | | | HR | 1898/9 | 64-70 | 18753-9 | 26918-23 (2) | 4/34 | 9/36 |
| | | | | | HR | 1903 | 74-5, 81-2, 171-4, 187-94 | 18763-4/70-1, 18834-45 | 26924-38 | 1/34 | 1/39 |
| | | | | | HR | 1904 | 83-90 | 18772-9 | 26939-46 | 11/34 | 4/37 |
| | | | | | HR | 1907 | 91-2 | 18780-1 | 26947-8 | 9/35 | 11/35 |
| | | | | | HR | 1909 | 99-100 | 18788-9 | 26949 | Pre '34 | 8/37 |
| | | | | | Pickering | 1909 | 140-3 | 18813-6 | 26950-3 | 4/34 | 2/38 |
| | | | | | HR | 1910 | 144-5 | 18817-8 | 26954-5 | 2/37 | 1/39 |
| 7 | 3 | 3/16 | Lav 1st | G | HR | 1900 | 58 | 18614 | (27401) | 5/55(1) | |

Notes    (1)     Written off as 18614, probably scrapped years earlier, but not included in 1935 withdrawal programme.
             (2)     Nos. 26916/9/29 never carried.

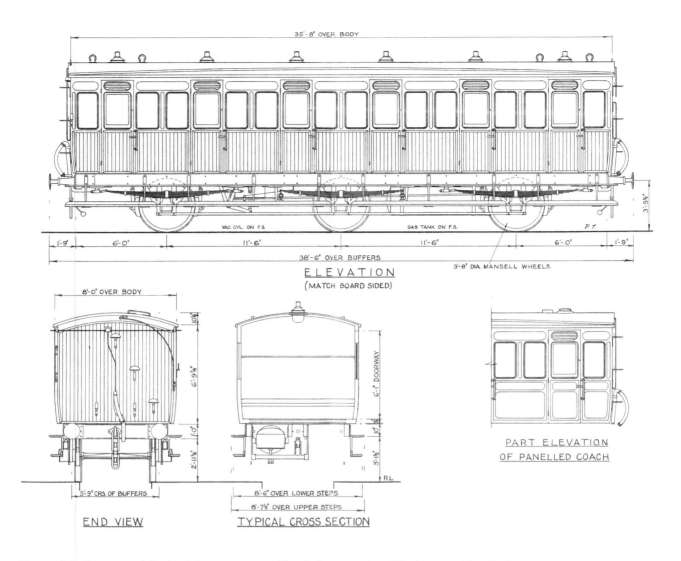

*Figure 24 - Drummond 6-wheel 6-compartment Third-class coach to HR diagram 22. (Author)*

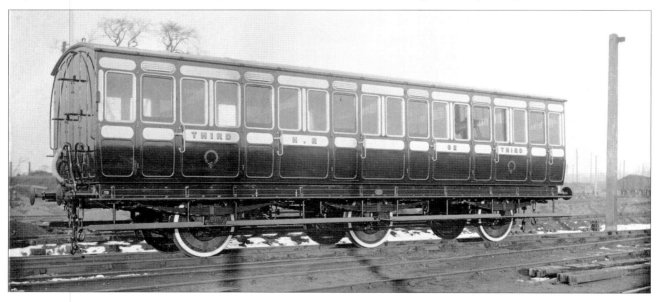

*Peter Drummond's design of low-arc roof 6-wheeled six compartment all Third No. 62 built by the HR at Inverness in 1897. This was photographed when new in green and white livery, equipped with dual brakes and oil lighting. (WG Chalmers collection)*

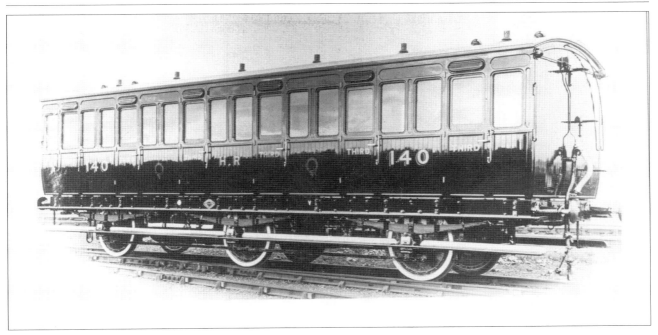

*The final examples were finished with vertical match boarding in lieu of the lower panels, gas instead of oil lighting and painted in all green livery, as exemplified by No. 140 built by RY Pickering in 1909. (RY Pickering, IR Steel collection)*

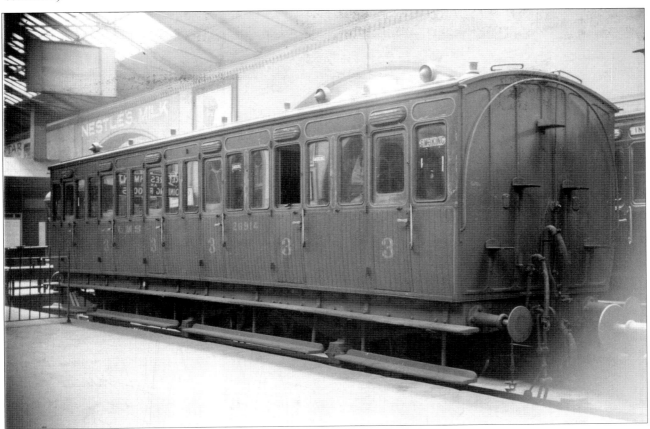

*No. 26914, formerly LMS first No. 18750 and HR No. 61, also built in 1897, at Inverness on 23 June 1938, two months before its withdrawal. Note that its lower panels have been replaced by vertical match boarding, but it still retains its Westinghouse brake pipes. The two end compartments are marked Smoking. (DLG Hunter)*

| | | | | | | | | | | | | | |
|---|---|---|---|---|---|---|---|---|---|---|---|---|---|
| **HR Drummond 6-wheel Cove-Roof Passenger Coaches** | | | | | | | | | | | | | |
| *1901* | *Diagrams* *1923* | *LMS* *ND* | *Descr-* *iption* | *Built* *by* | *Date* | *Cost* *(£)* | *HR* | *Nos* *LMS* *1st* | *2nd* | *Tare* *Wt* *(T-c)* | *Ligh* *ting* | *Withdrawal* *First* | *Last* |
| *58* | *22* | *22/45* | Lug/ compo | HR | 1908 | 690 | 86-7 | 18690-1 | 27233-4 | 16-0 | Gas | 8/37 | 11/41(1) |
| *59* | *23* | *23/46* | Compo/ coupe | HR | 1909 | 706 | 88-9 | 18692-3 | 27235-6 | 16-0 | Oil | 11/36 | 7/44(2) |

Notes    (1)     No. 27233 to Tredegar for workmen's set 2/39.

          (2)     No. 27236 to service stock as No. 297247 and subsequently preserved by SRPS, at Bo'ness.

Luggage Composites appeared from Lochgorm the next year, followed a year later by two coupé ended Composites provided with oil lamps. By the time these came to be built, not only had match boarding replaced the lower body side and end panels, but the roof profile of the new corridor coaches, see below, had also been adopted. It was not until near the end of 1921 that it was agreed to add steam heating fittings in carriage No. 86 working between Perth and Aberfeldy.

The minutes of the Traffic and Locomotive Committees also recommended to the Board the building of a pair of Third-class 6-wheel coaches as well and a general arrangement drawing for such was prepared showing a similar 36ft 2in long cove-roofed six-compartment design. In the event, however, they were constructed as the previous 35ft 8in long Third-class vehicles to diagram 22.

Following its withdrawal from revenue earning service, LMS No. 27236 (ex-HR No. 89) was granted an extension of life by being converted into travelling dormitory van No. 297247 for the Signal and Telegraph Engineer's Department at Inverness. Twenty years later, with the centenary of the Highland Railway impending, a proposal was made for its restoration and inclusion in the celebrations, but time was too short. Nonetheless, it was purchased and its slow renovation put in hand in 1966, being finished incorrectly as No. 17. It is currently in the custody of the SRPS at Bo'ness.

*One of the two Drummond cove-roof 6-wheel Luggage Composite to LMS diagram 22 in LMS livery seen at Inverness on 29 August 1938, and as it survived to that date it must be No. 27233 (ex-HR No. 86). By this time the beading round the match-boarding has been discarded and all the panels adjacent to the quarter lights plated over. (DLG Hunter)*

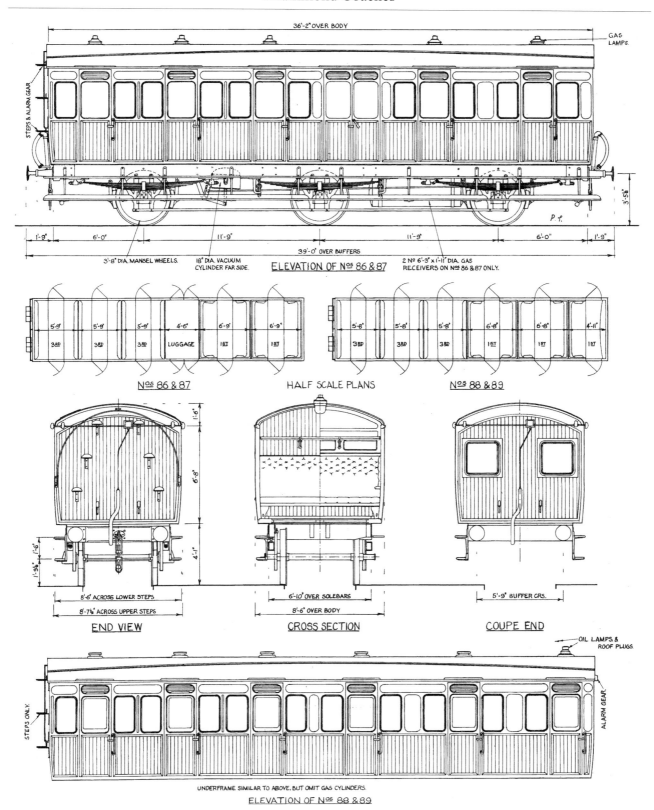

36'-2" OVER BODY

GAS LAMPS.

STEPS & ALARM GEAR

3'-5½"

1'-9"    6'-0"    11'-9"    11'-9"    6'-0"    1'-9"

39'-0" OVER BUFFERS

3'-8" DIA. MANSEL WHEELS.    18" DIA. VACUUM CYLINDER FAR SIDE.    ELEVATION OF Nos 86 & 87    2 Nº 6'-3" x 1'-11" DIA. GAS RECEIVERS ON Nºs 86 & 87 ONLY.

| 5-9" | 5-8" | 5-9" | 4-6" | 6-9" | 6-9" |
| 3RD | 3RD | 3RD | LUGGAGE | 1ST | 1ST |

| 5-8" | 5-8" | 5-8" | 6-8" | 6-8" | 4-11" |
| 3RD | 3RD | 3RD | 1ST | 1ST | 1ST |

Nºs 86 & 87    HALF SCALE PLANS    Nºs 88 & 89

1'-6"

6'-8"

4'-1"

1'-9½" 1'-6"

8'-6" ACROSS LOWER STEPS
8'-7½" ACROSS UPPER STEPS

END VIEW

6'-10" OVER SOLEBARS
8'-6" OVER BODY

CROSS SECTION

5'-9" BUFFER CRS.

COUPE END

OIL LAMPS & ROOF PLUGS

STEPS ONLY.

ALARM GEAR

UNDERFRAME SIMILAR TO ABOVE, BUT OMIT GAS CYLINDERS.

ELEVATION OF Nºs 88 & 89

*Figure 25,- Composite drawing of Drummond's 6-wheel cove roofed Composite coaches Nos. 86 to 89 to LMS diagrams 22 and 23. (Author)*

*Coupé ended Composite No. 89 to LMS Diagram 23 was converted for use by the Signal & Telegraph Engineer's Department, Inverness as No. (DM)297247. Here it is at Aberdeen on 10 July 1957. Later it was offered for sale and taken into preservation. (HC Casserley)*

*As can be seen of No. DM297247 at Inverness on 8 October 1965, some door handles were removed, two windows boarded up, external lighting fixtures removed, while a stove with pipe together with hand brake wheel were added. During repairs some of the panels next to the quarter lights have been plated over and the lower foot-boards curtailed. (Author's collection)*

## Drummond Bogie Low-Arc Roof Coaches

As well as renewing old 4-wheel coaches by replacing them with new 6-wheel coaches for routine work over the system as a whole, bogie lavatory stock, often Composite First and Third-classes, were required for front-line duties as through coaches from Edinburgh and Glasgow to Inverness. The bodywork was rested on a combination of steel section and timber under-frames mounted on Fox's 8-foot wheelbase pressed steel bogies. All had a tare weight of 22 tons 10 cwt, except the Brake Thirds which weighed a ton less.

In October 1899, the Traffic Committee had considered the possibility of rebuilding six Third-class carriages dating from 1863/4 as three coaches mounted on bogies at a cost of £1,534, but, perhaps wisely, discarded the idea. In 1900 thoughts were entertained of exhibiting one of the new bogie Composite coaches at the Glasgow Exhibition and it was found that the cost would be £126, but upon investigation of the conditions the idea was dropped.

### Composite carriages

All types of Composite carriage were 46ft 8in long over the body. The first two Composites Nos. 47 and 48 of 1898 to HR diagram 16 had internal corridors giving access to a pair of lavatories for the benefit of all passengers in the three First or four Third-class compartments. This arrangement provided seated accommodation for 19 First and 26 Third-class passengers.

Thereafter, to achieve greater seating capacity, designs with two pairs of lavatories only accessible to the immediately adjacent compartments were developed. Nos. 55 and 56 to HR diagram 18 had longer than usual compartments of just three First and three Third-class thereby offering seats for 22 First and 26 Third-class passengers. Of the remaining and bulk of the vehicles to HR diagram 17 all had two First-class and either four or four and a half Third-class compartments. This was achieved by incorporating either a luggage locker or a half Third-class compartment. In both cases seats were available for 14 First-class passengers, but either 38 or 43 Third-class passengers.

Internally the First-class compartments were upholstered with moquette velvet and panelled in sycamore and walnut. Photographs of Highland scenery and bevel edged mirrors were mounted on the partitions. The Third-class compartments were upholstered in rep with stained and varnished woodwork.

| | | | | | | | | | | | | |
|---|---|---|---|---|---|---|---|---|---|---|---|---|
| **HR Drummond Bogie Low-Arc Roof Coaches** | | | | | | | | | | | | |
| | Diagrams | | | Descr-iption | Type | Built by | Date | Cost (£) | | Nos | | Withdrawal | |
| 1901 | 1923 | LMS ND | | | | | | | HR | LMS | | First | Last |
| | | | | | | | | | | 1st | 2nd | | |
| 16 | 18 | | Lav/compo | H | HR | 1898 | | | 47 | 18654 | (19990) | 2/34 | 8/35 |
| | | | | | | | | | 48 | 18655 | 19991 | | |
| 31 | 40 | 40 | Bke 3rd | B | HR | 1898 | | | 13-14 | 18859-60 | 25698-9 | '36 (5) | 6/37 |
| 17 part | 19 part | 19/44C 87T | Lug/lav/compo | J | HR | 1898-9 | | | 49-54 | 18656-61 | 19966-71 (5) | 2/34 | 9/38 |
| | | | | | HR | 1901 | 900 | | 57-62 | 18664-9 | 19972-4 (1) | '32 | 9/51 |
| | | | | | Ashbury | 1902 | 1,115 | | 63-68 | 18670-5 | 19975-9 | 12/34 | 9/51 |
| 17 part | 19 part | 44C | Lav compo | L | Pickering | 1903-4 | 1,114 | | 69-80 | 18676-87 | 19980-9 (2 & 3) | '32 | By '51 |
| 18 | 20 | | Lav/compo | K | HR | 1899 | | | 55-56 | 18662 18663 | 18968 (4) | u/k | 9/51 |
| 29 | 37 | 37/79 | Lav/3rd | L | HR | 1899 | | | 71-73 | 18760-2 | 18971-3 | 11/36 | 9/51 |
| | | | | | HR | 1902 | 865 | | 156-64 | 18819-27 | 18974-82 | 12/34 | 9/38 |
| | | | | | Ashbury | 1902 | 1,030 | | 165-70 | 18828-33 | 18983-8 | 2/34 | 4/53 |
| | | | | | Pickering | 1903 | 1,025 | | 76-80 | 18765-9 | 18989-93 | 11/35 | 6/51 |
| | | | | | H Nelson | 1904 | 900 | | 83-98 | 18782-7 | 18994-8 | C'28 | 11/51 |

| | | |
|---|---|---|
| Notes | C | As a Composite |
| | T | As a Third |
| | (1) | No. 19972 never carried, it and No. 18671 both down graded to all Third-class Nos. 18613 & 18969. |
| | (2) | No. 18678 down graded to all Third-class No. 18970. |
| | (3) | Nos. 19982 & 19989 sold to War Deptartment in May 1945 for use overseas. |
| | (4) | As down graded to all Third-class. |
| | (5) | Nos. 19966/7/72 never carried. |

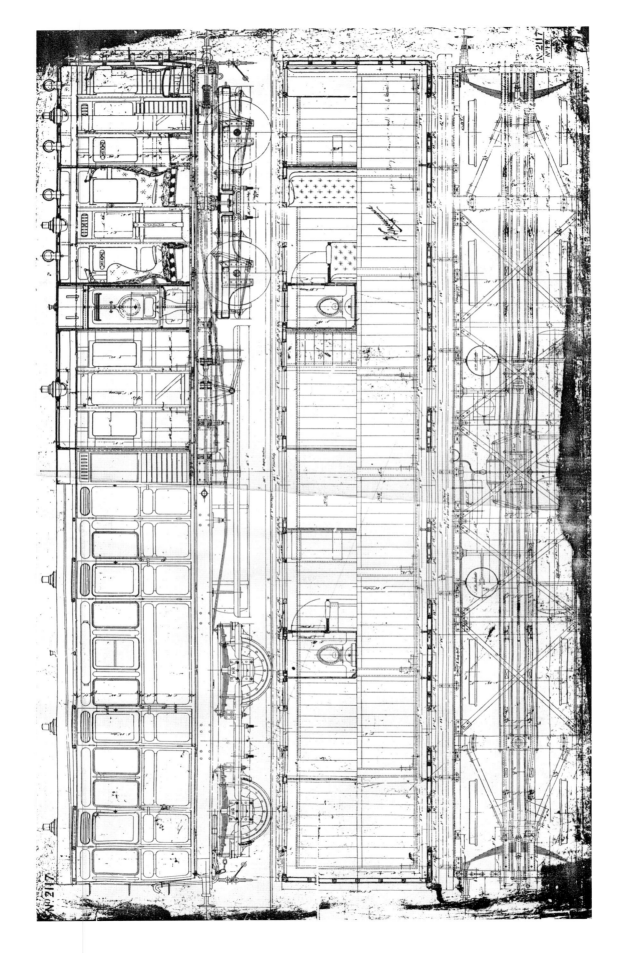

*Figure 26 - General arrangement drawing of a Drummond 46ft 4in bogie Lavatory Composite coach to HR diagram 17. (Highland Railway, author's collection)*

*Semi-corridor bogie Composite No. 47, as built in 1898 at Lochgorm to HR diagram 16 with internal access to a toilet for all passengers of both First and Third-classes. This was one of two of a type that was subsequently not repeated. (WG Chalmers collection)*

*Subsequent bogie Composite carriages had lavatories only accessible from four adjacent compartments, as shown here of No. 70 built by RY Pickering in 1903. This is the later version with a Third-class compartment in lieu of a luggage locker to be found on the earlier one. Nonetheless both were allocated to diagram HR 17. (R Pickering, author's collection)*

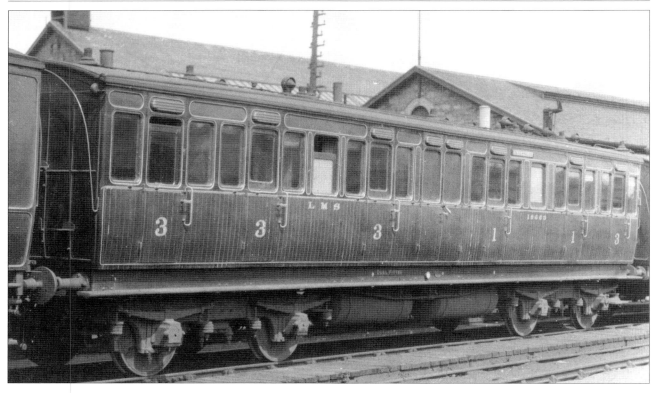

*Earlier production had included a luggage locker in the middle of the coach, as demonstrated by LMS No. 18660 (ex-HR No. 53) at Inverness on 19 July 1931 fully lined out in LMS livery. Its lower side panels had by that time been replaced by match boarding. (HC Casserley)*

### Third-Class Carriages

The seven compartment Third-class coaches with two pairs of lavatories were another two feet longer at 48ft 8in. They were built by both Lochgorm and contractors between 1899 and 1904. Examples remained in use until 1951.

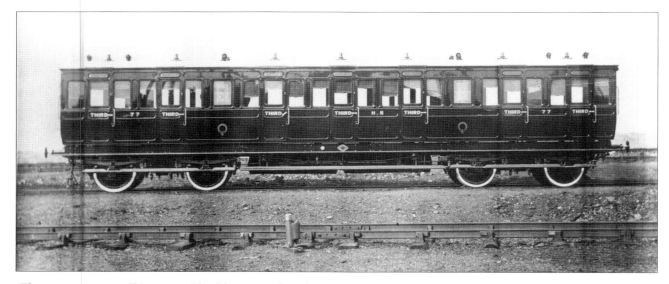

*The contemporary all Lavatory Third bogie stock to diagram 29 was built by both Lochgorm and contractors, No. 77 being supplied by RY Pickering in 1903 in the all green livery. (Author's collection)*

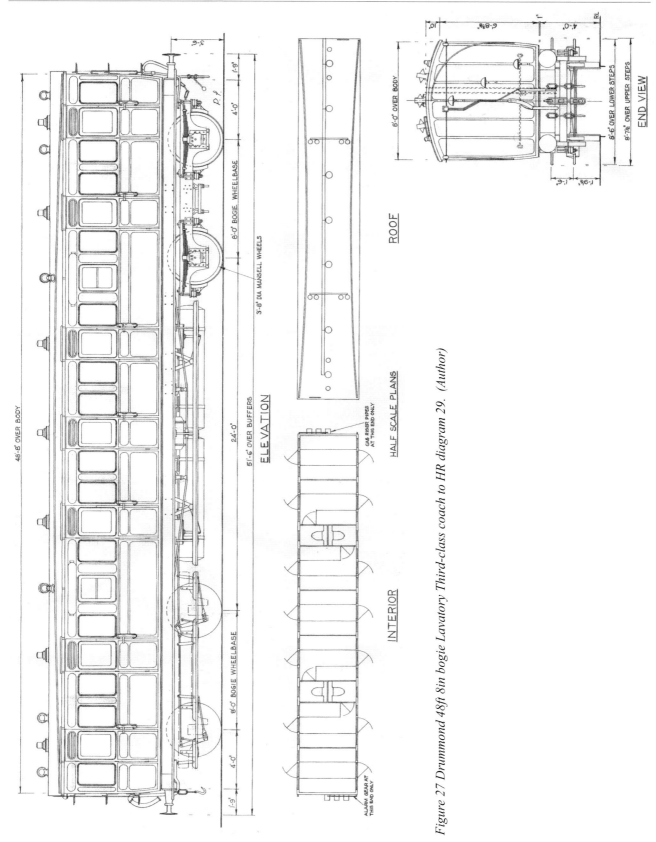

*Figure 27 Drummond 48ft 8in bogie Lavatory Third-class coach to HR diagram 29. (Author)*

*No. 96 was provided by Hurst Nelson the following year. The two end compartments were marked for smoking and were therefore fitted with pair of roof ventilators each. Otherwise ventilators were only fitted over the toilets. (AG Ellis collection)*

*LMS second series No. 18997, built as HR No. 97 by Hurst Nelson in 1904, was photographed at Inverness on 11 June 1938. Its panelling has survived remarkably well, with just a few lower panels repaired with horizontal boards. (DLG Hunter, HRS collection)*

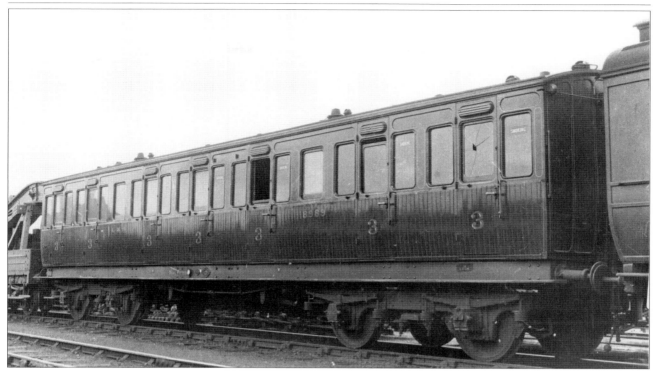

*LMS second series No. 18989 (ex-HR No. 76 and LMS first series No. 18765) however has had all its lower panels replaced, but retains a panelled end. The glass of the first door droplight has been broken and apart from a short length on the further bogie, the entire lower footboard has been removed. (WO Steel collection, courtesy RJ Essery)*

### Brake Third-Class Carriages

The Brake Third carriages, on the other hand had one pair of lavatories, six compartments and 9-foot brake compartment within the shorter 46ft 8in body. One of the latter became an Engineer's Department ballast brake van No. 297287 for the Highland Section. For this purpose many of the windows were boarded up and a stove added with projecting chimney, which one trusts was removed before moving out of a siding onto the main line.

*Brake Third (ex-No. 13) built in 1898 to diagram 31 relegated by 26 June 1938 to serving as a ballast brake van LMS No. 297287. Note the large letters E and H painted on the side. (DLG Hunter)*

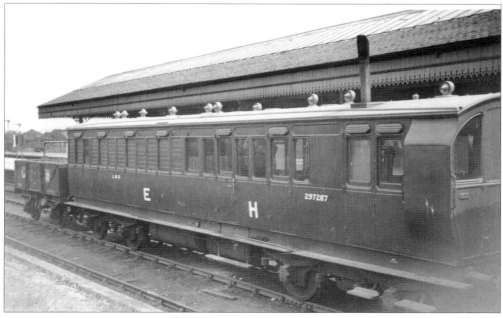

*No. DM 297287 still in service at Kyle of Lochalsh on 22 September 1960 by when the lookout had been re-clad with horizontal boards. (GE Langmuir, author's collection)*

### Director's Saloon

In May 1899 the directors of the neighbouring and rival Great North of Scotland Railway had travelled to Inverness and went on to inspect the recently opened Direct Line to Aviemore in their newly built First-class clerestory saloon carriage. Not to be outdone, in June 1900 Drummond was instructed to prepare a design and estimate of cost for a First-class saloon for use by the directors when undertaking inspections of the line, or other special occasions, as well as being available for hire by affluent families. In October they approved a bogie design at an estimated cost of £1,600 for construction in the Company's works, later adding the requirement for self-contained steam heating.

The clerestory vehicle was 48ft 8in long by 8ft 6in divided into a suite of compartments capable of seating 22 people. The central 22 foot long main saloon was panelled in sycamore and was furnished with a number of easy chairs with cushions and upholstered in mochette velvet, together with portable writing and lunching tables. Across the entrance passage was an 8 foot square smoking compartment looking out at one end with carved walnut panelling and provided with revolving easy chairs upholstered in Morocco leather. Beyond the main saloon in the opposite direction a central passage gave access to a toilet and wash-room after which there was a single compartment leading to the attendant's compartment. Across the other end of the vehicle was a luggage locker provided with double doors. Electric bells to summon the steward were fitted throughout the vehicle. Lighting was by Pintsch gas oil. The body was mounted on steel channel under-frames on Fox's pressed steel bogies and was dual braked.

This saloon is understood to have been fitted with telephone equipment which could be connected to the line-side circuits and is believed to have retained its two-tone livery until grouping. It was fitted with a steam heating supply from the locomotive in 1909. Its movements after 1923 are uncertain, but with its acceptance as an inspection saloon in 1934, it was given the number 45042 and may have been allocated to the Glasgow area, while Inverness gained a former North Staffordshire Railway 6-wheel director's saloon No. 45040. The HR saloon is presumed to have been withdrawn around 1947.

| HR Drummond Director's Saloon | | | | | | | | | | | | |
|---|---|---|---|---|---|---|---|---|---|---|---|---|
| Diagrams | | | Type | Built | Date | Cost | Length | | Nos | | | Drg |
| 1901 | 1923 | LMS | | by | | (£) | (ft-in) | HR | | LMS | | No. |
| | | ND | | | | | | | 1st | 2nd | 3rd | |
| 8 | 5 | 5 | H | HR | 1901 | 1,600 | 48-8 | 59 | 18615 | (823) | 45042 | 2527 |

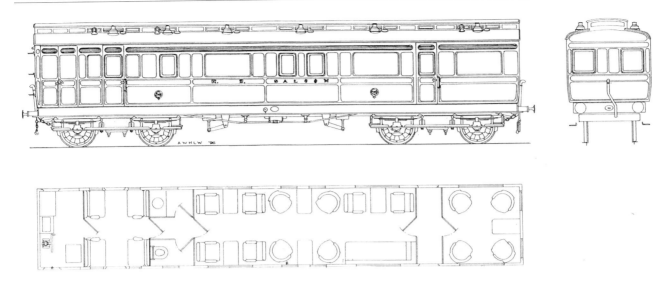

*Figure 28 - HR bogie directors'/family bogie saloon coach to diagram 8.  (AWH Wright)*

*HR director's saloon No. 59 built at Lochgorm to diagram 8 soon after its construction in 1901, painted in dark olive green with the waist and upper panels in white lined with gold.  (WG Chalmers collection)*

## Drummond Sleeping Cars

From early in 1905, the Company had started to review the sleeping car arrangements then still provided by the twenty year old Pullman cars now operating between Inverness and Glasgow.  They had in mind building and operating their own; by September going out for bids for two Composite sleeping cars with four First-class berths.  The limited sleeping accommodation provided in these, just four berths, suggests that the Pullmans were under utilised.

Hurst Nelson built two 50 foot long by 9 foot wide Composite carriage at a cost of £1,550 each.  Each of these contained: four First-class single berth sleeping compartments, pairs of which could be linked by a communicating door and upon which was mounted a bevel-edged mirror in the upper panel; an attendant's compartment; two and a half Third-class compartments with conventional daytime seating for twenty passengers; and a lavatory for each class of passenger.  The body was mounted on 49ft 4in long composite steel and timber under-frame and Fox's pressed steel bogies.  Recessed siide doors were provided at each end and an

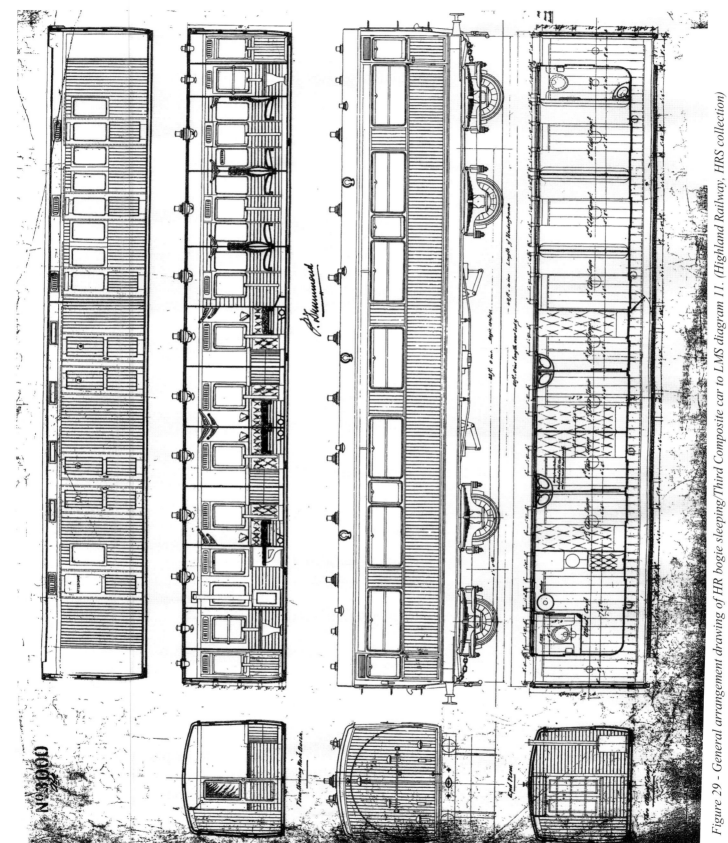

*Figure 29 - General arrangement drawing of HR bogie sleeping/Third Composite car to LMS diagram 11. (Highland Railway, HRS collection)*

| | | | | | | HR Drummond Sleeping Cars | | | | | |
|---|---|---|---|---|---|---|---|---|---|---|---|
| Diagrams | | | Descr-iption | Built by | Date | Nos | | | Tare wt (T-c) | Withdrawal | |
| DLGH | 1923 | LMS ND | | | | HR | LMS | | | First | Last |
| | | | | | | | 1st | 2nd | | | |
| 53 | 11 | - | Compo/ sleeper | H Nelson | 1907 | 8-9 | 18863-4 | - | 26-12 | | |
| - | - | 38/96 | BTK* | H Nelson | C'24 | - | 18863-4 | 6598-9 | | 11/36 | 3/51 |

Notes * Converted into Third-class corridor Brake circa 1924.

internal door across the corridor separating the classes.

Internally the lining to the corridor was in varnished cypress wood, the Third-class and attendant's compartments were finished in figured pine, while the sleeping compartments were in white teak. The couches in the sleeping compartment were fitted with woven wire mattresses with thick hair mattresses above. Patent wash-hand stand with flush out commode, towel racks, net racks and hat hooks, tumbler and bottle stands were provided in each compartment. The attendant could be summoned by means of electric bells, the knobs for which were conveniently placed in each compartment.

In the Third-class compartments the seats were formed again of wire covered in a thick coating of hair and upholstered in a corded cloth, known as rep or repp. Heating throughout the carriage was by means of a system of high pressure hot water circulating through small bore pipes which could be regulated in each compartment as required by the passengers. Externally the bodywork was of the current style with cove roof and vertical match boarding below the waist and all left as varnished teak, until painted green at some point during World War 1. Dual brake and passenger communication apparatus was fitted.

When first introduced, these vehicles usually worked on 10.30pm from Inverness and 10.0pm from Glasgow, arriving respectively at 8.42am and 5.10am. From 1 July 1913 the cost of a berth was increased from 5 shillings (25p) to 7 shillings and 6 pence (37½p). With such an early arrival in Inverness, a proposal was made that from October 1913 the sleeping car service should be extended to run north of Inverness on Thursday and Saturday mornings only. If implemented, the practice had ceased within two years. In July 1915 it was agreed to convert the cars to electric lighting. By May 1922 the numbers seeking berths must have increased, as costs were sought for converting the Third-class compartments into berths also, but by the following month it was decided not to proceed with this.

If the suggestion is that capacity of the existing sleeping cars was insufficient for the traffic offering, once the LMS took over, it was easy to transfer in larger sleeping cars for the Glasgow to Inverness service, rendering the by now seventeen year old cars redundant. Instead of being scrapped, however, the First-class sleeping and associated attendant's compartments were stripped out, making the half Third-class compartment full width and the remaining space converted into accommodation for a guard and luggage. This enabled them to serve out their time as a Third-class Brake Vans, LMS Nos. 18863 and 18864.

*The corridor side of bogie Composite Sleeping Car No. 8, one of two built for the HR by Hurst Nelson in 1907. Note that no gangway connections were at that time fitted. (HRS collection)*

*No. 8 again showing the compartment side with one of the lavatories and the two and a half Third-class compartments nearest the camera. The external finish was varnished teak. Note that access is by two doors only, one at each end. (Hurst Nelson, HRS collection)*

*By 1922 increasing demand for sleeping berths found these cars inadequate and with grouping they were replaced by the LMS, who then stripped out the sleeping accommodation and converted the vehicles into Brake Thirds, and if not already present adding corridor connections. (HS Orbach)*

| | Diagrams | | Descr-iption | Built by | Date | Cost (£) | Length (ft-in) | HR | Nos | | Tare wt (T-c) | Withdrawal | |
|---|---|---|---|---|---|---|---|---|---|---|---|---|---|
| DLGH | 1923 | LMS ND | | | | | | | LMS | | | First | Last |
| | | | | | | | | | 1st | 2nd | | | |
| 62 | 35 | 35 | 3rd saloon | Pickering | 1907 | 1,040 | 46-4 | 195-196 | 18846-7 | 973, (974) | 22-0 | 9/34 | 11/35 |
| 63 | 41 | 41/112 | BLT | HR | 1907 | 772 | 46-8 | 15-16 | 18861-2 | 25696-7 | 23-10 | 4/51 (2) | 6/55 |
| 56 | 24 | 22/36 | CK TK(1) | H Nelson | 1910 | 1,550 | 50-8 | 14-15 | 18627-8 | 19992-3 18598-9(1) | 24-7 | 9/51 | 9/51 |

**HR Later Drummond Non-Corridor Bogie Coaches**

Notes     (1) Down graded to all Third-class.
               (2) No. 25679 converted to weighing machine van No. 354909 and withdrawn 5/63.

### Later Drummond Non-Corridor Bogie Stock

As well as corridor bogie stock (see below), the latter non-corridor Drummond carriages adopted the cove roofed profile and amounted to three types of just two vehicles each, as shown in the table above.

In parallel with the development of the sleeping cars, plans for a pair of Third-class bogie saloon carriages for excursion traffic were undertaken. In 1907 RY Pickering built two such saloons 46ft 4in long by 8 feet wide to LMS diagram 35, each seating fifty passengers. Within there were two large open compartments with long bench style seats along each side and across each end, and long folding tables down the centre. The longitudinal benches made it difficult to look out at the passing scenery through the large windows without twisting one's body round. A lavatory and separate wash room were entered from the short passageway between the saloons.

Like the sleeping cars, the exterior was in varnished teak attached to teak framing and white roof, although they had vertical ends. Internally the lining to the compartments and lavatory was finished in varnished figured yellow pine. The seats were formed of wire covered in a thick coating of hair and upholstered in autumn tint coloured corded cloth and above which were net racks. The windows were provided with sprung roller blinds, while the ceilings were painted white. Within the wash room there was a wash-handstand with enamelled hopper, towel rack, hat hooks and water bottle. These saloons were equipped with dual brake and associated passenger communication apparatus and Pintsch oil-gas lamps with globes opened from inside.

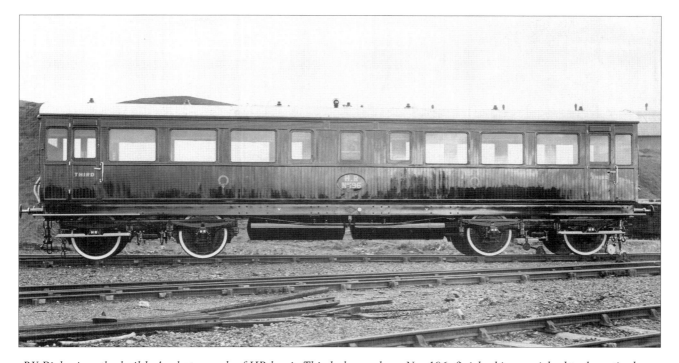

*RY Pickering, the builder's photograph of HR bogie Third-class saloon No. 196, finished in varnished teak vertical match-boarding. (RY Pickering, IR Steel collection)*

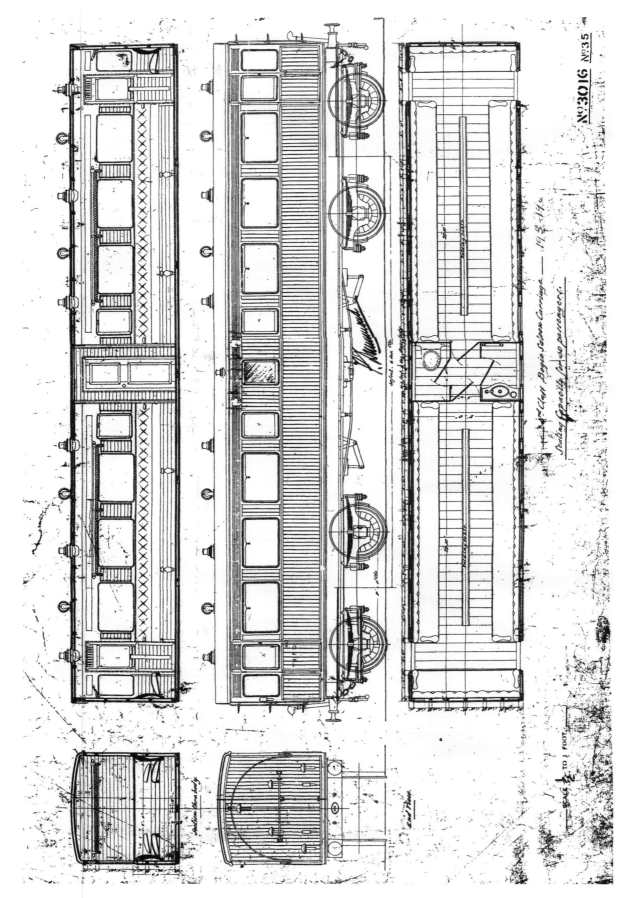

*Figure 30 - HR general arrangement drawing of bogie Third-class saloon coach to LMS diagram 35. (HRS collection)*

### Third-class Brake

The same year two more bogie Brake Third-class coaches to LMS diagram 41, Nos. 15 and 16, were also added, but this time with a cove, rather than low-arc roof. They were dual brake fitted and had five instead of the six compartments of their predecessors nine years earlier, thereby affording greater luggage capacity, but again the lavatories were reached from just two compartments.

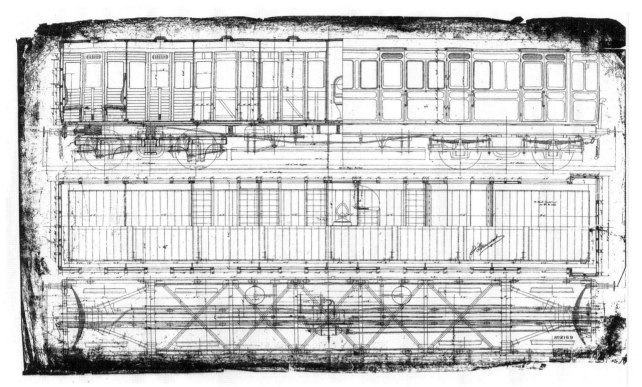

*Figure 31 - General arrangement drawing of a Drummond bogie cove-roofed Lavatory Brake/Third-class coach. (HRS collection)*

*Bogie Lavatory Brake Third No. M25697, ex-HR No. 16 built at Lochgorm in 1907, seen at St Rollox on 21 June 1949. Following nationalisation its LMS second series number has had the prefix M applied. Repairs to the lookout have been carried out in horizontal boarding; nonetheless, it was withdrawn in April 1951. (HC Casserley)*

*Following withdrawal from revenue earning service No. 25697 was given a further lease of life by being taken into departmental stock as No. 354909 and employed as one of W Pooley & Son's weighing machine repair vans until May 1963. (I Peddie)*

*HR bogie Luggage Composite No. 15 as built at Lochgorm in 1909 for use on trains with a through coach to Thurso. Note the First-class coupé end and that despite the pair of double doors, the far end is for luggage only and does not incorporate facilities for a guard. (Author's collection)*

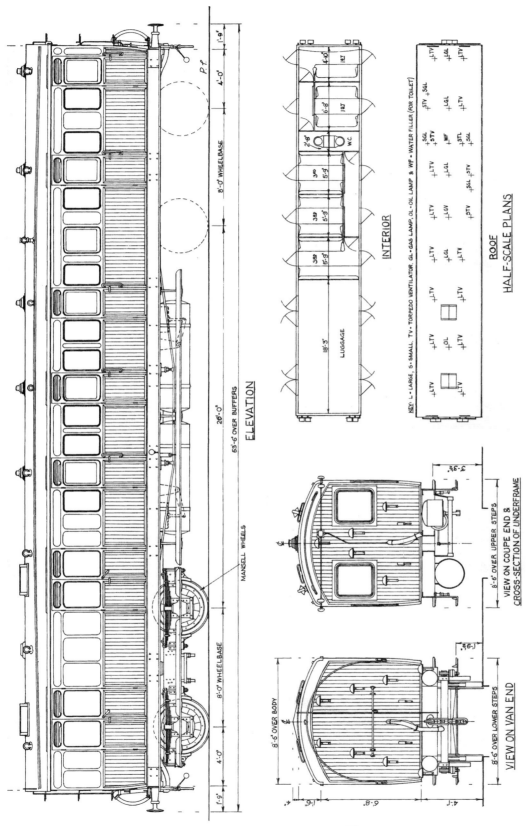

### Thurso Composites

In 1909 the need was identified for two semi-corridor Luggage Composites specifically for the through coach from Inverness to Thurso. These were designed by Drummond to LMS diagram 24 with one full First-class compartment and a coupé both with access by internal side corridor to a lavatory. A second corridor on the opposite side gave access to a another lavatory for three full Third-class compartments, beyond which was a large luggage compartment with two double doors on each side. Despite the presence of short lengths of corridor, one side was a mirror of the other, apart from the hanging of the doors. These vehicles were built by Hurst Nelson for £1,040 each, fitted with Hurst Nelson's own design of bogie in lieu of the Leeds Forge type, and put into service in May 1910. In their final years, the First-class compartments were down-graded and they both lasted until September 1951.

*Figure 32 - Drummond bogie cove-roof corridor Lavatory/ Luggage Composite (Thurso) coach to LMS Diagram 24. (Author)*

*No. SCM18598 (ex-HR No. 14) looks smart when captured at Aviemore on 14 August 1951, by when it had been fitted with Iracier axle-boxes. (AG Ellis collection)*

### Corridor Stock

Up until the middle of the first decade of the 20th century the Highland had survived without corridor coaches of its own. Even so when it did finally embrace them, initially the corridors were merely internal to the coach with gangway connections to adjacent coaches permitting movement along the train not present. Although envisaged from the outset, they were only added later at a cost of £50 and became routine for additional stock from 1908. By this time the vertically match boarded lower sides had been adopted and the roof profile that had changed to a low elliptical shape, sometimes known as a 'cove roof'. As built most, if not all, of this type adopted large panes of glass to the corridor sides, but these were later altered to double panes. All were dual brake fitted, while Iracier axle-boxes provided from 1912.

### Corridor Connections and Dining Cars

According to the Stephenson Locomotive Society, the Highland had considered the introduction of dining cars in April 1898, but the matter was not pursued. Unless the Midland Railway practice of allowing passengers to remain at their seats throughout the journey was adopted, however, the introduction of dining cars would have presumed the use of corridor coaches of which the Highland had none at the time. It was not, therefore, until February 1922 when the Caledonian Railway proposed the introduction of a dining car between Glasgow and Aviemore that the possibility was revisited. In April it was agreed, to run, as an experiment, a dining car between Glasgow and Aviemore on the 11.50am train from Perth returning on the train that had started from Inverness at 3.30pm. Many of the through coaches from other companies

*A publicity photograph showing a train composed of examples, apart from the rear brake van, of the Highland's corridor stock posed on the original line to Forres, Elgin and Keith headed by 4-6-0 Castle class No. 149 Duncraig Castle. The carriages are a Brake Composite No. 18 to LMS diagram 25, built in 1912; a Third to diagram 36; two Composites, the second to diagram 6; and a Composite or all Third-class. Such a train was unlikely in service because they probably would have contained other companies' through coaches from south of Perth and would also have included more vans. (Author's collection)*

were by then corridor coaches equipped with gangway connections, as were a few of the Highland's. Nonetheless, the need to fit up another three vans and three carriages with gangway connections at estimated cost of £423-12-0 was identified.

This was no sooner agreed than a proposal from the GNSR was received to run a restaurant car it had hired from the NER on the 8.5am from Aberdeen to Inverness, returning at 12.50pm. With grouping soon to be implemented the other companies in the Western group were first consulted before agreeing to accept it from 10 August 1922. With the Pullman car providing dining facilities for passengers on the 4.30pm from Aviemore to Glasgow, the East companies, not to be outdone, introduced their own dining car for their portion from Blair Atholl.

## Composite Coaches

The first batch of four corridor Composite coaches to LMS diagram 12, built by Brush Electrical in 1907, had three First-class and four Third-class compartments with lavatories at each end in a 50 foot long body and a total tare weight of 25 tons 13 cwt. Each compartment had doors to the outside on one side and access to the corridor on the other, but there were only two external doors, one at each end of the corridor. Gangway connections were not fitted until 1909. Steam heated and initially gas lit, towards the end of its life one coach was down-rated by the LMS to all Third-class as No. 3385.

To afford greater compartment space, all subsequent Composite coaches were mounted on 52 foot long under-frames and each had four external doors to

| | Diagrams | | | | | | Lengt | | Nos. | | Withdrawal | |
|---|---|---|---|---|---|---|---|---|---|---|---|---|
| | *192* | *LMS* | *Descr-* | *Built* | *Date* | *Cost* | *h* | | | *LMS* | | |
| *DLGH* | *3* | *ND* | *iption* | *by* | | *(£)* | *(ft-in)* | *HR* | *1st* | *2nd* | *First* | *Last* |
| *54* | 12 | 12/28 | CK TK (1) | Brush | 1907 | 1,700 | 50-0 | 10-13 | 18623-6 | 4984-6 3385 (1) | 9/47 10/46 | 2/55 |
| *55* | 6 | 6/29 6/84 | CK TK (1) | H Nelson | 1912 | 1,477 | 52-0 | 16-7 | 18629-30 | 3399(1) 4991 | 7/51 | 1/55 |
| | | | | Pickering | 1914 | 1,570 | | 7, 23/4, 33, 81-2 | 18622/33-4/40/88-9 | 4992-7 (2) | 6/44 | 10/55 |
| | | | | Pickering | 1918 | | | 25-6 | 18635-6 | 4998-9 | 4/51 | 4/51 |
| *57* | 25 | 25/54 | BCK | H Nelson | 1912 | 1,275 | 50-0 | 18-9 | 18631-2 | 7398-9 | 10/51 | 5/51 |
| *52* | 7 | 7/32 7/85 | CKLug TKLug | Pickering | 1916 | 1596-10-0 | 52-0 | 1-5 | 18616-20 | 4987-90 3398(1) | 5/46 | 12/52 |

Header: **HR Drummond Bogie Corridor Composite Coaches**

Notes  (1)  Down graded to all Third-class.
(2)  One 1st compartment of No. 4996 converted to Third-class.

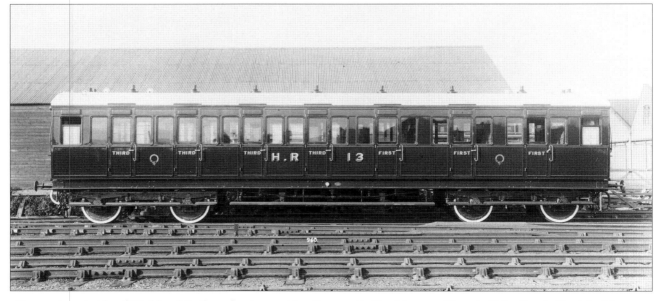

*Compartment side of Highland Railway bogie corridor Composite No. 13, one of four built by Brush Electrical in 1907. (Author's collection)*

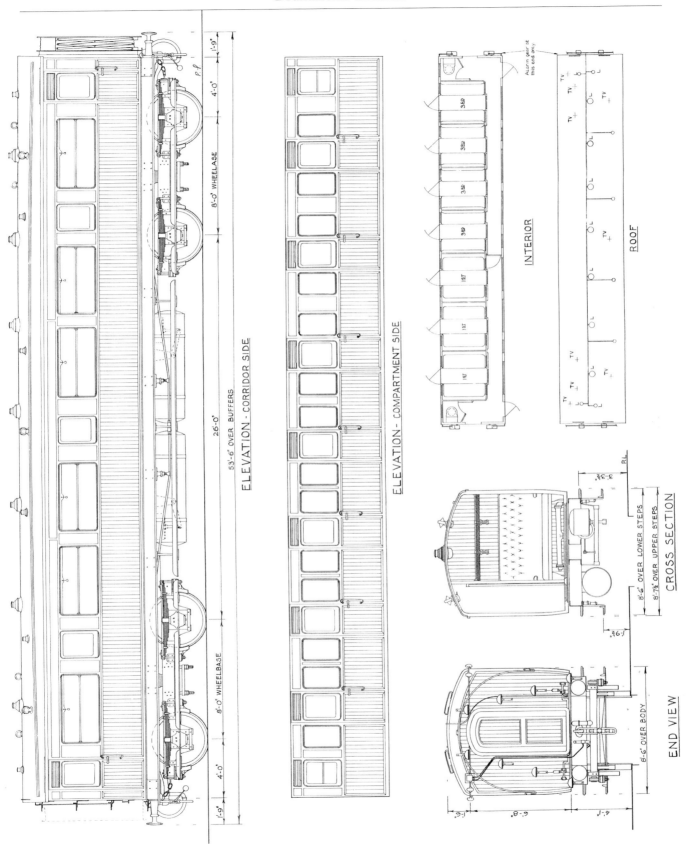

*Figure 33 - Drummond 50 foot bogie corridor Composite coach with two doors on the corridor side to LMS diagram 12.  (Author)*

*The corridor side of No. 12, showing that gangway connections have yet to be fitted. With only two doors on this side, access and egress was somewhat restricted, a deficiency remedied on subsequent production. (AG Ellis collection).*

*Ex-HR bogie corridor Composite in BR livery as No. SC4986 (ex-HR No. 12/LMS 18625). By this time the large corridor windows have been replaced by smaller pairs of lights. Note the four patches on the roof covering openings for the original gas lamps. (D Horne, courtesy Transport Treasury)*

the corridor side. The next batches to LMS diagram 6 were two constructed by Hurst Nelson in 1912, followed by six by RY Pickering two years later and finally two

more of them in 1918, which were electrically lit from the outset.

The final design of Composite coach to LMS

*The next batch of bogie Composites had four doors on the corridor side, as depicted of No. 16 built by Hurst Nelson in 1912 to LMS diagram 6, and must have been one of last gas lit coaches acquired by the company. (AG Ellis collection)*

*By early British Railways' days, No. M4994, ex-HR No. 24 built by RY Pickering in 1914, has found its way to Gloucester, by when its large corridor windows had been replaced by a pair of smaller ones. (LRGP, HRS collection)*

*Sister coach No. SC4993M (ex-HR 23) even achieved BR's carmine and cream livery. Note the steam heating pipe below the running board. (Author's collection)*

diagram 7 one of the Third-class compartments was replaced by a luggage locker with double doors. Five carriages of this type were supplied by RY Pickering in 1916. Again LMS No. 18619 was down-graded to all Third-class No. 3398. Nonetheless, the last batch of just two composite coaches acquired by the Highland reverted to the earlier style of three first and four third class compartments, i.e. without a luggage locker.

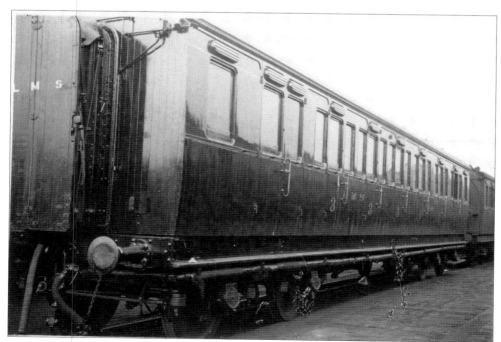

*Supplied during World War 1, carriages in Highland livery to diagram 7 seem to have escaped the camera. LMS No. 4988 (HR No. 2 and LMS 1st series No. 18617) was photographed on 12 April 1939 at Inverness with the lavatory and the luggage locker compartment next the camera. (DLG Hunter)*

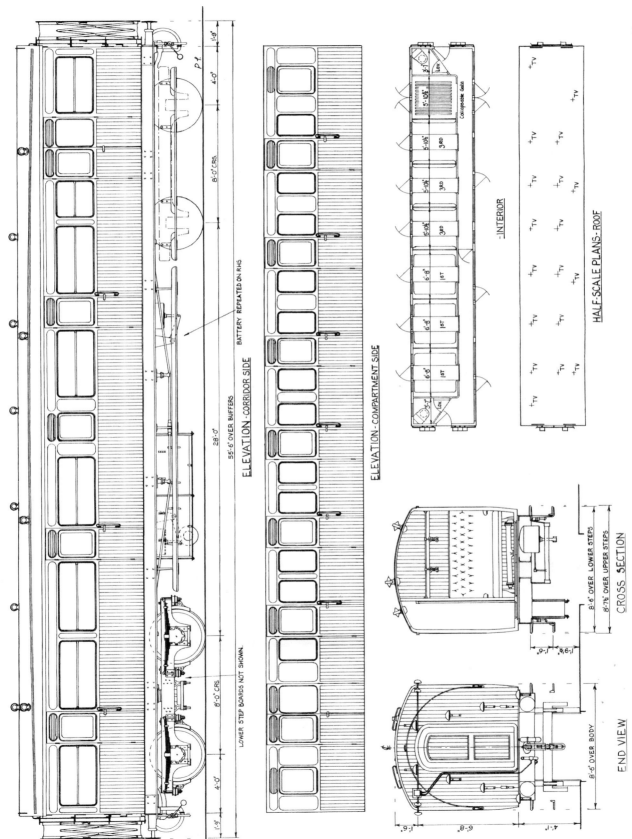

ELEVATION - CORRIDOR SIDE

ELEVATION - COMPARTMENT SIDE

- INTERIOR

HALF-SCALE PLANS - ROOF

CROSS SECTION

END VIEW

LOWER STEP BOARDS NOT SHOWN.

BATTERY REPEATED ON RHS

55'-6" OVER BUFFERS

*Figure 34 - 52 foot bogie Luggage/Composite coach to LMS diagram 7. The official drawings suggest that the corridor side originally had large windows; if so, each of these was also changed to a pair of smaller ones. (Author)*

*No. M4988 again, this time at St Rollox on 13 December 1952 marked up for scrapping. (JL Stevenson)*

### Brake Composites

Just two Brake Corridor Composites were built by Hurst Nelson in 1912 to LMS diagram 25. In these two and a half First and two Third-class compartments were provided along with two lavatories, accommodation for the guard and luggage on a 50 foot under-frame. These were gas lit and originally had the large corridor windows, together with two windows on the brake end each of which reached out into the lookout. Although the ends were framed for gangway connections, these were not at first fitted.

*The Highland only ever had two bogie Corridor Brake Composite carriages. No. 18 was built by Hurst Nelson in 1912, initially with gas lighting and without gangway connections. Note the company initials and number repeated on the guard's lookout. (Author's collection)*

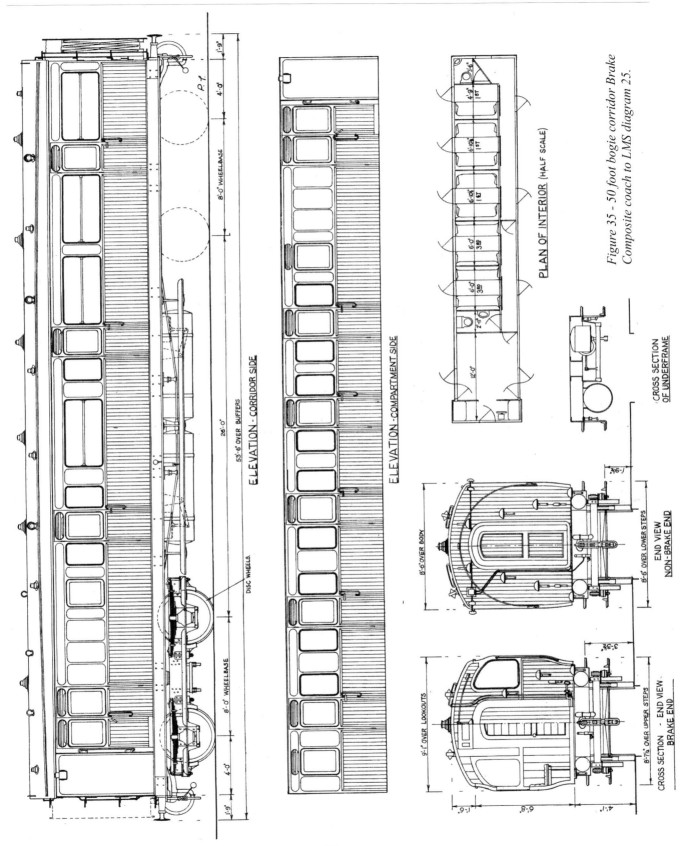

PLAN OF INTERIOR (HALF SCALE)

ELEVATION - CORRIDOR SIDE

ELEVATION - COMPARTMENT SIDE

CROSS SECTION OF UNDERFRAME

END VIEW NON-BRAKE END

CROSS SECTION - END VIEW - BRAKE END

*Figure 35 - 50 foot bogie corridor Brake Composite coach to LMS diagram 25.*

*By 11 June 1938 LMS No. 7399 (HR No.19 and LMS 1st series No. 18632) at Inverness has been altered by provision of small corridor windows and electric lighting. (DLG Hunter)*

### Third-Class Coaches

Between 1909 and 1911 RY Pickering supplied six all Third-class corridor bogie coaches with seven gas lit compartments and lavatories at each end on a 50 foot under-frame, followed a year later by two more from the Hurst Nelson stable but these were electrically lit from the outset. There were three doors down the corridor side and gangway connections were fitted from the beginning. The final four delivered in 1917 by Pickering, however, had four doors to the corridor and were electrically lit. Nonetheless, both types were accorded to LMS diagram 36 and had a tare weight of 26 tons 5 cwt.

*Above and opposite top - Third-class corridor carriages were introduced in 1909 and had three doors on the corridor side. RY Pickering supplied the first batch of six over an extended period of two years. These two views show No. 101 as built, fitted with large windows and gas lighting. (RY Pickering, author's collection)*

*This cruel enlargement of LMS No. 18795 (ex-HR No. 106) at Carlisle is included to demonstrate that the large corridor windows and gas lighting continued into 1926. (AG Ellis collection)*

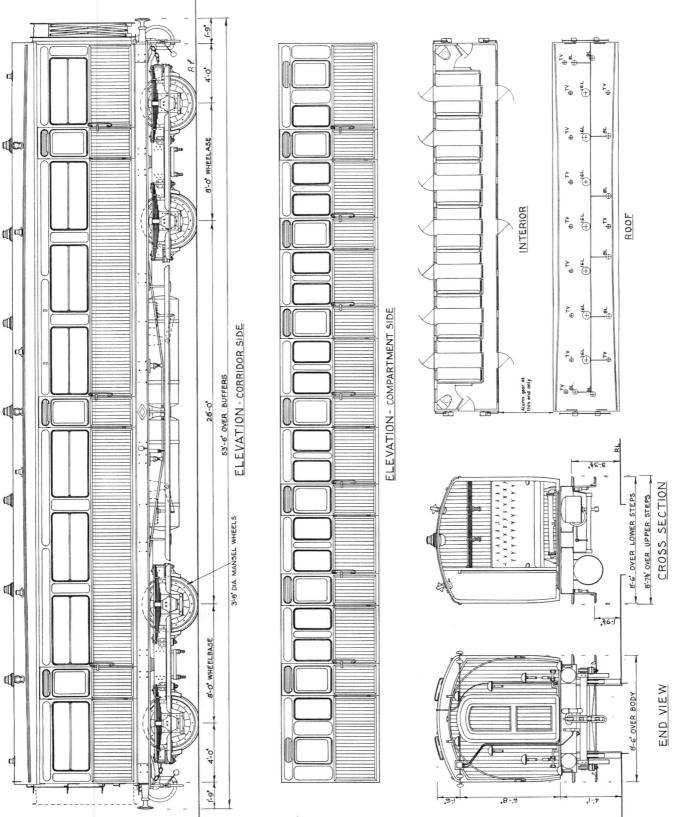

ELEVATION - CORRIDOR SIDE

ELEVATION - COMPARTMENT SIDE

INTERIOR

ROOF

CROSS SECTION

END VIEW

*Figure 36 - 50 foot bogie Third-class coach to LMS diagram 36 with three doors on corridor side, large windows and gas lighting.  (Author)*

# Drummond Coaches

**HR Drummond Bogie 50 Foot Corridor Third-Class Coaches**

| Diagrams | | | Built by | Date | Cost (£) | Nos | | | Withdrawal | |
|---|---|---|---|---|---|---|---|---|---|---|
| DLGH | 1923 | LMS ND | | | | HR | LMS | | First | Last |
| | | | | | | | 1st | 2nd | | |
| 60 | 36p | 36/65p | Pickering | 1909 1910-11 | 1,225/ 1,200 | 101-102 103-106 | 18790-5 | 3386-91 | 7/35 | 2/55 |
| | | | H Nelson | 1912 | 1,330 | 107-108 | 18796-7 | 3392-3 | 7/39 | 2/55 |
| 61 | 36p | 36/65p | Pickering | 1917 | 1,559 | 109-112 | 18798-801 | 3394-7 | 10/54 | 11/55 |

*A detail of the right-hand portion of BR No. SC3387M (ex-HR No. 102). (H Orbach, HRS collection)*

*The corridor side of No. SC3391M (ex-HR No. 106) with three doors at Corkerhill on 21 December 1952, having been converted to electric lighting and narrow windows, while Iracier axle-boxes have been fitted. (JL Stevenson)*

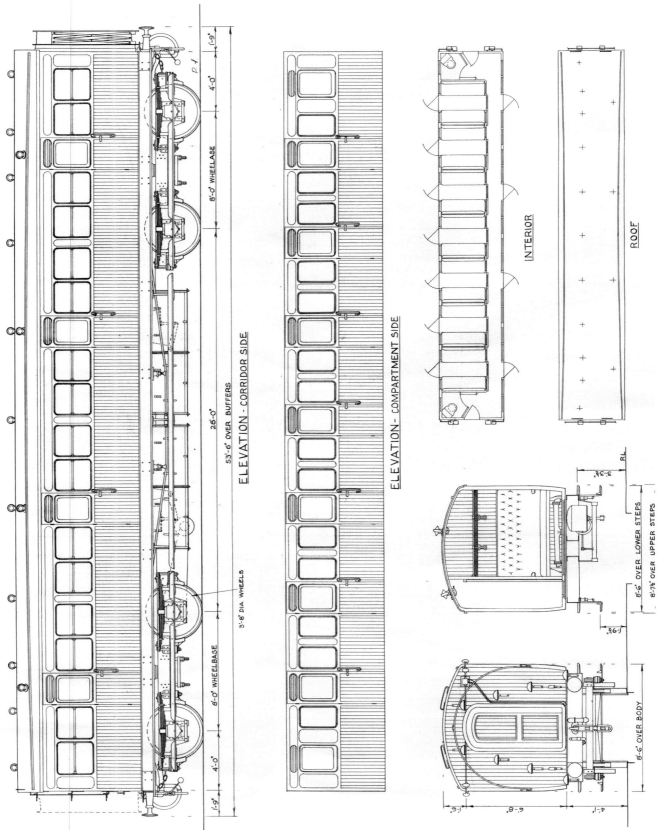

ELEVATION - CORRIDOR SIDE

ELEVATION - COMPARTMENT SIDE

INTERIOR

ROOF

*Figure 37 - 50 foot bogie Third-class coach to LMS Diagram 36 with four doors, twin-windows on corridor side, battery boxes for electric lighting and beading omitted from the edges of the vertical match-boarding. (Author)*

*The last four corridor Third-class carriages to LMS diagram 36 had four instead of three doors to the corridor, but were otherwise similar to the immediately previous with electric light, although it is uncertain whether they originally had wide or narrow windows. No. 3395 was seen at Inverness on 12 April 1939. (DLG Hunter)*

*Freshly repainted in unlined carmine No. SC3394 (ex HR No. 109/LMS 18798) waits at the head of a train at Buchanan Street station in early BR days. (JL Stevenson)*

# Non-passenger coaching stock

Non-passenger coaching stock is not a term the Highland Railway would have recognised, but it is a useful one to distinguish this class of vehicle from passenger carrying coaches, yet capable of being run in passenger trains; subsequently such vehicles were separately identified by the LMS. As railway business grew the extra revenue to be earned by conveying high value and/or perishable goods by passenger train was recognised. There was considerable traffic in such items as sundry parcels; bicycles; horses and carriages and in due course motor cars; milk; game - venison, grouse; fish; dogs; hens; small animals - pigs, calves each in a jute sack with their heads sticking out; and prize cattle. Indeed, this was sufficiently extensive that the railway companies found it worth attracting and catering for by the provision of appropriate services and in many cases special vehicles, such as Passenger Brake, Mail, luggage, prize cattle and meat vans; horseboxes, open and covered carriage trucks; and open fish trucks. In recognition of their status from 1912, all were painted green, rather than red oxide.

On the whole Passenger Brake Vans and Post Office vehicles usually reflected current passenger coach construction practices and to some extent horseboxes, whereas others such a passenger luggage, meat and prize cattle vans; carriage trucks and fish trucks developed out of goods wagons with increasing attention paid to suspension, buffers and brake gear necessary to run in passenger trains according to the regulations pertaining at the time, some travelling at express speeds. In reviewing below those possessed by the Highland, it will, therefore, be found that they originate from both the coach and wagon diagram books.

## Rib-Sided Passenger Brake Vans

In early 1903 an old I&AJR Passenger Brake Van, the spare tool van, found at the back of the engine shed Perth was mentioned in the *Locomotive Magazine* for that year and then broken up. It was reported to have been built by Brown Marshall & Co. of Birmingham with a total length 20ft 10in, 10ft wheel-base and tare of less than 9 tons. It shows sprung buffers with wooden ends; side lookouts and access steps at one end; a dog box at opposite end; rails on the roof to enable luggage to be carried outside; and spigot type lamp irons. It was suggested that Newall's 'chain' brake was fitted, but there is no evidence of this in the photographs; also that the side lookouts had been added later, but it seems that these form part of the original construction.

Orders for two brake vans had been placed with Wright & Sons in August 1861 at £216 each.

| Rib-Sided Passenger Brake Vans | | | | | | | | | | | |
|---|---|---|---|---|---|---|---|---|---|---|---|
| Diagrams 1901 | 1923 | Type | Built by | Date | Wheels | Length (ft-in) | Nos. HR | 1st LMS | Tare wt (T-c) | No. dupl'd | Wdn |
| - | - | - | Wright (2) Brown M | C'61 | 4 | c17-6 | u/k | - | 9-0 | | Last 1903 |
| 32 | 44p | A | HR | 1870 reb't 1900 | 4 | 20-6 | 1-10, 24-28' 80 | 7370-2/6/ 80-90, 7443(1) | 10-0 | '08-'12 | c'23-'26 |
| 33 | 44p | B | HR | | 4 | 20-6 | 11-12 | 7377? | 9-5 | '08-'10 | C'23 |
| 35 | 47 | D | Midland 6 @ £328 | 1873 | 6 | 24-1 | 29, 36-38 Or 31-38? | - | 11-10 | | To service stock |

(1)     Only Nos. 7376 & 7389 was actually carried.

*This page and opposite - The I&AJR 4-wheel Passenger Brake Van built by Brown Marshall found lurking in 1903 at the back of Perth locomotive shed as a spare tool van. The man sitting on the roof at the top of the steps is not thought to have been representative of actual practice. (Author's collection)*

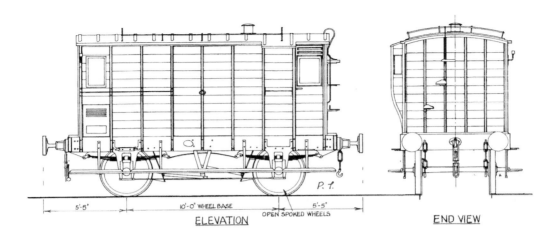

5'-5"    10'-0" WHEEL BASE    5'-5"
OPEN SPOKED WHEELS
ELEVATION                    END VIEW

*Figure 38 - I&AJR rib-sided Passenger Brake Van.  (Author)*

The bulk of subsequent construction to diagram 32 was also of rib-sided form and on four wheels, but longer at 20ft 6in long over headstocks and body. Some of these vans seem to have survived for a remarkably long time, six being heavily rebuilt from 1907 with panelled sides at a cost of £115 each for continued use on short branch lines. Instead of side lookouts, Nos. 11 and 12 had roof lookouts at one end; one of which was used on the Aberfeldy branch. These and subsequent Jones brake vans included at one end of the van a low level locker stretching from one side of the vehicle to the other with external doors with ventilation holes and an internal lift flap, in which to place dogs. These of course were more likely to be working sheep dogs, than domestic animals. All 4 and 6-wheel Passenger Brake Vans until Jones' retirement had guard's lookouts at one end with low-arc roof continuing over the lookout.

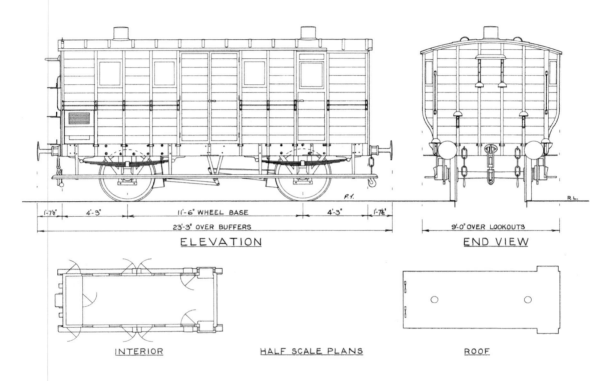

*Figure 39 - I&AJR 4-wheel rib-sided Passenger Brake Van to diagram 32.  (Author)*

*The grounded body of I&AJR rib-sided Passenger Brake Van No. 26 at Killiecrankie on 28 October 1939.  (DLG Hunter)*

*Another grounded body of a rib-sided Passenger Brake Van in use beside the track as a bothy at an unknown location. (HRS collection)*

No. 5, built in the early 1870s, like others during the first decade of the 20th century, was rebuilt at Lochgorm in the fully panelled style. After withdrawal as LMS No. 7371, it ended up on its wheels beside the track at Inchlea between Dalwhinnie and Newtonmore as the signalman's bothy until 1965, when it was rescued and restored by WEC Watkinson. After residing on the Strathspey Railway, following renovation it moved in 2005 to Bo'ness and is now on display in the Museum of Scottish Railways.

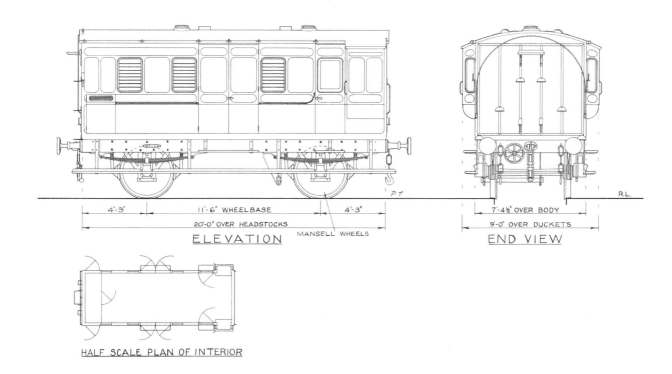

*Figure 40 - Jones 4-wheel Passenger Brake Van rebuilt in panelled form. (Author)*

*Above* - Restored Highland Railway 4-wheel Passenger Brake Van No. 5 on display at Shildon Wagon Works on 30 August 1975. *(Author)*

*Left and opposite top* - The interior of HR Brake Van No. 5 following restoration, showing the guard's seat and lookout and the dog box across the other end. *(Author)*

## Jones 6-Wheeled Passenger Brake Vans

31ft 6in long Passenger Brake Vans to two different diagrams were built on David Jones' standardised 6 wheel under-frame with 21 foot wheel base. The bodywork panelling was of the typical form with the three centre arc to the top of the upper panels. All were oil lit, vacuum and hand braked and are presumed to have been built by the HR at Inverness. The wheel diameter is not precisely known, but will have been of typical coach size of 3ft 6in plus. Likewise, it may be that spoked wheels were fitted rather than the wooden centred Mansell type usual for passenger carrying vehicles. Many were withdrawn from revenue earning service around 1925 to 1926, soon after the take over by the LMS. Some of these, however, found further use by being transferred to departmental stock,

when in LMS days they will have been renumbered in the 2972xx series, while the rest were broken up.

The older of the two diagrams was the Type F to HR diagram 37, of which there were a total of seven vehicles. Three were built in 1884 and the rest in 1888. These had two sets of double doors on each side, as well as the guard's entrance adjacent to the lookouts at one end. Their tare weight was 12 tons 15 cwt. Of the LMS numbers only No. 7404 was carried.

The second and more numerous version, with a total of twenty five examples, was the Type C to HR diagram 34 were built from 1892 onwards. In this design, the double doors were repositioned, so that one set also served as the guard's entrance. Their tare weight was 13 tons and some were steam heated. Only LMS Nos. 7384-6, 7410/320 were carried, of which Nos. 7386 and 7420 were allocated Nos. 34283 and 34282 respectively in second series, neither being formally withdrawn until

| HR Jones 6-wheel Passenger Brake Vans | | | | | | | |
|---|---|---|---|---|---|---|---|
| | Diagrams | | Type | Date | Length | Nos | |
| 1901 | LMS | | | | (ft-in) | HR | 1st LMS |
| | 1923 | ND | | | | | |
| 37 | 49 | - | F | 1884 1888 | 31-4 | 39-45 | 7402-8(2) |
| 34 | 45 | 45/125 | C | 1892 1894 u/k | 31-4 | 46-57 13-21/7 31-4, | 7409-20 (1) 7378--86 7394-7, |
| 36 | 48 | - | E | | 27-1 | 30 | (7393) |

*Behind the 0-4-4T Drummond passenger tank No. 25, named Strathpeffer, with the branch train from that place arriving at Dingwall on 21 September 1912, is the sole example of a 27ft 1in long 6-wheel Passenger Brake Van to HR diagram 36, No. 30. Following it are one of the two oil-lit coupé Composites, a Drummond Third and a Jones Third, all 6-wheel. (WF Jackson, courtesy University of Glasgow)*

May 1951, although presumably scrapped many years earlier.

One final example No. 25 was only 27ft 1in long, Type E to diagram 36 with a tare weight of 12 tons, and is thought at times to have worked on the Strathpeffer branch.

*A Jones 6 wheel Passenger Brake Van to diagram 37, on 14 June 1938 towards the end of its days as LMS No. 297293 in departmental service. Several of this or similar types found employment as tool vans in the thirties. (DLG Hunter)*

*Figure 41 - Drawing of Jones 6 wheel Passenger Brake Van to diagram 34. (Author)*

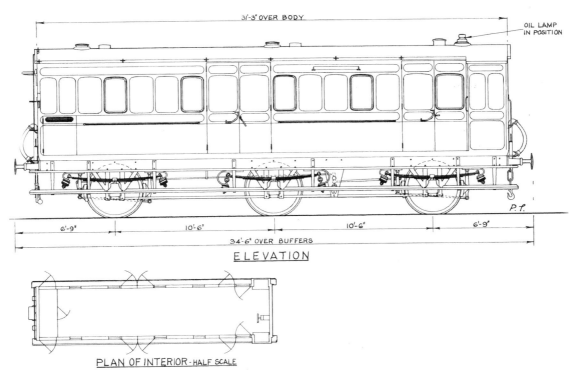

| HR Drummond 6-wheel Passenger Brake Vans | | | | | | | | | | | | | |
|---|---|---|---|---|---|---|---|---|---|---|---|---|---|
| Diagrams | | | Type | Built by | Date | Cost (£) | Length (ft-in) | Nos. | | | Tare wt (T-c) | Withdrawal | |
| 1901 | 1923 | LMS ND | | | | | | HR | LMS | | | First | Last |
| | | | | | | | | | 1st | 2nd | | | |
| 38 | 46 | 46/126 | G | HR | 1900 | 600 | 35-8 | 22-3, 35, 58-62 | 7387-8/98, 7421-5 | 34284-86, 34287-9 | 14-5 | u/k | 5/55 |
| | | | | | 1902 | | | 63-68 | 7426-31 | 34290-2 (1) | | c'26 | c'40 |
| | | | | | 1903 | | | 28 | 7391 | (34293) | | | 5/55 |

(1)     Only LMS Nos. 34284/6/8/90-2 in 2nd series were actually carried.

Although allocated an LMS number, this was never carried.

### Drummond 6-Wheel Passenger Brake Vans

Concurrent with Drummond's 6-wheel passenger coaches fifteen panelled Passenger Brake Vans of similar style were built. Most seem to have been dual braked, but a few were vacuum braked with only Westinghouse pipe. Brake van lookouts were of the

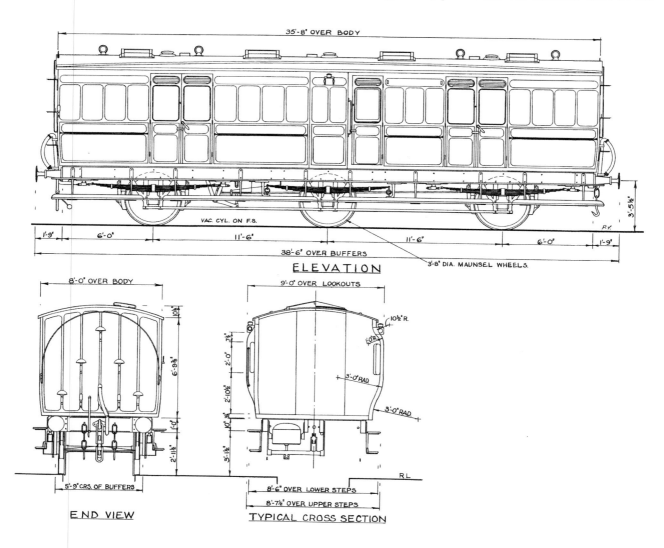

*Figure 42 - Drummond 6-wheel Passenger Brake Van to diagram 38. (Author)*

*Drummond's version of a 6-wheel Passenger Brake Van to diagram 38, No. 67 was built at Lochgorm in 1902. Renumbered by the LMS as 7430, it nonetheless failed to be allocated a second series number in 1933. (HRS collection)*

*One of these vans in due course found its way into the breakdown train at Hurlford, where it was seen on 29 July 1950. By then numerous patch repairs to the panelling had been undertaken. (JL Stevenson)*

double ogee section in end view, see page 151. Six similar, but match-boarded sided vehicles without lookouts were produced as road vans.

### Drummond Bogie Passenger Brake Vans

Low-Arc Roof Bogie Passenger Brake Vans

In 1904 a bogie version of the Drummond low-arc roof Passenger Brake Van was introduced for use on main line trains. The first batch built by RY Pickering in 1904 was definitely fully panelled in the same style as the contemporary coaches with tumble home to both the sides and ends, measuring 46ft 8in long by 8 feet over the body and 9 foot over the lookouts. From 1907, however, the body sides and ends were vertically planked and drop-lights added in the double doors. It is seems likely that Nos. 73 to 76 and possibly No. 77 were initially panelled above the waist line and only vertically boarded below. These vans had longitudinally centrally placed side lookouts and dual brakes, while from 1907 outside steam pipes were fitted. In the absence of any form of windows, apart from the guard's door, it is not surprising to find roof lights shown on some of the drawings, but if provided they are difficult to discern on photographs and anyway they may well have been

suppressed later and the double doors glazed. Prompted by the Board of Trade, in 1911 fifty Passenger Brake Vans were fitted up with fire extinguishers and tools for use in an emergency at a cost of £3 each.

Repairs during their life led to the panelling of the sides, but not necessarily the ends, being replaced by full height vertical planking and sheet metal covering to the lookouts; and the removal of the lower foot boards, leaving a short length on the outer end of the bogies.

Drummond low-arc roof vans were originally gas lit, but all were in due course converted to electric. Sometime between 1934 and 1941 LMS No. 33698 (ex-HR No. 77) was renumbered as 31947, indicating that it had been fitted with gangway connections. Late in life Nos. 33692/5/6 were rebuilt and allocated to Beattie's bread traffic for a steady passenger train traffic of bread steam-baked in Dennistoun in Glasgow which supplied much of rural Scotland. The conversion consisted of stripping out the guard's equipment and fitting a four-spoked hand brake wheel of about 18 inch dia. below the solebar, while the upper foot board was removed between the double doors. On 20 February 1942 LMS No. 33695 (ex-HR No. 74) was sold to the LNER for £402 for the same purpose. It was given the number 301

| | | | | | | | HR Bogie Passenger Brake Vans | | | | | | |
|---|---|---|---|---|---|---|---|---|---|---|---|---|---|
| | *Diagrams* | | *Built by* | *Date* | *Cost* | | | *Nos.* | | *Tare* | *Drg* | *Withdrawal* | |
| *DLGH* | *1923* | *ND* | | | *(£)* | *HR* | | *LMS* | | *wt* | *No.* | *First* | *Last* |
| | | | | | | | *1st* | *2nd* | | *(T-c)* | | | |
| 64 | 50 | 50/127 | Pickering | 1904 | 645 | 69-72 | 7432-5 | 33692/3 | | 22-0 | 2785 | C'28 | 13/62 |
| | | | HR | 1907 | 607 | 73-76 | 7436-9 | 33694-7 | | | | 10/42 | 9/54 |
| | | | HR | 1909 | 670 | 77 | 7440 | 33698* | | | | u/k | |
| 65 | 50 | 51/128 | HR | 1911 | - | 78 | 7441 | 33699+ | | u/k | 3966 | 4/51 | - |
| | | | HR | 1913 | 800 | 79 | 7442 | - | | | 32?? | C'27 | - |
| | | | Pickering | 1917 | - | 81/2 | 7444-5 | 32898/9 | | | | | |
| | | | HR | 1915 | 720 | 83 | 7446 | 32897 | | | | | |

Notes    *      Renumbered 31847 in the corridor series between 1934 and 1941.
          +      Renumbered 31952 in the corridor series by 12/33.

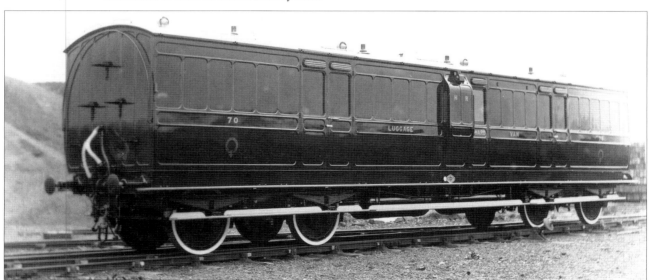

*No. 70 was an example of those supplied by RY Pickering in 1904 fully panelled and lettered Luggage Van. (RY Pickering, author's collection)*

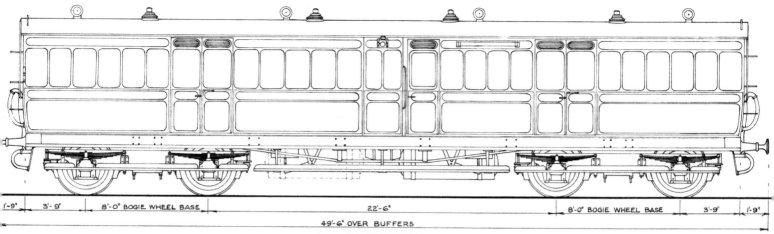

1'-9" | 3'-9" | 8'-0" BOGIE WHEEL BASE | 22'-6" | 8'-0" BOGIE WHEEL BASE | 3'-9" | 1'-9"

49'-6" OVER BUFFERS

ELEVATION

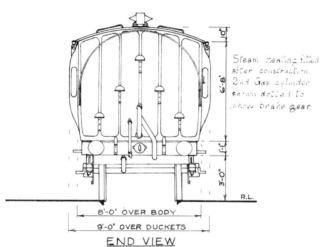

1'-0"

6'-8"

1'-4"

3'-0"

R.L.

Steam heating fitted
after construction.
2nd Gas cylinder
shown dotted to
show brake gear.

8'-0" OVER BODY

9'-0" OVER DUCKETS

END VIEW

*Figure 43 - Drummond bogie panelled Passenger Brake Van to LMS diagram 50. (TW Bourne)*

*LMS No. 33693 largely still in its original panelled state on 11 June 1938. A note at the bottom right hand corner reads: Load 6 tons (Evenly distributed). (DLG Hunter)*

*Note that the end of BR No. M33694 is vertically planked with edge beading and the framing allows for the fitting of a gangway connection. (HS Orbach)*

*LNER No. 301, formerly HR No. 74 used for the Beattie's bread traffic from 1943 to 1947. (HRS collection)*

in the ex-North British van series to LNER Southern Scottish Area diagram 316B and finally withdrawn in May 1947.

### Cove Roof Bogie Passenger Brake Vans

The vans to the final Drummond design with cove roof, perpetuated by his successors, for new construction from 1911 were capable of being fitted with gangway connections. With square ends they are thought to have been 46 feet long and again 8 feet over the body and 9 feet over the lookouts. The first batch was gas lit

subsequently converted to electricity, the rest being electrically lit from the outset; all had Iracier axle-boxes. In 1913 two vans were equipped with sliding doors for luggage, instead of a pair of double doors, but later altered to double doors, and electric light was adopted.

Both low-arc and cove roofed types were dual braked. In 1923 both versions were accorded to LMS diagram 50, but a distinction was made in the Northern Division book of 50/127 for vehicles with the low-arc roof and 51/128 for those with gangway connections.

*During World War 1, RY Pickering supplied two bogie Passenger Brake Vans of revised design with cove roof, strip windows below the cantrail, fully vertically match board sides and framed to accept gangway connections and in this case a pair of sliding doors for loading luggage. No. 82 was built in 1917 and is fitted with Iracier axle-boxes. (Author's collection)*

*On 17 April 1949 a rather tatty LMS No. 32898 (ex-HR No. 81) waits in line outside St Rollox Works for overhaul; by June it was back in service. As sister to No. 82, this too will originally have had sliding doors which have clearly been altered to a pair of conventional doors. (JL Stevenson)*

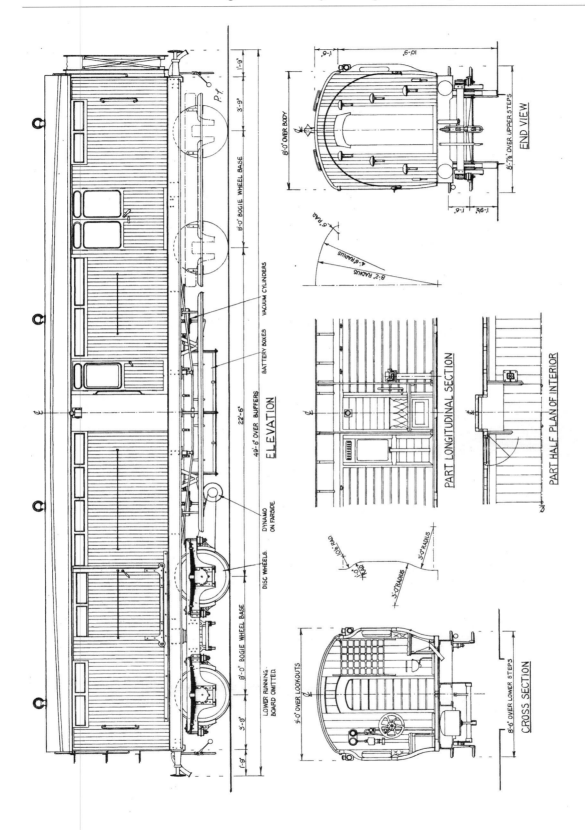

*Figure 44 - Cove-roof corridor Passenger Brake Van to LMS Northern Division diagram 51. (Author)*

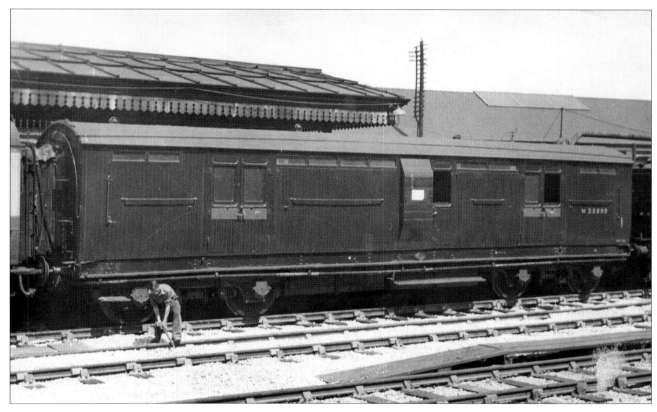

*The same van as seen at the foot of page 111 following its visit to the works and now with the prefix M applied to its number 32898 and appears to be on former Great Western territory.  (LGRP, author's collection)*

## Passenger Brake Vans Converted from Post Office Vans

In 1914 the idea of converting three redundant 6-wheel vehicles to HR diagram 42 Post Office Vans Nos. 7, 8 and 9 into parcels or luggage vans was first mooted. By 1917, during the period of acute shortages during World War 1, however, the vans involved were changed to the bogie vans Nos. 5, 6 and 10 to HR diagram 41 that were taken in hand. Thereafter no fresh diagram appears to have been issued for this major reconstruction and change of use and they escaped the attention of the LMS, although by 1923, Nos. 7, 8 and 9 were shown to be mounted on bogies (diagram 54). They were, nonetheless, completed as Passenger Brake Vans with facilities for a guard. The rebuilding seems to have consisted of removing the original panelling and re-cladding in the current fashion of vertical match boarding, but with straight sides and with the addition of side lookouts for the guard. The beading on the ends, however, still exhibited the Jones style of vertical rectangular panels.

Photographs suggest that at first they were used on the line to the North from Inverness. The LMS first renumbered the vans 7371, 7372 and 7375, only the last also receiving No. 33691 in the 1933 renumbering

scheme.  Withdrawal dates are not known, but two presumably went before 1933, while No. 33691 survived into the mid 1950s and possibly received BR's carmine livery.

| HR Bogie Passenger Brake Vans | | | | | |
|---|---|---|---|---|---|
| Converted by | Date | Drg No. | HR | Nos. LMS 1st | 2nd |
| HR | 1917/8? | 3528 | 5/6/10 | 7371/2/5 | 33691 |

## Early Mail Vans

From the outset constituents of the Highland Railway undertook to convey the mails, the Inverness & Nairn entering negotiations with the Inspector of Mails in Edinburgh prior to opening of the line in November 1855. Initially the mail was even carried on goods trains. With the extension of the line, in September 1858 the I&AJR invested in a Post Office Mail carriage from Brown Marshall at a cost of £210, while by the beginning of 1862 one additional Third-class carriage was being fitted up for the conveyance of mail bags.

With the completion of the line from Forres to

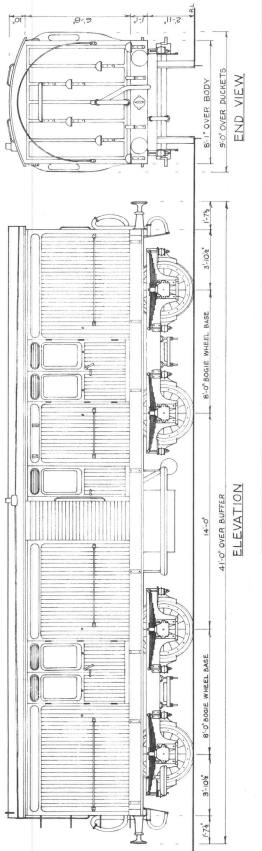

*Figure 45 - Bogie Passenger Brake Van converted from Post Office Vans. (TW Bourne)*

**Right** - *HR 38 foot bogie Passenger Brake Van No. M33691 at Birmingham New Street on 5 May 1954. It is just possible to discern Iracier axle-box covers on the original print. (SNJ White collection)*

114

*Another view of No. M33691 in the 'Coffee Bay' at Birmingham New Street.   (JE Cull)*

Perth the mail was diverted from the route via Aberdeen and the provision of a sorting carriage on the main line from Inverness began in June 1864.  Following the opening of the line to Wick in 1874 by independent companies, but worked by the Highland, difficulties arose over agreeing terms, only finally settled by arbitration.  A sorting carriage had been added to the train from Inverness to Bonar Bridge from July 1875, but the dispute reignited over renewing the contract in 1881.

*Diagrams 39 and 40*

By 1864 there were four Mail Vans.  These 4-wheel vehicles appear to have been similar to the 24 foot long coaches.  According to the diagrams Type A Nos. 1 and 2 had two sliding doors per side and were placed in duplicate stock in 1914.  Type B Nos. 3 and 4 each had a single door per side and some form of clerestory, the first of which disappeared from the lists prior to 1901.  No. 2 had been reclassified as a parcel van by 1923 and probably quickly succumbed as none were renumbered by the LMS, suggesting the rest had already been withdrawn by 1923.

*Diagram 43*

Type E Nos. 11 and 12 were 6-wheeled versions of diagram 40 and were likewise extinct prior to grouping in 1923.

| **Early HR Post Office Mail Vans** | | | | | | | | | |
|---|---|---|---|---|---|---|---|---|---|
| *Diagrams* | | *Type* | *Wheels* | *HR Nos.* | *Size l x w (ft-in)* | *Tare wt (T-c)* | *Brake* | *Drg No.* | *Remarks* |
| *HR 1901* | *LMS 1923* | | | | | | | | |
| 39 | 52 | A | 4 | 1, 2 | 24-3 x 7-11 | 9-10 | V, WP | 1152 | SP, wdn c'23 |
| 40 | | B | 4 | 3,4 | 24-1 x 7-11 | 9-10 | V, WP | | |
| 43 | | E | 6 | 11, 12 | 30-0 x 7-3 | - | V | | Used as stores van |

By September 1881 the Post Office were seeking to attach the exchange apparatus to the existing 20 year old 4-wheel travelling Post Office Vans, but these were too weak to allow this to be fitted. In the interim two second-hand, possibly 6-wheel, vans were bought from the Caledonian Railway at a cost of £100 each. As partners in the West Coast Joint Committee, the LNWR and Caledonian Railway had agreed in 1879 to contribute stock to form a postal train to run throughout from London Euston to Aberdeen. In doing so, the LNWR considered that the former Scottish Central Railway vans, CR Nos. 6 and 7 dating back to 1860, at a little over 20 feet were too short for such long journeys and were therefore not taken into joint stock. However, once replacement vehicles became available from 1881, the SCR vans were surplus and could be offered to the Highland.

## Jones 37ft 9in Mail Vans

In 1884 the PO was also complaining that, with the impending introduction of the parcel service, the vans operating on the Down night mail between Perth and Inverness were too small. As a consequence in October two 37ft 9in foot long vans were ordered off the Midland Carriage Co at a cost of £565 each. A further van was required in 1888 and built at Lochgorm at a cost of £500. In August 1890 it was proposed to extend the use of the sorting carriage in the Down mail from Tain to Helmsdale, requiring an additional large Mail Van from 1 July 1891, while one more appears to have been under construction in December 1896.

*Diagrams 41 and 42*

The 1901 diagram book shows that Type C Nos. 5, 6 and 10 to diagram 41 were mounted on 6-foot wheelbase

| HR Jones Post Office Mail Vans | | | | | | | | | |
|---|---|---|---|---|---|---|---|---|---|
| Diagrams | | Type | Wheels | Nos. | | Built | Size l x w | Tare wt | Remarks |
| HR 1901 | LMS 1923 | | | HR | 1st LMS | | *(ft-in)* | *(T-c)* | |
| 41 | | C | 6/bogie | 5, 6 10 | - | 1881 1891 | 37-9 x 8-1 | 18-0 | Rebuilt as pbv '17, see above |
| 42 | 54 | D | 6/bogie | 7-9 | 7364-6 | 1885/9 | 37-9 x 8-1 | 18-0 | SH, wdn c'14 |
| 43 | - | E | 6wh | 11, 12 | - | 1894 | 20-0 x 7-3 | 20-0 | Became stores van |
| 44 | | F | Bogie | 13, 14 | - | 1894 | 37-9 x 8-1 | 18-10 | Parcel vans, No. 13 wdn c'14 |

*Corkerhill's tool van No. 354398 in August 1950 converted from a former Highland 37ft 9in bogie Post Office Mail Van to HR diagram 41, showing the recess within which the pick up gear was originally fitted and the opening in the end for the Lansdowne gangway connection. (CJB Sanderson)*

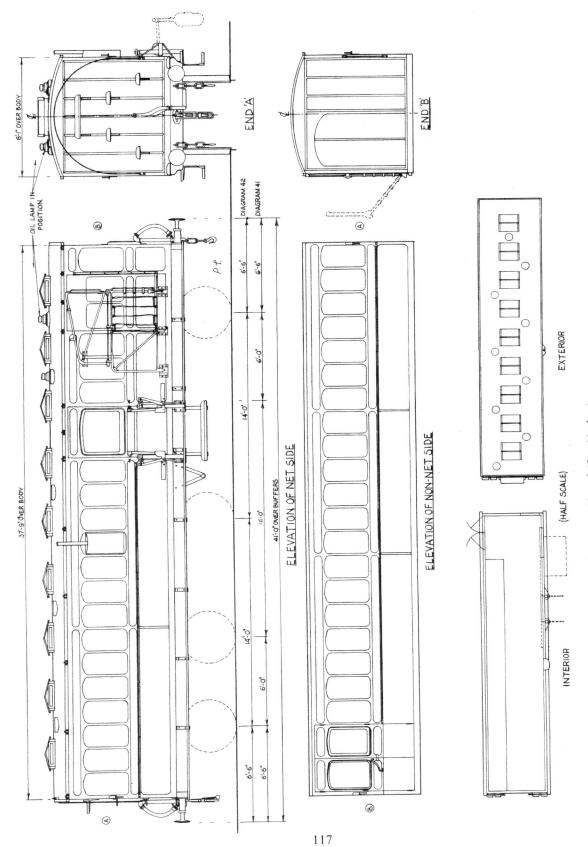

*Figure 46 - Jones 6-wh/bogie Post Office Van to diagrams 41 and 42. (Author)*

*By the same photographer, possibly on the same occasion, the opposite side of apparently the same or very similar vehicle, but numbered 354958. Both sides have vertical match boarding in place of the original lower panels. (CJB Sanderson)*

bogies and Type D Nos. 7, 8 and 9 to diagram 42 were 6-wheeled, whereas only the latter are listed in the 1923 book but are shown fitted with bogies, although only No. 10 was renumbered into the LMS lists. This suggests that, like the contemporary passenger coaches, all 37ft 9in long by 8ft 1in Post Office Vans built in the 1881 to 1891 period had originally been mounted on 6-wheel Cleminson under-frames with 14ft 3in plus 14ft 3in wheelbase and over the years all may have been re-mounted on bogies.

The vehicles had vacuum brake gear added, including alarm gear on the end with steps. 3 foot wide Lansdowne offset gangways were fitted at the net end only. Inside there was a bench for most of the length on the side away from the net apparatus. Opposite the bench and about half way along a sealing wax pot was let into one of the upper panels. Originally oil lit, they were later altered to gas with naked jets, requiring a large longitudinal cylinder to be fitted on the non-net side, if not both. In gas lit days at least, a lamp was

mounted low down on the waist forward of the forward door pointing towards the traductor arms and the Garratt's bag receiving net apparatus.

*Diagram 44*

Diagram 44 for Post Office Parcels Vans Nos. 13 and 14 Type F built in 1894 shows a 37ft 9in long by 8ft 1in wide vehicle mounted on 7ft 6in wheelbase bogies. They had two sliding doors and offset Lansdowne gangway connections, but without any exchange apparatus.

**Later Mail Vans**

All the 20th century Mail Vans were bogie vehicles with 46ft 8in long by 8 foot wide bodies with offset Lansdowne gangway connections at both ends, vacuum braked fitted and, apart from initially No. 3, all electrically lit from new. Confusingly all these vans are covered by LMS diagram 55, which actually shows No. 3.

| Later HR Bogie Post Office Vans | | | | | | | | | |
|---|---|---|---|---|---|---|---|---|---|
| | *Diagrams* | | | *Nos* | | *Built* | *Drg No.* | *Wth'n* | *Remarks* |
| *HR 1901* | *LMS 1923* | *NDiv* | *HR* | *LMS 1st* | *2nd* | | | | |
| 45 | 55p | 55/130 | 3 | 7367 | - | 1901 | 2485 | 5/63 | Parcels Van Type G, SH |
| | 55p | 130 | 13, 14 | 7368/9 | - | 1914/5? | 3411 | c'31 | 7368 to tool van No. 3548615 |
| 66 | 55p | 130 | 5, 6, 10 | 7361-3 | 30321-3 | 1916-7? | 3446 | 13/61 | Iracier axleboxes |

*Drummond Parcel Sorting Van*

A Parcel Sorting Van No. 3 to HR diagram 45 was added to stock in 1901, having been built at Lochgorm, to work on the 6.25 am mail train from Perth as far as Inverness and return over-night. It was of typical early Drummond style fully panelled with low-arc roof, roof lights and a pair of wide sliding doors on both sides with benches between the doors on the gangway connection side. A sealing wax pot was let into one of the upper panels at the left hand end on both sides. Later the lower panels were replaced by vertical match-boarding and it worked out its time as tool van No. 191467 until finally withdrawn from departmental service in May 1963.

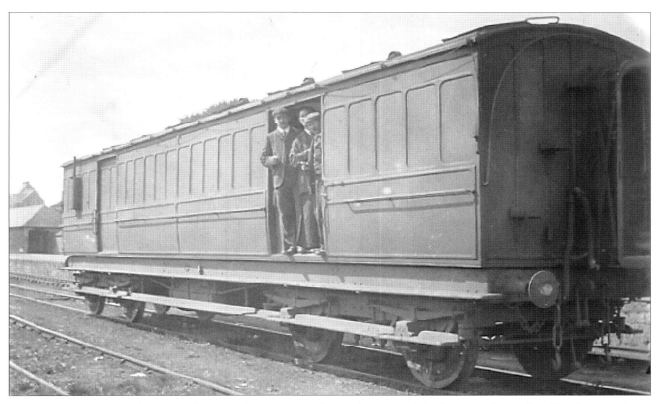

*Parcel sorting van No. 3 pausing between duties at an unknown location while three members of staff look out at the cameraman. The presence of a gas cylinder suspended from the under-frame, the rings for the Harrison passenger alarm gear still attached to the cantrail and a full set of step boards all suggest this is fairly early in its life. (J Roake collection)*

*Another Highland Post Office Van that found its way to a breakdown train on the G&SW Section was former Drummond Post Office Sorting Van No. 3, which became a tool van for the Loco Dept at Ayr. No. DM191467 was photographed there on 1 July 1957. (HC Casserley)*

*Yet another ex-HR PO vertically planked Parcels Van built at Lochgorm in 1915 turned up at Ayr, this time the Smith version as the next number 191468. By 12 May 1958 when this photograph was taken a further window has been inserted in way along the side. (FW Shuttleworth)*

### Smith Parcel Sorting Vans

By June 1913 the Post Office were complaining, yet again, that the existing sorting vans were worn out and in need of replacement, to which the Company would not concede, but proposed to overhaul and to proceed with their gradual replacement.

Nonetheless, perhaps due to an increase in mail for the Fleet, two Parcel Sorting Vans, to drawings signed by FG Smith, were built at Lochgorm in 1915. These were an up-dated version of No. 3 with cove roof profile, lights in the eaves instead of the roof, electric lighting and vertically match-boarding. Internally, as well as the usual benches along one side and shelves on the other, it included a toilet. Heating was by overhead pipes below the roof. One ended up as the tool van No. 191468 at Ayr MPD until at least 1958.

### Post Office Sorting Vans

The final three Post Office Sorting Vans were built at Lochgorm in 1916 and remained in service until 1961, the last being withdrawn in May 1963, having spent their entire lives working between Perth and Inverness, extending to Dingwall in November 1917 and Helmsdale from 6 August 1923. As such these became familiar to the post-war enthusiast as the last, and possibly only, Highland vehicle they encountered in regular service. These followed similar constructional features with two large sliding doors, two pairs of traductors and one collecting net all on one side, with associated Lansdowne gangways in the ends. The other side was plain with a central door, a small low level hatch and drop light to the toilet towards the left hand end. The collecting net was removed during the fifties, but the traductors remained in position. Internally on the side opposite to the pick-up gear five fixed stools faced the letter racks at the left hand end, a door in the centre, with more racks and a toilet in the right hand corner. On the other side, between the pick-up gear numerous pegs were attached to the sides upon which to hang mail bags. Heating was again by overhead pipe. Unlike perhaps other TPOs, the Highland vans seem to have been painted in plain dark olive green until repainted by the LMS in lined crimson lake.

Line-side mail exchange standards were located at up to seventeen sites, viz: Murthly; Dunkeld, 310 yards in advance of starting signal; Ballinluig, 323 yards in advance of starting signal; Pitlochry; Struan; Dalwhinnie; Newtonmore; and Kincraig, 100 yards in rear of home signal; Aviemore; Dunphail; Fort George (Gollanfield); Clunes; Muir of Ord; Conon; Novar

(Evanton); Delney; and Nigg. They were all on the Down side only so there was no need to turn the vans for the Up journey. By March 1937 only those on the main line continued in use, less Murthley and Struan and of these only Dunkeld, Ballinluig and Kincraig survived to September 1956.

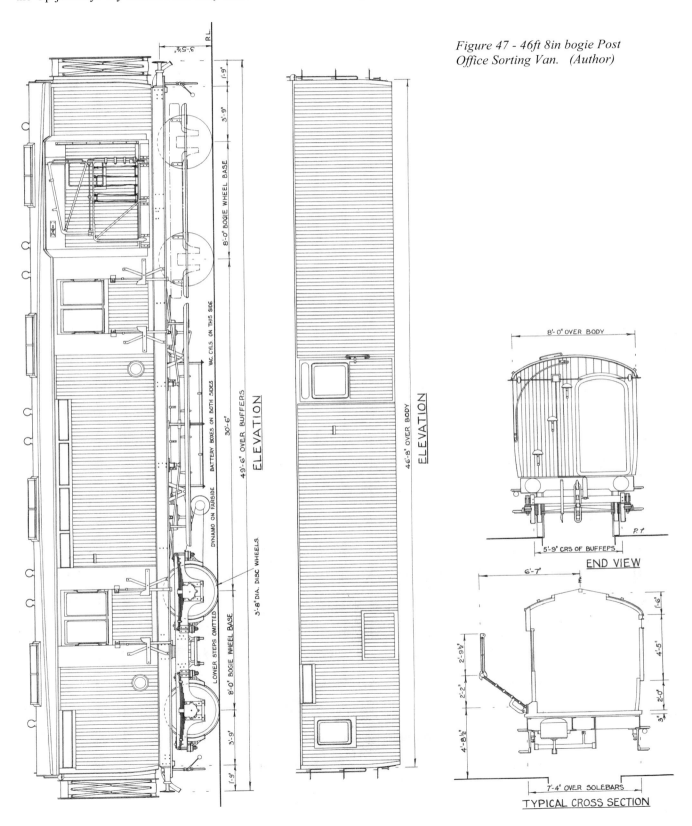

*Figure 47 - 46ft 8in bogie Post Office Sorting Van. (Author)*

By July 1924 it is reported that old Post Office Vans Nos. 3, 7, 8, 9, 13 and 14 were lying at Inverness out of use and suffering from exposure to the elements. Interestingly, as seen above, at least three of these subsequently found further use as breakdown vans on the Northern Division. The newer Highland sorting carriages, however, continued in use until taken out of service in 1961, to be replaced by BR Mark 1s, prior to the cessation of the service on the northern section from 4/5 November 1967 and the southern section after 7 October 1978.

*Pick up net and off sides respectively of Post Office Mail Sorting Van LMS No. 30323 (ex-HR No. 10) during an interval at Dingwall on 23 June 1938. (DLG Hunter)*

*At the northernmost point on its journey at the time, No. M30323 having been dropped off the morning train from Inverness to Wick waits at Helmsdale to be picked up for its return south on 15 June 1949. Note the late posting box to the right of the left hand door, the royal cipher at mid-point and the traductor arms and pick-up gear still in position.*
*(HC Casserley)*

*During its brief morning lie over at Dingwall an unidentified PO Sorting Van waits at Dingwall on 21 September 1960. Note the low level hatch for loading from the off side and on the end the off-set Lansdowne gangway connection unique to PO vehicles. (GE Langmuir)*

*No. M32323 at Aviemore on 24 May 1959 on its way south to Perth. By now the pick-up gear and one of the set of traductor arms has been removed, while* ROYAL MAIL *and a crown have been applied along both sides. (JL Stevenson)*

## Luggage Vans

Despite some having goods wagon diagrams, certain 4-wheeled vehicles, such as: covered and luggage vans with close doors; valuable cattle vans; meat vans and fish trucks, appear from early days to have been set aside for use in passenger trains, rather than being limited to being worked in goods trains, and as time passed received the necessary refinements to allow them to continue in passenger service. These were improved running gear; and in due course a minimum wheel base of 10 feet, although a minimum of 11 feet seems to have been preferred by the neighbouring Caledonian and North British companies; through pipes for continuous brakes, or even full vacuum and occasionally Westinghouse brake gear; steam heating pipes; long buffers and screw-link couplings. As such they will have been painted green in the Highland period and, initially at least, crimson lake once the LMS took over,

although how long thereafter they will have remained in front line duty is uncertain. Usually the hand brake lever, initially on one side only, will have operated on only a single brake block. Once full vacuum brake equipment was added, brake blocks would have been power operated on all four wheels, often as clasp brakes.

The covered vans with close doors were for the conveyance of luggage often in passenger trains. The limitations of early brake power came under review in December 1867, when amongst other things, Stroudley was instructed to fit continuous brakes to closed vans for use on the 4.4pm Up and 3.0am Down trains between Inverness and Perth. At that time this must have meant the Newall brake. Later some were fitted with vacuum brake cylinders and, by 1916 at least, were not allowed into goods train circuits, while those without automatic brake were barred from passenger trains between Inverness and Perth. Only those that reached the LMS are clearly identifiable, as set out below:-

| Later HR Passenger Luggage Vans | | | | | | | | | | |
|---|---|---|---|---|---|---|---|---|---|---|
| Diagrams | | | Nos. | | Built | Size | Wheel base | Drg No. | Last wdn | Remarks |
| HR 1901 | LMS ND | HR | 1st | LMS 2nd | | L x w (ft-in) | (ft-in) | | | |
| W8 | | 769-780 | (7463) | (37893-5) (38286-8) | 1891 | 16-0 x 8-0 | 9-0 | | 6/38* | |
| | W11 | 285-294 | 7457 | 37896/7 (38289) | 1907 | 16-0 x 7-6 | 9-0 | 2313 | 5/55* | |
| | W9 | 772/4 | 7462/4 | 37898/9 38290/1 | 1918 | 18-0 x 7-6 | 11-0 | 3103 | 12/51* | 4 ton capacity |

*Photographs of Highland luggage vans seem to be rare; this rather poor image, however, shows 18 foot long luggage van LMS No. 7464 in crimson lake livery. It was built in 1918 with an 11 foot wheelbase and allocated to LMS diagram 9 in the wagon series which shows that these were fitted with vacuum brake and Westinghouse pipe. (WO Steel collection, courtesy RJ Essery)*

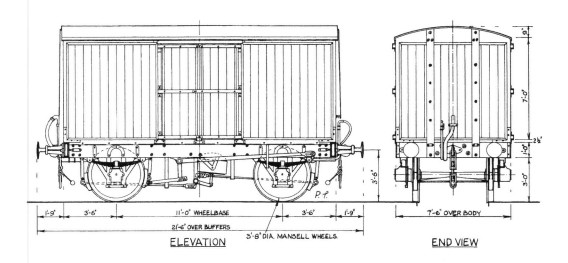

*Figure 48 - 18 foot Passenger luggage van to LMS wagon diagram 9. (Author)*

## Horse Boxes

In 1855 the I&NR order for two horseboxes at a cost of £212 went to Mr William Watson, millwright of Errol. In addition, it is known that I&AJR had three horseboxes as early as February 1857. When in 1878 six more were acquired from Metropolitan Carriage & Wagon at a cost of £202-15-0 each, two of the existing fourteen were cast aside.

The design of later horse boxes passed through a couple of identifiable phases. Both were without windows as horses tend to get frightened if they can see the countryside passing by while they are stationary, but the train is on the move. The 1901 carriage diagram book contains only one style of horse box, diagram 46, which was 18ft 1in long with a space for three horses and a small compartment for the grooms and attendant staff, together with an additional compartment where equipment and hay could be placed, hence its name as the luggage or fodder compartment. So they could look after their charges during the journey, sliding panels between the groom's compartment and the horse box afforded visual, face to face contact.

In January 1903 Drummond introduced a 19ft 8in version, which was adopted over the years for the replacements to the earlier design as and when they became life expired. As might be expected the first new boxes Nos. 1 to 6 were allocated for through or long journeys and were labelled "To be returned to Inverness".

Moveable partitions were provided inside to create three stalls. Both types had full vacuum and Westinghouse brake gear, while steam heating pipes were added to all horseboxes from 1913 at a cost of £2 each. The lower running numbers of LMS diagram 56 will have been renewals for earlier horseboxes withdrawn, whilst the higher numbers are likely to have been additions to capital stock. There are numerous variations in the detail of the body cladding, with a

| | | | | | | | Built | Size | Wheel | Tare | Last wdn |
|---|---|---|---|---|---|---|---|---|---|---|---|
| *Diagrams* | | | | *Nos.* | | | | | base | wt | |
| *HR 1901* | *LMS 1923* | *ND* | *HR* | *1st* | *LMS* | *2nd* | | *L x w (ft-in)* | *(ft-in)* | *(T-c)* | |
| 46 | 57 | - | 1-25, 105 | 7532-3 | | - | | 18-1 x 8-0 | 11-0 | 9-5 | Pre '33 |
| 59 | 56 | 56 | 1-6 | 7521-6 | | 43785-7 | 1903 | 19-8 x 8-9 | 11-0 | 10-0 | 9/36 |
| | | | 26-31 | 7540-5 | | 43788-91 | 1911 | | | | 11/47 |
| | | | 14, 20 | 7534-5 | | 43792 | 1914 | | | | 11/47 |
| | | | 22-24 | 7536-8 | | 43777-8 | 1921 | | | | 3/56 |
| | | | 7-11, 25 | 7527-31/9 | | 43779-84 | 1923 | | | | 8/55 |

**HR Horseboxes**

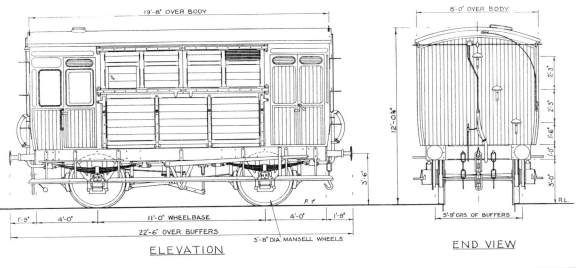

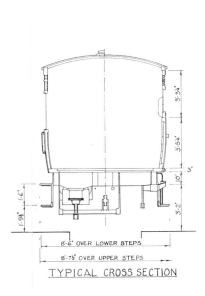

*Figure 49 - Drummond 19 foot horsebox to LMS Diagram 56. (Author)*

*HR horsebox, possibly No. 43783, ex-HR No. 11 built in 1923, to LMS diagram 56 as the leading vehicle behind an LMS Stanier 4-6-0 Black 5 recently arrived at Inverness, probably on 23 June 1938. Note the panelling on the ends and horizontal planking on the compartment doors. (DLG Hunter)*

tendency for increasing amounts of vertical planking in lieu of panelling, as with the passing of time construction practice became more utilitarian for both new build and maintenance repairs.

Following World War 1, road vehicles of all types began to replace horse power for commercial purposes and consequently the need for railway horse boxes gradually declined, so the LMS let the fleet reduce by natural wastage.

## Valuable Cattle Vans

Prize cattle heading for agricultural shows warranted something better than an ordinary cattle truck, so rather than hire in from another company, in April 1900 the Board agreed to build two valuable cattle vans. To wagon diagram 22, these followed the usual pattern of a drover's compartment between and with access to two cattle boxes. Externally each box was accessed by a pair of doors on each side consisting of a falling door, to

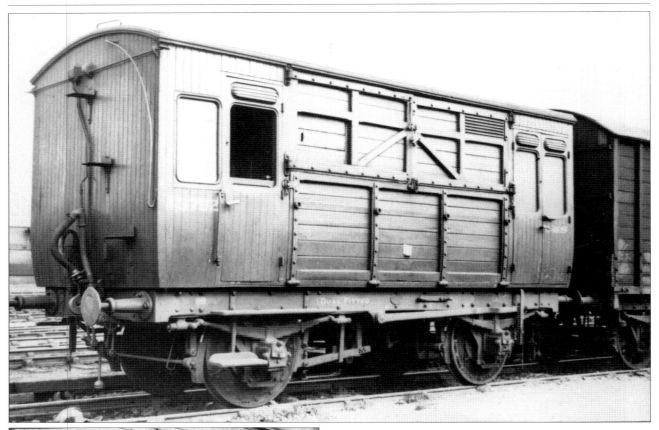

**Top -** *LMS second series No. 43792, formerly HR No. 14 built at Lochgorm in 1914 with a high proportion of vertical match boarding photographed in 1935. Note the two forms of brake hose and Mansell wheels. (LGRP, author's collection)*

**Left -** *Close-up of the door to a 19ft 8in horse box No. M43784. Note the sliding shutter in the upper leaf of the horse door and hand-brake lever below foot-board. (Author's collection)*

provide a ramp up for the animals, closed at the top by side hung double doors. To afford better ventilation these vans had narrow clerestories for much of the length of the roof, causing the hole for the oil lamp to be displaced to one side. The drover's compartment was fitted with a quarter-light and a bucket pointedly placed under the single seat, or was this for cattle feed? In the clerestory over the compartment was a 40 gallon water tank from which to quench the animals thirst.

23ft 6in long the body was mounted on a flitched under-frame with a 13 foot wheelbase. As built in 1900, they were equipped with Drummond's patent each side brake and pipes for vacuum and Westinghouse. Steam pipes were not added until 1920, when the cost for fitting had risen to £13-5-0 each. The last was allocated a second series LMS number, but was withdrawn in May 1933 before this could be applied.

| HR Valuable Cattle Vans | | | | | | | | |
|---|---|---|---|---|---|---|---|---|
| Diagrams | | | Nos. | | Built | Size | Wheel base | Last |
| HR 1901 | LMS ND | HR | 1st | LMS 2nd | | L x w (ft-in) | (ft-in) | wdn |
| W22 | W22 | 2365-6 | 7847-8 | (43999) | 1900 | 23-6 x 8-6 | 13-0 | 5/33 |

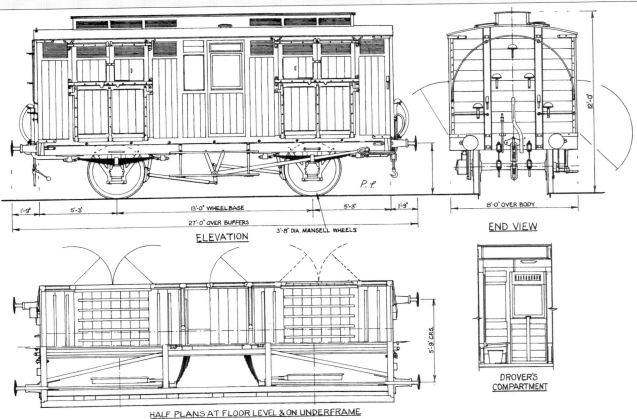

*Figure 50 - Drummond valuable cattle van to diagram 22. (Author)*

## Carriage Trucks

With, until the mid-twentieth century, such poor conditions and torturous roads in parts of the Highlands the railway was called upon perhaps more than most to provide transport for road vehicles. Indeed from time to time it offered a ferry service over particularly difficult terrain, or to bypass ferries where no highway existed. As early motorcars reached its territory it is known to have run such a service from Blair Atholl over the Hill to Inverness and another from Strathcarron to Kyle of Lochalsh, avoiding the ferry at Strome.

### Open Carriage Truck (Type A)

Again the I&AJR had three carriage trucks in February 1857 and presumably these were of the open type. By

1901 diagram 47 indicates fourteen 18 foot long trucks of the usual form with a side bar on each side against which to secure adjustable cross bars and leather straps to tie the vehicle down. All were built by HR at Lochgorm Works and in due course vacuum automatic brake fitted and Westinghouse piped. A hand lever applied the brake to the left hand wheel. It is unclear whether this was on both sides of the truck from the outset, but, if not, a second is likely to have been added later. The trucks were fitted with Mansell wheels. Two forms of wheel plate are apparent, one consisting of short plates just at each end, while the other had turned up lips on each side and stretched from one end to the other. Both projected over the headstocks to assist the wheels bridge the gap to the end dock.

| HR Open Carriage Trucks | | | | | | | | | |
|---|---|---|---|---|---|---|---|---|---|
| Diagrams | | | | Nos | | Built | Size | Wheel base | Tare wt | Last wdn |
| HR 1901 | LMS 1923 | ND | HR | 1st | LMS 2nd | | L x w (ft-in) | (ft-in) | (T-c) | |
| 47 | 58 | 58 | 1-20, 32-3 | 7504-20 | 41893-8 | 1899-1920 | 18-0 x 8-0 | 11-0 | 6-10 | 5/65* |

Note:    *    Not found during census, so written off.

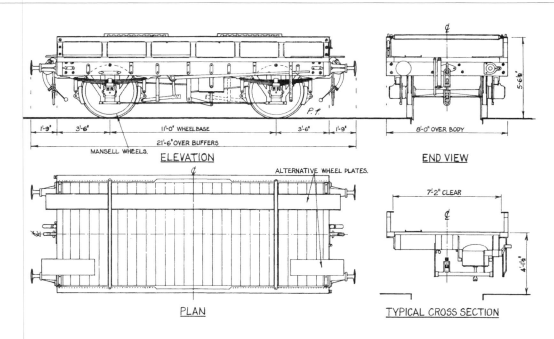

*Figure 51 - 18 foot open carriage truck to diagram 47. (Author)*

*18 foot long open carriage truck No. 41897 (ex-HR No. 2 and LMS 1st No. 7505) was built at Lochgorm in 1920. The longitudinal position of the two cross bars between the side rails, to which the number has been applied, together with stout leather straps were used to secure the road vehicle on the truck. Ignoring one written off as lost in May 1965, this was the last of the type being withdrawn in November 1957. (DLG Hunter)*

## Covered Carriage Trucks

By 1878, if not before, the Highland had acquired covered carriage trucks, purchasing two that year from the Metropolitan Carriage & Wagon Co for £170-7-6 each. Diagram 48 of the 1901 book shows Nos. 15 to 20 as 18 foot long covered carriage trucks.

By 1902 the availability of 24 foot long underframes, recovered from old rib-sided coaches, prompted the construction of longer trucks, particularly for motor vehicles then coming into vogue, and these were outshopped from Lochgorm in batches over the coming two decades, initially at a cost of £112/116 each.

The first batches appear to have had arc roofs (LMS diagram 59), but it was realised that taller vehicles could be accommodated, without fouling the loading gauge, if a high elliptical roof was adopted (LMS diagram 60). Then in 1911, by using sliding doors instead of a pair of cupboard doors, the trucks could also be used to convey fish (LMS diagram 61). These cost £170 per van.

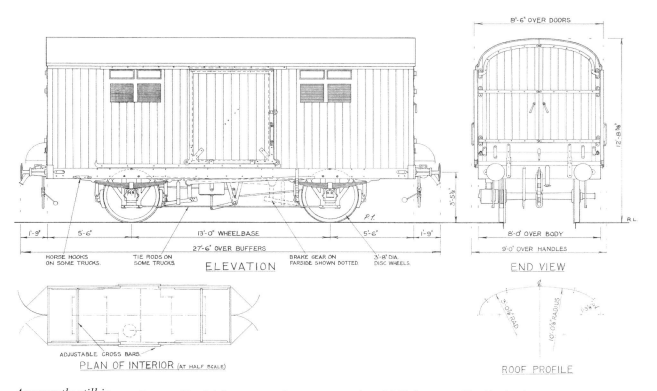

Figure 52 - 24 foot covered carriage truck to LMS diagram 61. (Author)

*Apparently still in revenue earning service, 24 foot long covered carriage truck No. M37197, ex-HR No. 45 built in 1912 and earlier LMS No. 7498, survived to be nationalised and was not withdrawn until February 1955. The cross within a circle indicated that the vehicle was not permitted on the Metropolitan Widened lines of London Transport.*

131

**HR Covered Carriage Trucks**

| Diagrams | | | HR | Nos. | | Built | Size | Wheel base | Tare wt | Drg No. | Last wdn | Remarks |
|---|---|---|---|---|---|---|---|---|---|---|---|---|
| HR 1901 | LMS 1923 | ND | | 1st | LMS 2nd | | L x w (ft-in) | (ft-in) | (T-c) | | | |
| 48 | - | - | 15-20 | - | - | | 18-0 x 8-0 | 11-0 | | | u/k | |
| - | 59 | 59 | 23-38 | 7478-91 | 37189-95 | 1904-10-18? | 24-0 x 8-6 | 13-0 | 9-0 | 2732 | 2/37 | Low arc roof & cupboard doors |
| | | 60 | 15-18, 21-22 | 7472-7 | 37196-99 | 1921 | 24-0 x 8-6 | 13-0 | 9-0 | 3259 | 3/56 | Elliptical roof & cupboard doors |
| | | 61 | 39-50 | 7492-7503 | 37492-99 | 1912 | 24-0 x 9-0 | 13-0 | | 3328 | 2/55 | Elliptical roof & sliding doors |

**Right -** *End view of a covered carriage truck, possibly No. 297223. (I Vaughan)*

**Bottom -** *By 26 August 1938 LMS No. 297223 had found further use in departmental service acting as a tool van for the Signals & Telegraph Engineers Department, later at least at Irvine. (DLG Hunter)*

## 11-Ton Meat vans

Until the 1880s dead meat had been conveyed to London in hampers covered with cloths, but in April 1881, to meet the demands of his customers, the Goods Manager requested well ventilated vans with hooks upon which to hang the carcasses. In response Jones built twenty vans at a cost of £150 each, plus £5 to make them suitable for working in passenger trains. Ten further vans were added in 1891. These 17ft 6in long by 8 foot wide vans

were initially fitted with Mansell wheels, although some were later changed for eight open-spoked ones; through vacuum brake pipe and originally with hand brake lever on only one side. The over-sail at the ends of the clerestory provided ventilation to the contents at a high level. Originally the louvred vents in lower body side extended in three panels for the full width each side of the door. Subsequently those adjacent to the door were sealed up by extending the vertical match boarding of the sides down to kerb level.

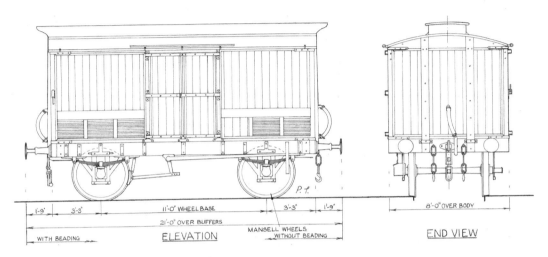

**Above** - *Figure 53 Jones 11-ton meat van to HR wagon diagram 21. (Author)*

**Right** - *A Jones meat van with clerestory roof No. 2521 in the latter years of its life. The hand brake is on the far side only and smaller diameter spoked wheels have been fitted. (CP Keane, J Suter collection)*

| HR 11-Ton Meat Vans | | | | | | | | | |
|---|---|---|---|---|---|---|---|---|---|
| Diagrams | | Nos. | | Built | Size | Wheel base | Tare wt | Drg No. | Remarks |
| HR 1901 | LMS ND | HR | 1st LMS | | L x w (ft-in) | (ft-in) | (T-c) | | |
| W21 | - | 2320-39, 2515-24 | | | 17-6 x 8-0 | 11-0 | 7-0 | | Jones clerestory design |
| - | 62 | 2794-2803 2894-23 | Possibly 7848-7880 | HR 1904 HR 1906 | 17-6 x 8-0 | 10-0 | 7-0 | 2918 | Drummond design |
| - | 63 | 2804-68 | | Pickering, 1911 | 17-6 x 8-0 | 11-0 | 7-0 | 3295 | Drummond design |

When in April 1904, the construction of another ten meat vans was sanctioned at a cost of £155 each, but qualified by the need to make them suitable for other purposes, Drummond prepared his own design. Another twenty to be built in the workshops were ordered in May 1906 at an estimated cost of £160, including dual brakes. Difficulty was experienced in sourcing the oak scantlings and the use of steel underframes was briefly considered, but American oak with flinched steel plates was eventually chosen, together with disc wheels. They were piped for both vacuum and Westinghouse brake, but fitted with hand brake on both wheels actuated by Drummond's patent each side system.

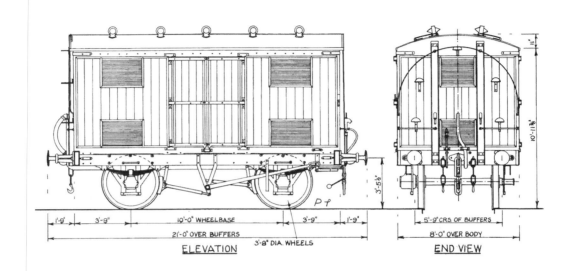

ELEVATION

END VIEW

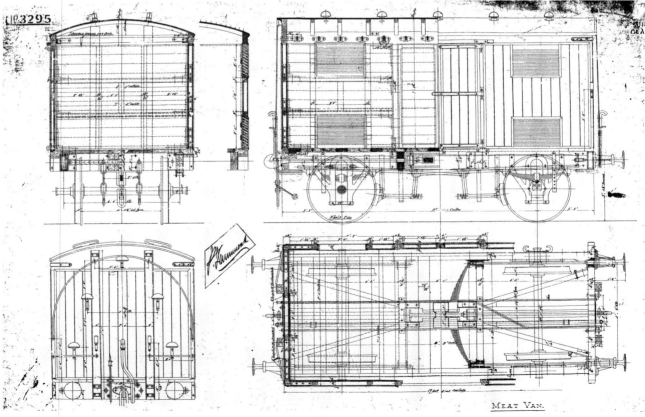

MEAT VAN.

***Opposite middle -*** *Figure 54 Drummond meat van with 10 foot wheelbase to LMS diagram 62. (Author)*

***Opposite bottom -*** *Figure 55 Meat van to LMS diagram 63 with 11 foot wheel base in accordance with the latest requirements of the Caledonian and North British railways. (Author's collection)*

In February 1911 the construction of twenty more was authorised, but with an 11-foot wheelbase and omitting the louvres in the ends. Again they were dual piped, but provided with simple hand brakes on each side actuating on one wheel per side. Instead of undertaking this in the workshops, however, the order was placed the next month with RY Pickering at a price of £178 each.

Two general arrangement drawings and two LMS diagrams exist for Drummond style meat vans, the first with a 10 foot wheelbase and the second 11 foot, which latter wheelbase was definitely adopted for the Pickering vans, but which vehicles, if any, had the shorter wheelbase is uncertain. Both were conceived as having 8-ton capacity, but are shown as 11-ton on the LMS diagrams, like the earlier Jones vans.

By June 1909 meat vans Nos. 2321, 2329, 2330, 2334, 2515, 2516, 2518, 2519 and 2522 had been fitted with divisions and until the end of September were exclusively reserved for the traffic originating at Keith.

*HR 8-ton 17ft 6in long meat van as new, one of twenty built by RY Pickering in 1911 with an 11 foot wheel base. Although piped for both vacuum and Westinghouse brake, only a single hand lever can be applied to one brake block per side. Safety chains are still being provided. (Author's collection)*

*Much later in life an unidentified meat van has gravitated to being an Engineer's tool van. (Author's collection)*

### Open Fish Trucks

In the 1890s, depending on the season and competition from other railway companies and points at which catches were landed, 12,000 to 17,000 tons of fish was generally being carried annually by the Highland Railway. Originally fish traffic was variously despatched in boxes, barrels, or alive in tanks. The first two were conveyed in open fish trucks sheeted over, or, as has been suggested, covered in peat turves. The Highland had three types all 18 feet long. First of 100 fish trucks were introduced on the line in 1872 and they were not to be used for other traffic without the authority of the Traffic Manager. The earliest had 4-plank sides and central falling doors and curved ends (Figure 56). From December 1892 Westinghouse pipes were to be fitted to fish trucks for through running to foreign companies.

Of the total of 300 by the turn of the century, the 1901 wagon diagram 12 - Type K refers to a Jones design of 8 foot width with curved ends, although some square ended fish trucks existed perhaps following repair. From 1896, as the Jones type wore out, they were replaced by similar vehicles with straight ends (LMS Northern Division diagram 64) but of the Drummond width of 7ft 7in overall (Fig 57). A variation of the latter had full length drop-sides, thereby enabling them out of season to double up as an open carriage truck if the occasion demanded (Fig 58). If not fitted from the outset, lamp brackets will have soon been provided. Later full brake rigging and steam pipes will also have been added.

Known numbers in HR (Nos. 1874 to 2146) and LMS 1st series (Nos. 7547 to 7845) have a few gaps, but

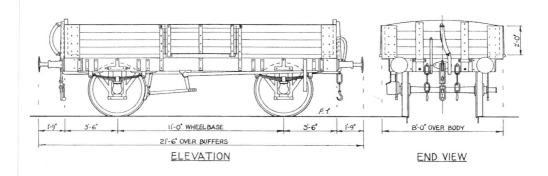

ELEVATION    END VIEW

*Figure 56 - Jones open fish truck to HR wagon diagram 12. (Author)*

| HR Open Fish Trucks | | | | | | | |
|---|---|---|---|---|---|---|---|
| | Nos. | | Built | Wheel | Tare | Drg | Last |
| HR | LMS | | | base | wt | No. | wdn |
| | 1st | 2nd | | (ft-in) | (T-c) | | |
| 1847 | 7547- | 40978 | HR | 11-0 | 5-18 | 2654 | 12/56 |
| - | 7845 | -99 | | | | | |
| 2146 | | | | | | | |

each was probably at one time allocated to a truck since withdrawn, while not all LMS 2nd series (Nos. 40978 to 40999) were actually carried. Of those trucks allocated 2nd series numbers, all were 7ft 7in wide and building dates range from 1897 to 1916, suggesting, as one might expect, that the earlier 8 foot wide Jones version was extinct by 1933. Except for those achieving the 2nd LMS number being of the more modern two designs, it is not possible to determine which type any number applies to unless photographs are available.

By May 1903, new Fish trucks Nos. 1847, 1848, 1849, 1850, 1851, 18952 and 2146 fitted with continuous brakes and oil boxes were not allowed to be used for goods traffic and must be retained for Passenger Traffic only. On the other hand meantime all other fish trucks could be used for conveyance of light loads of general goods between local stations, or for hay and wool traffic to foreign stations, load not to exceed 6 tons, in December 1911 amended to 4 tons; but on no account were they to be employed in carrying stones, coal, lime, or any other mineral traffic.

During the summer in anticipation of the fishing season, the Weekly Notices would require that all fish trucks currently in goods circuit to be removed and confined to passenger traffic. In 1903, those located north of Dingwall were to be sent to Wick and Thurso, while those at stations south of Dingwall were to be forwarded to Kyle of Lochalsh; by June 1913 altered to those trucks south of Tain.

On the other hand, the amount of traffic in passenger's luggage generated by the change over of holiday lettings at the end of September led to instructions being issued, from 1900 at least onwards until perhaps 1914, as follows:

**CHANGE OF MONTH TRAFFIC**
**Where Luggage Vans cannot be provided, Fish Trucks thoroughly cleaned and provided with covers to keep the Contents dry, to be used for stations having large quantities of Luggage for Edinburgh, Glasgow or Dundee to load direct into fish trucks.**

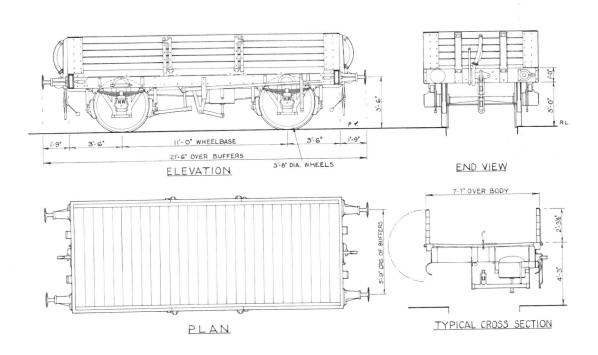

*Figure 57 - Drummond open fish truck to LMS carriage diagram 64. (Author)*

*The '80 28.5.54' painted on the solebar indicates that ex-HR open fish truck No. M40993 has recently been overhauled by BR, after which it survived until December 1956. Formerly HR No. 2096 built by the company in 1912, its first LMS No. was 7795. Alterations include smaller diameter wheels, note the joggled keep plates; hand brake lever and push rods; and the removal of Westinghouse brake pipe. On this and the truck below the four side planks appear to have been replaced by five narrower ones and in the case of the above intermediate washer plates added.*

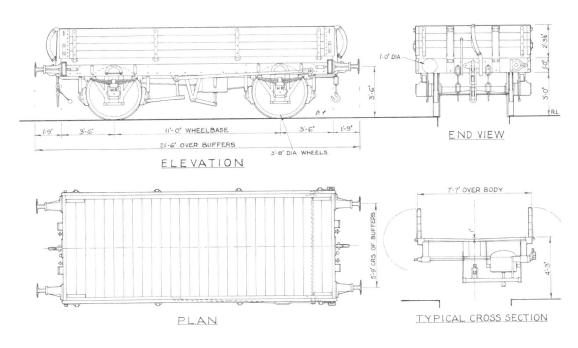

*Figure 58 - Drummond open fish truck with drop sides also to LMS carriage diagram 64. (Author)*

**Opposite bottom** - *Looking up at the corner of an unidentified 4-plank open fish wagon on 12 April 1939. Note the lamp bracket on the end, clasp brakes and HR axle-boxes. (DLG Hunter)*

**Above** - *Formerly LMS first No 7566, No 40981 was built at Lochgorm in 1904 as HR No. 1867 with drop-sides. It is still fitted with dual brake pipes and Mansell wheels, being withdrawn in May 1944. (AB McLeod, HRS Collection)*

The original promoters of the eventual Highland Railway network envisaged the creation of the line being as much if not more for the conveyance of goods and minerals, as it was for the more glamorous movement of passengers. So, even the company's front line express passenger engines had occasionally to take their turn at hauling the humble goods train. Here Drummond 4-6-0 Castle class No. 149 Duncraig Castle, fitted with Westinghouse pump, runs the last length along Caledonian route from Stanley Jct into Perth in around 1923. Behind No. 149 is a mixed train containing a wide variety of types of wagon from various companies, including a few vans. Apart from the brake van at the rear, no Highland wagon is identifiable, although the first is a Caledonian 4-plank end door mineral wagon followed by a private trader's wagon. (HL Salmon, courtesy Stephenson Locomotive Society)

# Goods Wagons

## General Review

Outgoing goods traffic on the Highland Railway derived from a thriving trade in timber; farm produce; livestock; malt whisky in barrels and spent mash as cattle feed; quarried stone; wool; and tweed. Incoming included coal; malting barley and yeast; and general merchandise, including more domestic items for shop & hotel supplies – wines, spirits, laundry, cigarettes, drapery and household goods.

To convey these, like contemporary carriages, very early wagons were constructed using guard irons mounted on the outside of the solebars and carrying springs, while the solebars were of timber. Some early wheels were of cast iron with a multitude of radial webs on the inside like the underside of a mushroom.

*Building Styles*

Wagons provided during Jones' tenure of office can be identified by the inverted 'tee' shaped crown plates to the guard irons, the horizontal leg of the left hand of which was extended in each direction to provide horse or towing hooks (Fig 59.9). The outside width over the body planking or sheeting was usually 8 feet. Except for vans and cattle and sheep trucks, the headstock did not extend the full width of the body as was more usual later; instead it was curtailed in line with the outside of the solebars with a wrap round corner plate. On vans etc. the vertical corner posts were spliced on an inclination with the end of the headstock. The drawbar front plates on the headstocks were often elliptical and the base of the buffer guides circular with four fixing bolts around the periphery (Fig 59.11). Generally Jones seems to have used 3ft 8in diameter wheels, although the smaller 3ft 2in are to be found, perhaps due to renewals later in life.

*Above right - much of its existence the Highland Railway used open spoked wheels of either 3ft 8in or 3ft 2in diameter with grease lubricated axle-boxes on goods stock, as seen on the Strathspey Railway at Aviemore on 25 August 1974. (Author)*

*Right - Just as at in 1903 an I&AJR 4-wheel Passenger Brake Van had been found lurking at the back of Perth shed, so it appears that at about the same time one of the same company's 3-plank drop side, but fixed end, wagons supposedly built in 1858 was also unearthed. Discounting the paper cut out company initials and builder's plate, which may or may not represent underlying features: the self-contained buffers, which might indicate former dumb buffers; the outside guard irons and unusual cast wheel centres with multiple radial webs are worthy of note. (WG Chalmers collection)*

*Inset - A HR wagon ticket for wagon No. 2727 and sheet No. 177 for a journey from Perth to Blairathole on 19 March 1886. (Author's collection)*

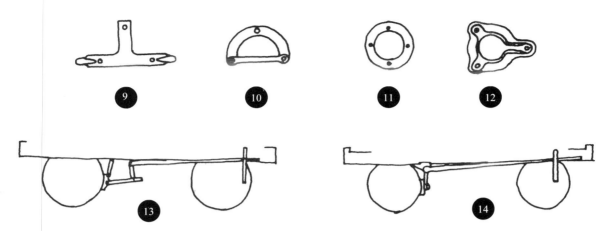

*Figure 59 - Distinguishing features of Jones and Drummond wagons. (Author)*

Drummond wagons on the other hand had full width headstocks with banding at the ends to limit splitting, diamond shaped drawbar front plates and three bolt fixing to the buffer guides (Fig 59.12). Semi-circular crown washer plates over the wheels replaced the inverted tee (Fig 59.10). The width over the bodywork was generally 7ft 7in, or occasionally 7ft 6in.

As might be expected, when the new Locomotive Superintendent arrived on the scene in the form of Peter Drummond, he quickly asserted that the existing stock of goods vehicles was in an unsatisfactory condition and that out of a total of 1,971 cattle, mineral

*The later style of three-bolt buffer adopted by Drummond and subsequently, as applied to double deck sheep van LMS No. 284555. (WO Steel collection, courtesy RJ Essery)*

and merchandise wagons about two thirds would require rebuilding. In February 1915 the shortage of wagons became so acute that resort had to be made to hiring wagons from various sources until 1920, while in addition hundreds were lent by NB, GE and SECR.

In August 1920 six 30-ton bogie wagons and thirteen 10/12-ton wagons from the Government's wagon pool built up during the war were made available to the Highland on hire. With the Ministry of Transport's approval, bolsters were made and fitted to four of the bogie wagons at a cost of £80 each to make them suitable for conveying long timber.

### Drawings and diagrams

The situation with regard to drawings and diagrams is generally as already described for coaches with wagons included in the 1901 diagram book. In the case of wagons, however, as life expired vehicles were renewed by new construction, the displaced vehicles' number was reused, a new diagram was apparently not always issued even if of different form. As with carriages, the LMS Northern Division issued a series of larger diagrams for the few remaining ex-Highland wagons still in use. The contents of the various books are listed in Appendix 2.

### Buffers

As originally conceived the line eastward from Inverness was to be connected to the Great North of Scotland Railway which was advancing in stages from Aberdeen. In 1857 the GNS made it plain that they would only accept for onward transmission goods wagons fitted with sprung buffers and, after consulting with the Engineer and despite Mr Allan's reservations, the I&AJR agreed to go along with this. As a result the Highland had only a few wagons with dumb buffers, mainly ballast wagons and a few early service vehicles. An exception to this was a later batch of mineral wagons to be worked up the main line from collieries in the south, together with early bolster wagons for local traffic. Despite this, dumb-buffered wagons were in common use elsewhere and as late as September 1915 the North British was urging the Highland to continue to accept dumb buffered wagons until the end of the year.

### Miscellaneous

The Highland had adopted the double horn attached to the solebar, usually above the left-hand wheel, for use when towing wagons by rope attached to a horse, capstan, or more controversially to an engine on an adjacent track. At some point in the first decade of the 20th century closed loops had briefly been fitted instead, a practice depreciated by the Traffic Department and reversed at the end of December 1907.

### Common User Arrangement

On 5 June 1916, following the lead set in England, the CR, NB and GSW signed up to a Common User Agreement to form a common pool of ordinary wagons and, by much reducing empty running and affording greater flexibility, thereby improve their utilisation. This had been initiated between the GN, GC and GE railways on 13 December 1913 with unfitted medium and high-sided open wagons. The advantages in the supply of wagons were such that, under the pressures of World War 1, the scheme was widened until from 2 January 1917 all companies, including the Highland, partook. The common use of wagon sheets followed on 14 February that year.

The process was obviously found to be generally beneficial and was therefore continued following grouping on 1 January 1923. One unfortunate result was that, among the vast hordes of wagons elsewhere, the Highland's small stock of wagons became widely dispersed, which, apart from the clearly identifiable double-deck sheep vans and 6-wheel goods brake vans, led on the whole to a failure by those whose might have been interested to make any note of them.

### Brakes

Like most other Scottish companies, the Highland Railway used the long handled brake lever on one side only acting through a cast iron fulcrum attached directly to the solebar to the right of the left-hand wheel (Fig 59.13). The brake block was suspended on a hanger also attached to the solebar adjacent to the fulcrum. The braking force was applied through a drop-arm off the side lever acting on a short push rod pressing a single cast iron brake shoe onto the tread of the wheel. Re-adjustment of the block for wear was achieved by a series of closely spaced holes in the push rod, although some Drummond 9 foot wheelbase vehicles had a cast iron shoe attached directly to the drop arm, adjustment being by means of a range of holes (Fig 59.14).

By 1896, the Board of Trade was pressing the company to provide brake levers on both sides of the wagon, although it was to be November 1911 before the Regulations were implemented and, due to the outbreak of World War 1 and other extenuating circumstances, 1938 before all wagons had to comply. The easiest way to achieve this on existing wagons was to add another separate set on the opposite side, which was put in hand over a number of years at a cost of £1 per wagon and this was still on-going in 1908.

In the interim, various ideas were developed in an attempt to meet the proposed requirements for a right hand lever brake of like pattern on both sides that could only be released from the side on which it was applied. Amongst the inventors was Peter Drummond, who devised mechanism consisting of the usual right-hand lever one side, acting on only one brake block, at the upper end of which was an elongated hole. The slot thus created engaged with a short cranked lever at one end of a cross-shaft located just short of the headstock under the solebar. On the opposite side of the cross-shaft now at the left hand end of the wagon was another similar short lever, which meant that by raising up either short lever, the long lever was pushed down thereby applying the brake. This, however, did not comply with the regulations, which required a downward movement and both sides to be right-handed. Nonetheless, a few wagons had the Drummond system fitted, see Figure 62, page 147 and Figure 78 on page 172. Following an accident on 29 January 1906 at Curzon Street, Birmingham, however, in which a man's hand was trapped when unwittingly it was applied from both sides at the same time, the Highland was obliged to remove them promptly and fit a conforming system.

## Numbering

Like the Highland's carriages, the first wagons were numbered in the order of their being taken into stock, but in one combined sequence of all types, except goods brake vans and road vans, which had their own series. Later, as early wagons were renewed the replacement vehicle took its number, unless they were additions to capital stock, when they would have been allocated new numbers at the high end of the list.

### LMS Renumbering of Goods Stock

When in 1923 the London Midland & Scottish Railway took over the Highland Railway's rolling stock, it received 2,718 revenue earning wagons and 114 service vehicles, for which the number series 292000 to 299999 was available, i.e. 8,000 numbers. However, before going on to see how these numbers were allocated, we can dismiss as contenders passenger luggage vans, fish trucks, meat vans and the two valuable-cattle vans. As noted above, these joined other non-passenger coaching stock in the range 7361 to 7848 (and possibly up to 7880) in the LMS's first numbering series for coaching stock.

Initial study of the limited evidence available, largely photographic, suggests that rather than being allocated at random or by adding 294000 to the Highland's numbers, wagons were in fact placed in distinct groups. For instance, all goods brake vans, other than those transferred to service stock, fall within the 2940xx series, whilst the numbers for double-deck sheep vans so far found are all in the group 2945xx. However, as there were 292 livestock vans at the grouping, the range for them was presumably a little more extensive. The 296xxx series seems to have been reserved for mineral and open wagons, although it is

possible that they were by then on loco coal duties. The 12-ton open wagons built in 1914 and 1915 so far found fall within the range 296738 to 296873.

The next group, 297xxx, contains all the service stock allocated to the Highland Section, including vehicles transferred from revenue-earning stock after the grouping. Examples exist of foreign vehicles being allocated the number of a vehicle of Highland origin which it replaced, whilst HR vehicles transferred to other sections for non-revenue earning purposes were renumbered in that section's block of numbers within their group. Wagons etc. of different types were numbered in distinct batches, starting with 29700x for cradle bolster wagons. Single bolster wagons known carry numbers from 297053 to 297129, which presumably includes a number of rail and timber wagons from former revenue-earning stock. These are followed by two-plank drop-side ballast wagons from 297184 to 297217, of which there were 54 in 1923. Various mess vans without facilities for a guard, crane runners etc. are to be found between 297223 and 297247. Finally, ballast brake vans and tool vans equipped to carry a guard fall within Nos. 297267 to 297299. Nonetheless, readers will appreciate that there are obvious gaps in the above review of the LMS's practice in renumbering HR wagons.

### Livery

As previously mentioned with respect to coaches, the livery of HR wagons has been fully explored in *Highland Railway liveries* by H Geddes and E Bellass, where details of painting, lettering, devices, number & builders' plates will be found.

### Wagon sheets

Like other railways, the Highland maintained a stock of over 2,000 wagon sheets, or tarpaulins, for protecting goods in open wagons, especially in view of the small number of covered vans then available. Their maintenance was a constant task for which the company had its own factory, where new sheets were made and existing repaired and redressed, although sometimes new sheets were bought in.

## 8-Ton Open Wagons

By far the largest type of wagon was the ordinary open wagon. Equating it to the horse drawn vehicles of the day with which both customers and staff would have been familiar, it was equivalent to the horse drawn cart and, apart from timber wagons, not too many alternatives were available at the time. So until more sophisticated types were developed to meet specific demands, the open wagon had to suffice, sheeted if necessary. By far the largest proportion of the Highland's goods stock, therefore, was open wagons,

| HR 8-Ton Open Wagons | | | | | |
|---|---|---|---|---|---|
| Diagrams | | Nos. | Type | Size L x W/wb (ft-in) | Lochgorm Drg No |
| HR 1901 | LMS N Div | | | | |
| 1 | | 1-20, 27-83, 126-283, 1322-75, 1497-1546 | A | 15-6 x 8-0/9-0 | |
| 6 | | 344-684, 1152-1176, 2158-2287, 2367-2514, 2737-2738 | C | 15-6 x 7-7/9-0 | |
| 14 | | 833-841 | D | 15-0 x 8-0/9-0 | |
| 15 | 5 | 993-1092, 1184-1221 | E | 15-0 x 7-7/9-0 | 1834 |
| 16 | 7 | 1222-1291 | F | 15-6 x 7-7/9-0 | 3053 |
| 19 | | 1376-1476, 1547-1746 | B | 15-6 x 8-0/9-0 | |

amounting to over 70% at grouping.

The order for some of the first goods wagons and vans, consisting of twenty wagons for £1,383, together with two horseboxes for £212 and six timber trucks for £437, went to Mr William Watson, millwright of Errol in Perthshire. The order was completed in July 1855, but, as the I&NR was not yet connected with the rest of the rail network, delivery, along with other items of plant, was delayed due to a lack of shipping.

In 1858 a hundred open wagons, measuring 12ft 10in by 7ft 6in by 1ft 4in internally, were supplied at a cost of £65 each. Later wagons became almost universally 8-ton 4-plank with a body height of between 2 foot and 2ft 2in, varying in length from 15 foot to 15ft 6in with a 9 foot wheelbase. Those built under Jones' tenure were 8 foot wide, while Drummond reduced this to 7ft 7in.

The company seems to have been constantly short of them, even as early as December 1857 the twenty six on hand were deemed inadequate for the traffic offering and the next month twenty five more were ordered from Brown Marshall & Co at a price of £78 to £79 each, and again a hundred from Bray Waddington at £88-17-6 each in 1861. Subsequently Lochgorm Works seems most of the time to have been building batches of 100 wagons, renewing existing and

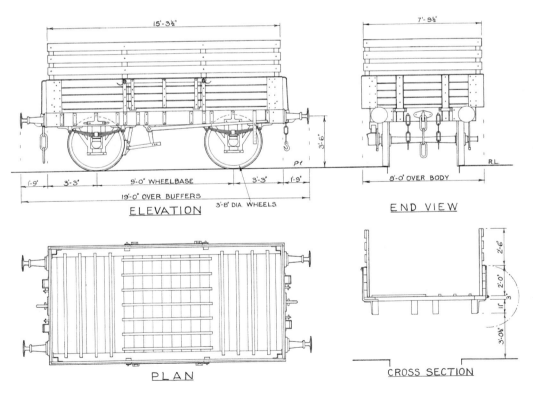

*Figure 60 - Jones 15 foot 4-plank open wagon to HR diagram 19 fitted up with flakes for carrying sheep. (Author)*

*Jones 4-plank open wagon No. 2462. Note the inverted tee washer plates on the solebar over each wheel, the left hand one combined with a double horned horse hook, the side rail supported on six brackets off the solebar and the corner plate folded round from the headstock to the ends of the solebar. (JP Richards, author's collection)*

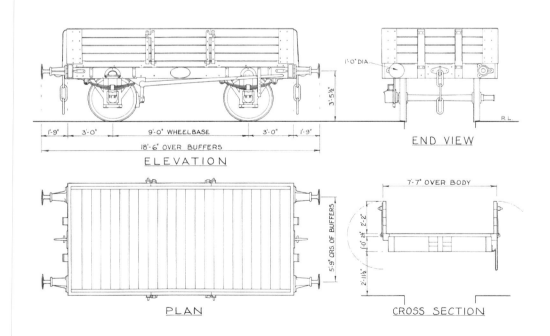

*Figure 61 - Drummond 15 foot 4-plank open wagon to HR diagram 15. (Author*

*With full width headstocks, No. 2252 appears to be a Drummond wagon to diagram 6, but it is fitted with inverted tee washer plates and may therefore have been a reconstruction reusing old parts. (WO Steel collection, courtesy RJ*

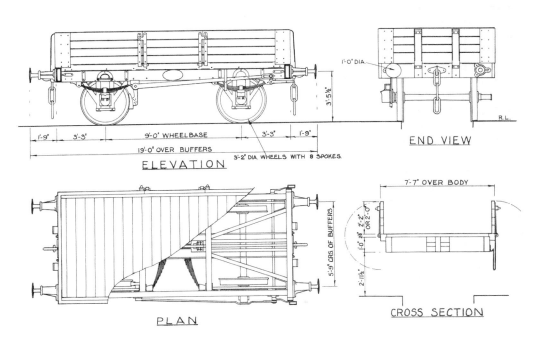

*Figure 62 - Drummond 15ft 6in 4-plank open wagon, equipped with Drummond's patent brake, to HR diagram 6 or 16. (Author)*

repairing this class of wagon. Even if fittings and wheels etc were bought in, building new wagons in the workshops naturally distracted resources from the all important task of keeping the existing fleet in good repair. In such circumstances, in August 1871 it was expedient to offer the Duke of Sutherland £50 each for four wagons acquired by him the previous November from Ashbury for working the line between Golspie and the new but temporary station at West Helmsdale.

By 1901 the width of wagons to diagrams 1, 14

*Drummond's patent brake highlighted in white applied to 15 foot long 4-plank wagon No. 1003 to diagram 15. (WG Chalmers collection)*

and 19 suggest they were constructed by Jones, whereas diagrams 6, 15 and 16 are for wagons of Drummond origin; while those to diagram 19 may have had fixed sides, perhaps only on one side. During November seed potatoes in jute sacks would be loaded in open wagons surrounded by straw to protect from the frost.

**Covered Goods Vans**

Although always relatively few in number, even as early as October 1858, Ashbury were offering to supply ten covered goods vans with the sheeting on the roof covered with strong canvas and fitted with brass hinges, third class handles, spring bolt locks & keys to doors at a price of £96-5-0 each. In January 1867 Stroudley was authorised to build 25 close vans, two of which were

fitted with Newall's continuous brake, and nine were still in hand the following year. 41 covered goods vans to be supplied by Midland Wagon Co in 1874 at cost of £102 each.

Authority was granted in March 1906 for the construction of seventeen close vans in the workshops. Drummond's first design of covered goods van to diagram 29 was 16ft 3in long of vertical match-board cladding and close fitting doors and although provided with screw couplings for possible use in passenger trains was only fitted with a simple hand brake operating on one wheel. Although automatic vacuum braking might have been fitted subsequently, 9 foot wheelbase would have precluded these vans' inclusion in fast running trains.

| HR Covered Goods Vans | | | | | | | |
|---|---|---|---|---|---|---|---|
| *Diagrams* HR 1901 | *Diagrams* LMS N Div | *Nos.* | *Load* | *Type* | *Description* | *Size L x W/wb (ft-in)* | *Lochgorm Drg No* |
| 4 | | 284-295, 781-786 | 8T | Q | Covered goods van (Old) | 16-0 x 8-0/9-0 | |
| 8 | | 769-780 | 8T | S | Luggage van | 16-0 x 8-0/9-0 | |
| 13 | | 1747-1787 | 8T | R | Covered goods van (Old) | 16-0 x 7-7/9-0 | |
| 29 | 11 | 1123-1137 | 8T | S | Covered goods van (new) cupboard doors | 16-3 x 7-6/9-0 | 2313 PD |
| | 8 | ? | | | Covered goods van 6 No. | 24-0 x 7-6/13-0 | 3322 |
| | 10 | 1158-1189 | 10T | | Covered goods van sliding doors | 18-0 x 7-6/11-0 | 3307 |

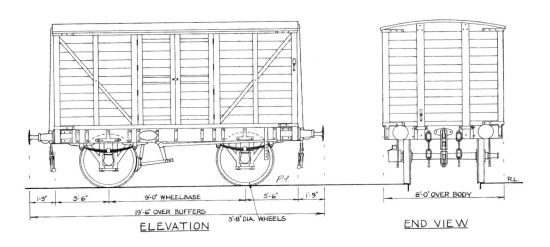

*Figure 63 - Jones 16 foot outside framed covered goods van to HR diagram 4.  (Author)*

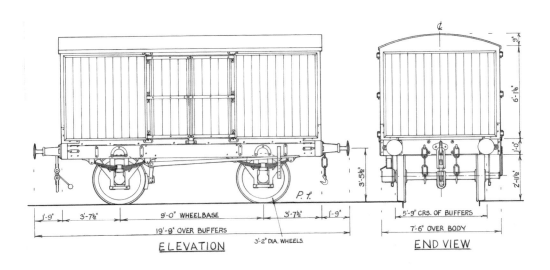

*Figure 64 - Drummond 16ft 3in 8-ton covered goods van to HR diagram 29.  (Author)*

In September 1911 RY Pickering undertook to build for delivery by end of January 1912 ten covered goods vans on timber under-frames with 3ft 2in diameter spoked wheels mounted in oil axle-boxes with HR cast on the covers, at £120 each. At about the same time the suggestion was made that the 24 foot long under-frames from old 4-wheel carriages be re-used to create more covered goods vans at a cost of £120. The existence of LMS diagram 8 would suggest that some at least some were converted.

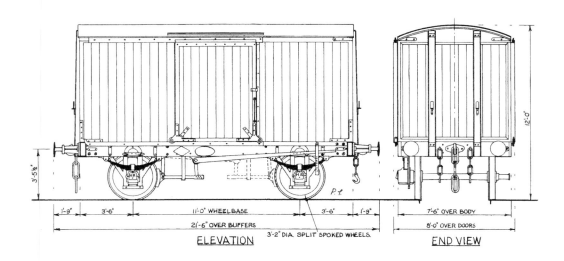

*Figure 65 - 18 foot 10-ton covered goods van with sliding doors to LMS diagram 10. (Author)*

*18 foot long covered goods van No. 1168 with sliding doors supplied by RY Pickering in 1911. (WO Steel collection, courtesy RJ Essery)*

| 6-wheel Road Vans | | | | | | |
|---|---|---|---|---|---|---|
| Diagrams | | HR Nos. | Tare wt. | Description | Size L x W/wb | Lochgorm |
| HR 1901 | LMS N Div | | | | (ft-in) | Drg No |
| 31 | 22 | 1-6 | 13T 15c | | 35-8 x 8-0/23-0 | 2776 PD |
| | 21 | | | 2 sliding doors | 35-8 x 8-8/23-0 | 3306 PD |

## Road Vans

Small packets and parcels for wayside stations were either carried in the guard's van, if the van was large enough, or alternatively in a dedicated covered goods van. Individual items would then be dropped off and collected from stations along the route. By May 1903 the magnitude of the traffic must have grown sufficiently on some lines to justify the building of six 6-wheel road vans specifically for the purpose at a cost of £330 each, with an extra £5 for vacuum brake pipe and hand brake. The under-frames of these vans to HR diagram 31 were the same as the contemporary Drummond 6-wheel coaches and resembled the Passenger Brake Vans, but without lookouts; they had vertical match-board sides and ends instead of being panelled. These were numbered in their own series of Nos. 1 to 6.

As well as diagram 22 for the above, the LMS diagram book has diagram 21 showing a similarly proportioned road van, but with a pair of 5 foot sliding doors.

## Mineral Wagons

As early as 1864, some 100 open wagons were tied up in the business of conveying coal from the collieries to the engine sheds for locomotive purposes. Five years later at the Board's request, Stroudley inspected 40 second-hand dumb-buffered coal wagons with a view to purchasing them from the Scottish Wagon Co, Edinburgh, to fulfill this duty. Financial constraints at the time, however, precluded this and even eight months later the opportunity to buy on hire-purchase was turned down. It was December 1880 before authority was given to Jones to build twelve 10-ton mineral wagons at a cost of £90 each for conveying loco coal from the Wishaw coal pits to Perth and onward transmission to the locomotive sheds.

If the numbers allocated to diagram 5 Type H are anything to go by, these 10-ton 6-plank coal wagons were multiplied over an extended period and they seem to have had long lives. The diagram shows them to be dumb buffered, which the early deliveries may have been. Photographs suggest that these wagons were

| Mineral Wagons | | | | | | | | |
|---|---|---|---|---|---|---|---|---|
| Diagrams | | Nos. | | Load | Type | Description | Size L x W/wb | Drg |
| HR 1901 | LMS N Div | HR | LMS | | | | (ft-in) | No |
| 5 | - | 316-343, 2308-2514, 2537-2636 | | 10T | H | Loco coal wagon | 15-6 x 7-9/9-0 | |
| 10 | 4 | 943-992, 2637-2736 | | 8T | G | 4pl mineral wagon | 15-0 x 7-7/9-0 | 1832 |
| 33 | 1 | 1497, 1507/22/75/87, 1634/57/8/60/89, 1703/3142, 2161/9/90, 2760-2793, 2824-2848 | 296939 | 16T | | 6pl coal wagon | 18-4 x 7-8/10-0 | 3185 |
| 34 | 2 | 2869-2918 | 296759 | 12T | | 7pl coal wagon | 17-0 x 7-8/10-0 | 2715 |
| | 3 | | 296738/60/95 296804/23/5/ 32/51/5/62/73 | 12T | | 6pl coal wagon (1914/5) | 15-11 x 7-4/9-0 | |
| 34 | 6 | 2919-3018 | | 12T | | 7pl end door mineral wagon | 16-6 x 7-10/9-0 | |

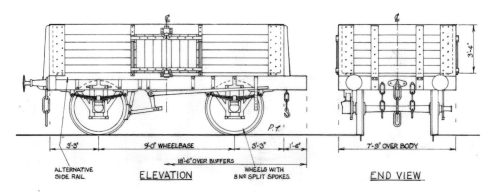

*Figure 66 - Jones 10-ton 6-plank mineral wagon to HR diagram 5. (Author)*

taken in hand over the years and often heavily reconstructed by the provision of sprung buffers, if not already so fitted after which it is uncertain whether they continued to be 18ft 6in over buffers as originally shown on the diagram. Other alterations were to the brake gear, including Drummond's patent each side brake; while some marked for locomotive coal appear to have had fixed sides, at least on one side.

*A glimpse of a Jones 6-plank loco coal wagon to HR Diagram 5 apparently with fixed sides. (WO Steel collection, courtesy RJ Essery)*

*An unidentified long lasting 6-plank loco coal wagon, by now reconstructed with sprung buffers. (DLF Gilbert, courtesy RJ Essery)*

Soon after Drummond's arrival he was granted authority in September 1898 to construct 100 8-ton coal wagons at a cost of £75 each. These will have been to HR diagram 10, adopting typical constructional features he brought with him from the Caledonian Railway. Note that compared with the not dissimilar contemporary 4-plank open wagon, the top plank is continuous with a pair of 3-plank side-hung doors and without an end-door.

Like many other railways at the time, in July 1900 consideration was given to investing in 30-ton bogie wagons for loco coal purposes. This was not followed through, but instead in October 1903 fifty 16-ton 18ft 4in long 4-wheel wagons were ordered from Hurst Nelson for £84 each to diagram 33.

When in 1908 twenty-five more of the same were required, these appear in fact to have been 12-ton

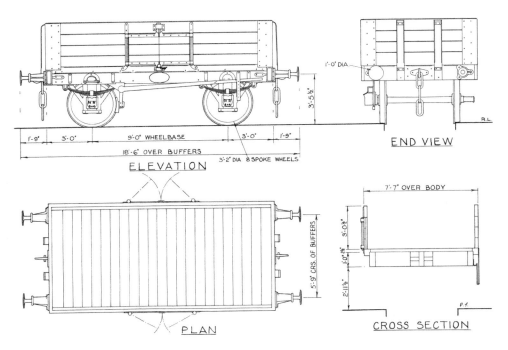

*Figure 67 - Drummond 8-ton 4-plank mineral wagon to HR diagram 10. (Author)*

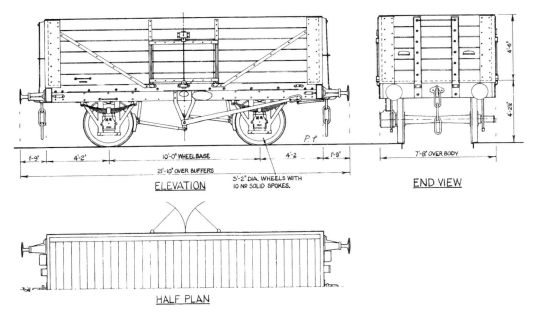

*Figure 68 - Drummond 16-ton 6-plank locomotive coal wagon to diagram 33. (Author)*

*A leap in capacity and size was made 1903 with the construction of 16-ton 18ft 4in long 6-plank loco coal wagons to HR diagram 33, No. 1657 being an example built by Hurst Nelson. (F Moore, HRS collection).*

*Another was No. 2773 out-shopped on 11 April 1904. (Author's collection)*

*Above* - In LMS service No. 296439 was, with ex-CR 15-ton 5-plank loco coal No. 343454, captured at Aberfeldy in June 1936. (WA Camwell)

*Right -* A decrepit HR 12-ton 7-plank mineral wagon No. 2872 which is believed to be to LMS diagram 2. (WO Steel collection, courtesy RJ Essery)

*Bottom* - Of similar form and in better condition No. 296759 was painted and lifted on 13 September 1935. (WO Steel collection, courtesy RJ Essery)

17 foot long vehicles to LMS diagram 2, albeit with seven rather than the six planks shown on the diagram, from Harrison & Camm at cost £94 each.

In September 1913 a change was made to 12-ton capacity and an order for fifty wagons was placed with Buchanan & Co at a price of £81-10-0 each. These are thought to be to LMS diagram 3. Only six months later an order for a further fifty to the Railway Clearing House Specification was awarded to RY Pickering for £77 each. LMS diagram 6 shows a 12-ton 6-plank end door mineral wagon with cupboard side doors. However, as no other mineral wagon diagram shows end doors, it seems probable that some, if not all, of these wagons in fact were the 7-plank end door mineral wagons with falling side doors supplied by RY Pickering in 1914. A year later fifty more were ordered from Pickering again, but at a cost of £88 each.

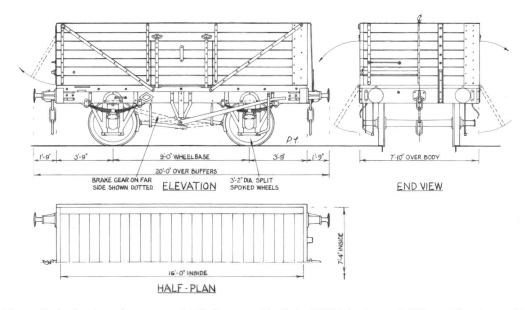

*Figure 69 - 12-ton 7-plank mineral wagon to LMS diagram 6 built by RY Pickering to RCH specifications. (Author)*

| Timber Wagons | | | | | | | | |
|---|---|---|---|---|---|---|---|---|
| Diagrams | | Nos. | | Load | Type | Description | Size L x W/wb (ft-in) | Drg No |
| HR 1901 | LMS N Div | HR | LMS | | | | | |
| 2 | - | 21-26, 94-103 | | 8T | M | Swivel timber wagon | 11-0 x 8-0/6-0 | |
| 7 | - | 680-768, 843-942 | | 7T | L | Timber wagon | 15-6 x 6-10/9-0 | |
| 35 | 25 | 908 | 297000/02 | 7T | | Swivel cradle wagon | 15-6 x 7-7/9-0 | 3458 |
| 36 | 26 | 3019-3038 | 297053/69/129 | 8T | | Swivel single bolster wagon | 15-6 x 7-7/9-0 | 3563 |
| 37 | 24 | 21-26, 94-103 | | 8T | | Swivel single bolster wagon | 11-0 x 8-0/9-0 | 2605 |
| | 19 | | | 10T | | Timber wagon | 15-6 x 6-10½/9-0 | 2773 |
| | 23 | | | 15T | | 6 wh rail & timber wagon | 25-1 x 6-11/19-0 | 2699 |

## Timber & Bolster Wagons

Wagons designed to convey timber were one of the first specialist types acquired by the I&NR, six timber trucks being supplied by Watson of Errol for the opening of the line 1855 for £437. In late 1863, the Railway Carriage Co was supplying 84 timber wagons at £79-18-6 each. The Highland soon had a stock of 200.

The allocation of low numbers sequences to HR diagrams 2 and 7 suggest that these vehicles were part of the original stock of wagons acquired on the capital account as the line was built and expanded. The duplication of the numbers of diagram 2 to Peter Drummond's version LMS diagram 24 indicates that they were replacements charged to the revenue account.

In July 1902 the Loco Supt submitted a design of 6-wheel wagon with flexible wheel base for carrying round timber etc and approval given for one to be built for trial; its existence is confirmed by LMS diagram 23.

*Figure 70 - 7-ton 2-plank timber wagon to HR diagram 7. (Author)*

***Bottom -*** *An old 7-ton 2-plank timber wagon No. 687 to diagram 7 with two cast-iron stanchion holders bolted to the sides. Note the wooden brake blocks and self-contained buffers. (HRS collection)*

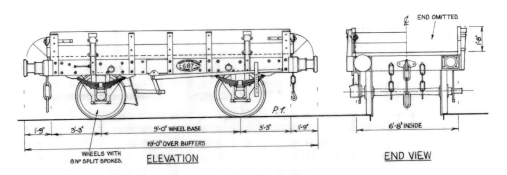

***Opposite bottom -*** *In 1914 RY Pickering supplied fifty 12-ton 7-plank end-door loco coal wagons, as shown by No. 2968 as new, although where the Highland would have found use for the end door facility is uncertain. (HRS collection)*

*A view of No. 873 updated with angle iron side supports, sprung buffers and improved brake gear showing upright poles inserted in the sockets to contain the load stacked up between. The adjacent Drummond wagon is connected by a screw coupling. (HRS collection)*

*LMS No. 297069 would appear to be a 7-ton timber wagon that has been heavily rebuilt as a 2-plank single bolster wagon with one of the two cast iron sockets moved to the centre and a bolster positioned between the sides. It was spotted at Inverness on 29 August 1938. (DLG Hunter)*

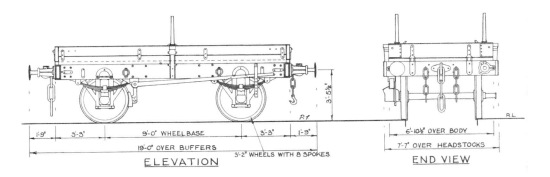

*Figure 71 - 8-ton 2-plank single bolster wagon. (Author)*

As time went on methods of repair of wagons became more desperate and diverse in the extreme. In this way we find that Sir Eric Hutchinson recorded a random collection of old timber wagons that had been through Lochgorm Works on numerous occasions, where they had been patched up as best they could to get wagons back on the road to meet the burgeoning demand especially during World War 1. For instance, in the photographs above and below all three examples are different, yet there is a cast iron socket bolted at the centre and on the outside of all, which one suspects came from the pairs originally attached to the outside of the timber wagons to diagram 7.

It will be noticed that none of the diagrams listed above refer to 'twin' bolster wagons, yet photographs of wagons lettered such exist and are

*LMS No. 297129 is an 8-ton version of single bolster wagon, by now in departmental service, with slightly lower 2-plank sides necessitating the cast iron socket being reduced in height. This wagon was seen on 23 June 1938. (DLG Hunter)*

*No. M297053, built at Lochgorm in 1912, survived to be photographed in Inverness sorting sidings on 20 July 1952. As can be seen, these wagons had one end fixed and the other open so that long rigid loads could be supported on a pair of wagons. These were fitted with screw couplings to limit longitudinal movement and during the LMS period lettered 'Twin'. (RE Wilson)*

*Swivel cradle wagon LMS No. 297002 at Inverness on 23 June 1938. (DLG Hunter)*

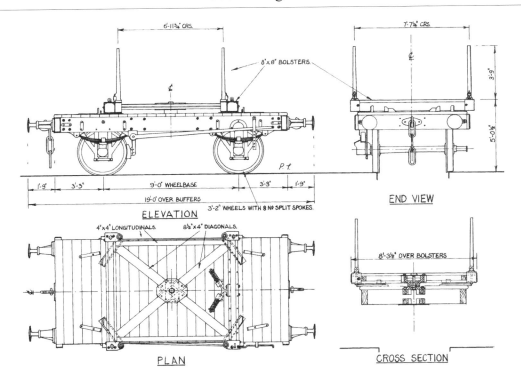

*Figure 72 - 7-ton swivel cradle wagon to LMS diagram 25. (Author)*

reproduced here. In July 1920 approval was given for the construction of twenty swivel bolster wagons at a cost of £235 each in the workshops. These were to LMS diagram 26.

Another design to LMS diagram 25 shows the whole cradle supporting four bolster pins was capable of rotating as the load on the wagon and its neighbour negotiate a curve, but the degree of movement is constrained by a bracket and pair of opposing springs attached to the inside of a bolster at one end and screwed to the wagon floor. Some at least were built at Lochgorm in 1916, but only two LMS, numbers are known, by then in departmental service, and it is uncertain whether there were any more.

*Looking down on the cradle with four posts, one in each corner. The degree of rotation is limited by stops on the floor of the wagon. (Author's collection)*

## Specially Constructed Vehicles

| HR 1901 diagram | Nos. | Load | Type | Description | Size L x W/wb (ft-in) |
|---|---|---|---|---|---|
| **Specially Constructed Vehicles** | | | | | |
| 20 | 2147 | 7T | N | Engine wagon (6 wheel) | 18-0 x 8-0/13-0 |
| 27 | | | P | Tar wagon (6 wheels) | 16-0 x ?/11-0 |

### Engine wagon

As early as October 1874 authority was given to the Locomotive Superintendent to build a special truck for the purposes of conveying locomotives between Lairg and Brora. As by then the line was already open to Wick, one assumes this may refer to road engines. No further details of this wagon have come to light.

A 6-wheel furniture truck to HR diagram 20 was approved for construction in October 1900 at a cost of £40. Other than HR Diagram 20 for No. 2147 (amended to 2146), an 18 foot long by 8 foot wide and 13 foot wheel base 7-ton capacity vehicle, no more details of this wagon have come to light.

### Traders' tank wagons

It would appear from the Board Minutes that the company provided for hire wagons, or just under-frames, to one or two local industries to which they attached their own tanks for the conveyance of liquid chemicals, oil or tar. Those known include the names shown in the table below.

For reasons unknown, however, it is not until February 1896 that a vitriol wagon is included under the Return of Rolling Stock. The North of Scotland Chemical Works, Forres was incorporated as John Burn Ltd in 1901 and wound up in 1925. When the plant was sold in 1925 it included three 6-wheel 10-ton rail tanks wagons, but presumably not those to diagram 27, Type P, unless the railway had relinquished ownership.

G & G Kynoch purchased the Morayshire Chemical Works, Burghead, from the bankrupt estate of William Adam and their business was later incorporated as the Banff & Morayshire Agricultural Co Ltd. Although in 1925 this became part of Scottish Agricultural Industries, it continued trade under its original name until 1943 when it was wound up. It is possible therefore that the tank wagon acquired by Kynoch in 1907 was the one supplied to Adam in 1900.

| Company | Location | Contact | Date | Product | Plant Provided by HR | Added |
|---|---|---|---|---|---|---|
| **Private Traders' Wagons** | | | | | | |
| Chemical Works | Forres | Mr Wilson | 1863 | Acid | Wagon | Tank |
| North of Scotland Chemical Works | Forres | The Manager | 1871 | Sulphuric acid | Wagon | |
| North of Scotland Chemical Works | Forres | John Burn | 1878 | Sulphuric acid | | Tank |
| Chemical Works | Burghead | Mr Adam | 1878 | Naphtha and creosote | | 2 tanks |
| Chemical Works | Burghead | Mr Adam | 1900 | | Wagon u/f | Tank |
| Chemical manufacturer | Keith? | for G&G Kynoch | 1907 | | Wagon u/f No. 5080 | Tank |

## Cattle Wagons

The seasonal movement of live stock, particularly sheep, was one of the most important traffics handled by the Highland Railway. Two cattle and sheep trucks were supplied in 1855 to the I&NR by Faulds for £174, while the I&AJR possessed ten cattle wagons by February 1857. The need for more with the completion of the through line to Keith was soon identified and thereafter regular additions were made to the stock of cattle wagons. Typically the Midland Wagon Co supplied 49 cattle wagons in 1874 at a price of £104 each.

In September 1857 consideration was given to providing roofs to cattle wagons, which implies that early cattle wagons were open. It would appear too that prior to 1866 the ends of cattle wagons were also open, because, in response to the Easter Ross Farmers' Club's request, Mr Stroudley was asked in September to investigate the cost of boarding up the ends and whether this would adversely affect the train's resistance. Later the Board of Agriculture Regulations would require that vehicles intended to convey horses, asses or mules should be fitted with spring buffers; a roof; a means of preventing animals slipping on the floor, such as battens, and be strewn with sand or litter; be ventilated and have a means of inspecting the floor; flush interior to prevent injury to animals; and falling loading doors.

The movement of animals was also subject to the Animal Diseases Act 1875. This required thoroughly washing out with water and the application of lime wash as a disinfectant, which usually disfigured the lower portions of the exterior as well. Two years later the Highland was prosecuted on two counts for failing to clean out and disinfect cattle wagons properly following markets at Muir of Ord. This arose due to a

| 8-Ton Cattle Wagons | | | | |
|---|---|---|---|---|
| Diagrams HR 1901 | Nos. | Type | Size L x W/wb (ft-in) | Drg No |
| Diagrams LMS N Div | | | | |
| 3 | - | 84-93, 104-125, 296-315, 817-832, 1093-1122, 1292-1321, 2288-2307, 2345-64 | U | 16-0 x 8-0/9-0 | 1226? |
| 18 | - | 1798-1846 | V | 15-8 x 7-7/9-0 | |
| - | 16 | 85 | | 15-9 x 8-0/9-0 | 2275 |

lack of an adequate water supply and resulted in the installation of hydrants at the loading bank at Inverness where wagons could be attended to prior to moving north. Following its failure to wash out trucks at Fort George before reloading with sheep on 17 July 1882, it was convicted of contravening the Contagious Diseases (Animals) Act of 1879 and fined £20. Lime wash was later found to rot the animals' hooves and, by virtue of Diseases of Animals (Disinfection) Order of 1926, was altered to a commercial disinfectant.

By 1899 consideration was being given to fitting ten cattle wagons with vacuum brake piping at a total cost of £55. These and others were obviously so treated, because later, as older wagons came into the workshops this equipment was transferred to 25 of the newer wagons.

Cattle sales occurred in the spring and sheep sales began in August. During the quieter times between seasonal livestock sales, however, cattle wagons tended to be used for the transport of other things such as empty barrels and timber, but with the approach of the next sale timely instructions would be issued for this to cease, as every available cattle wagons would be pressed into service coping with the movement of livestock. For instance, sheep sales were regularly

*Left - A Highland wagon label for the conveyance of livestock from Inverness to Forres on 16 October 1962 for Alex Grant. Wagon No. 891775 was a 12-ton cattle wagon of GW design built at Swindon in 1949 to BR diagram 1/352. (Author's collection)*

*Opposite page - At certain times of the year, the movement of livestock, especially sheep, resulted in substantial traffic on the Highland Railway. Here 4-6-0 Superheated Goods No. 81 heads a long train of cattle wagons and/or sheep vans near Drumochter Summit in 1923. One private trader's coal wagon has slipped in amongst the whitewashed vehicles. (LGRP, author's collection)*

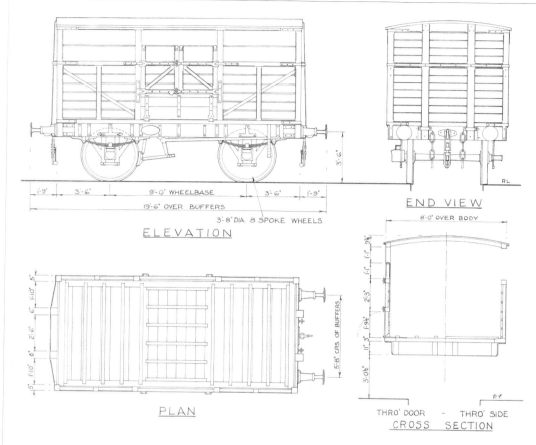

Figure 73 - Jones cattle wagon to diagram 3. (Author)

*Drummond cattle wagon No. 85 at Lichfield in 1928 still in pre-grouping livery, but no longer stained with whitewash. (Author's collection)*

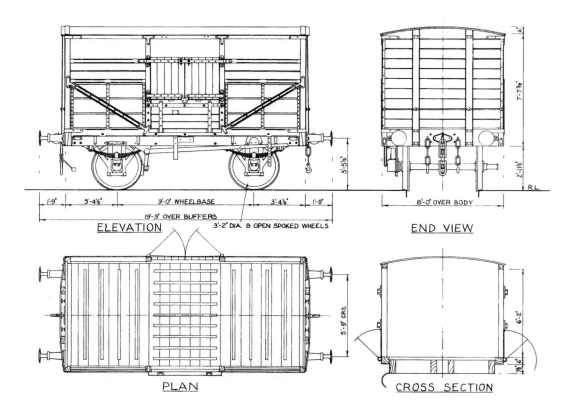

*Figure 74 - Drummond 8-ton cattle wagon to LMS diagram 16.  (Author)*

held at Lairg every August when over 30,000 sheep were sold in a single day.  In 1938 nine empty trains of trucks were on hand and sixteen special trains bringing livestock for sale were run.  By the end of that year, 17,600 trucks of livestock had been forwarded from stations in the district.  The aggregate numbers of animals dealt with during the year forwarded and received amounted to:

| | |
|---|---|
| Sheep | 863,371 |
| Cattle | 65, 041 |
| Pigs | 21,709 |

Another seasonal movement of the sheep was from the exposed uplands, typically in the west and intervening high ground, in the autumn for winter grazing on low lying more sheltered land in the east, returning the following spring.   The HR only charged carriage one way - the sheep in the spring were carried free, see *Highland Miscellany*, Oxford Publishing Co, 1985, plate 259.

Further peaks in traffic would occur in connection with military manoeuvres, when, whilst officers' chargers would be assured the privilege of a horsebox, other ranks' horses might have to be loaded into humble cattle wagons, if insufficient horseboxes were available.

**Sheep Vans**

With such a high proportion of sheep to be moved and with their height considerably less than that of cattle, it made much sense to the economically minded Highland to adopt double-deck sheep vans, although their flexibility in use would not be as great as cattle wagons. To access the upper deck, special portable gangway ramps, or ladders as they were referred to, were provided at the points of loading and discharge, not all GNSR destinations being so equipped.  Two sheep vans with a canvas covered roof were acquired in 1858/9 from Ashbury at a cost of £93-15-0 each, while in October 1862 twenty eight of the cattle wagons ordered from the Railway Carriage Co., Oldbury, for the opening of the Inverness and Perth line were to be made as double deck sheep vans at a cost of £114-17-0 each.

*The wintery scene of Kyle of Lochalsh station early in the twentieth century with snow capped Ben na Caillich in the background. A Jones 4-4-0 Skye Bogie class stands at the head of a train containing six livestock vehicles of which five are double deck sheep vans and at the tail of which is a side lookout goods brake van. There are two more sheep vans of Jones style in the left foreground with their doors open are in front of which are a couple of loading ramps and beyond a string of Jones open fish trucks. The steam ship against the quayside on the right may well have brought the sheep in from one of the Western Isles. (AA McLean collection)*

Ten more of these were obtained from the Midland Wagon Co for £115 in 1874.

Both Jones and early Drummond double-deck vans contained the beasts along the sides by closely spaced vertical iron bars to the sides and were planked across the ends, whereas later vans had planked sides more akin to cattle wagons. Jones vans, however, had no diagonal bracing to the sides and were equipped with double doors, whereas Drummond ones had bracing and single doors. Four Jones vans may have been internally divided to enable up to four different consignments to be loaded in one van. Presumably, despite the small dimensional differences, HR and LMS diagrams 17 represent the same type of vehicle.

| 8-Ton Double-Deck Sheep Vans | | | | | | | |
|---|---|---|---|---|---|---|---|
| Diagram | | Nos. | | Type | Sides | Size L x W/wb (ft-in) | Lochgorm Drg No |
| HR 1901 | LMS N Div | HR | LMS | | | | |
| 9 | | 787-816 | | X | Iron bars | 15-6 x 8-0/9-0 | |
| 17 | | 1477-1496, 1788-1797 | | Y | | 16-0 x 8-0/9-0 | |
| | 17 | | 294515 | | Iron bars | 15-9 x 8-0/9-0 | 2297 |
| | (17?) | | 294528/55 | | Planked | | |

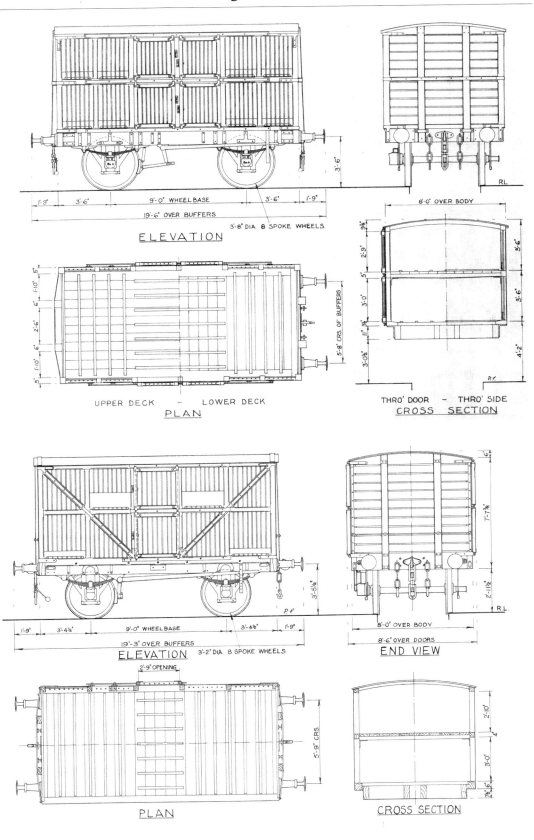

**Top -** *Figure 75, Jones 8-ton double-deck sheep van to diagram 17. (Author)*

**Bottom -** *Figure 76, Drummond 8-ton double-deck sheep van to diagram 9. (Author)*

Finally towards the end of the company's independent existence it changed the design of sheep vans to be more akin to the form of construction of cattle wagons with a pair of horizontal bars towards the top of each deck closing the gap above the planks and a door arrangement similar to cattle wagons. Nonetheless, no separate diagram seems to have been issued.

Highland sheep vans could carry about 100 sheep. The divided vans were also used to transport pigs. As well as having a regular year round traffic in

*Drummond double-deck sheep van LMS No. 294515 to diagram 9 photographed on 23 June 1938. Note the single door per deck, the closely spaced vertical iron bars along the sides, diagonal bracing and boards upon which to apply the inscriptions. (DLG Hunter)*

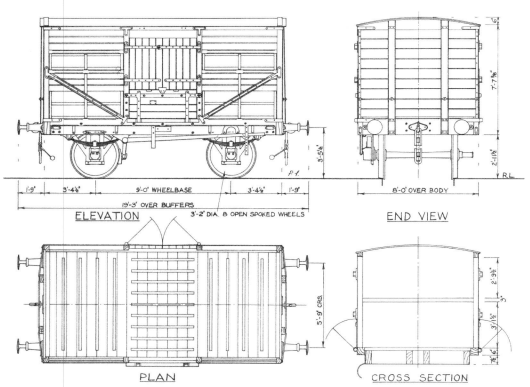

*Figure 77 - 8-ton double-deck sheep van with planked sides. (Author)*

*The final form of Highland double-deck sheep van with horizontal planks instead of vertical bars, as exemplified by LMS No. 294528 also on 23 June 1938. Note the falling lower doors and the height of the upper side-hung doors. (DLG Hunter)*

*Shunted to the end of the siding at Dingwall in August 1950 sheep van LMS No. 284555 looks a bit the worse for wear. (WO Steel collection, courtesy RJ Essery)*

*A detail of the under-frame of LMS No. 284555. (WO Steel collection, courtesy RJ Essery)*

sheep for slaughter, as noted above, the company offered farmers special rates to transport sheep from the lowland pasture to the uplands in the spring and to bring them back in the autumn, so it was worth while having special wagons for this traffic.

Nonetheless, to cope with the autumn sheep sales the Lochgorm Works used temporarily to fit up large numbers of ordinary open wagons with flakes (hurdles) to extend the height of the sides and ends, perhaps with a tarpaulin stretched over to provided cover, to carry the additional seasonal traffic, see Figure 60 on page 145. From November 1904, with the issue of revised Board of Agriculture Regulations, roofs to new livestock vehicles became obligatory; even so the Highland continued to use open wagons fitted with flakes, asserting that the wagons had been built prior to 1904. However, the Board of Trade did not accept that converted wagons were exempt and stopped the Highland from using them and threatened with prosecution for disregard of the Board of Agriculture Regulations. As a result of discussions with the Inspector of Agriculture Board improved wagons for the conveyance of sheep based on a Caledonian design was adopted in 1908. This consisted of drilling 5 inch diameter inspection holes at each end of the sides, but this not immediately implemented. By then their use was almost wholly confined to working between the Black Isle and Kyle of Lochalsh, for onward transportation by ship to Portree on the Isle of Skye for

sheep going to and returning from wintering in lowland pastures, with vans stored at Dingwall and Muir of Ord when not in use.

Those ordinary wagons known, between the summers of 1909 and 1916, to have been provided with ventilating holes and hence available to be fitted up with flakes for sheep traffic, are: 7, 15, 137, 556, 600, 665, 1174, 1254, 1401, 1464, 2378, 2450, all 400 - 499. To enable them to be readily distinguished, a triangular white paint-mark was applied at the upper corner of the box of each wagon. The practice of using flaked wagons to convey sheep continued until at least November 1927.

**Non-Revenue Earning**

It was not long before the railway found that there were frequent occasions when it was necessary to use wagons for its own internal purposes for which no revenue was generated, the most obvious of which was work on the track somewhere out along the line. At first the company's wagons were used on an unofficial basis, but it was soon recognised that the Engineer's, and subsequently other departments, needed to have wagons dedicated to their use without resorting to taking revenue earning vehicles from the Traffic Department. Hence was born the description non-revenue earning vehicles. Quite often such wagons were former revenue earning vehicles from which a little extra use was obtained before they were finally retired and scrapped.

*Ballast Wagons*

A dozen purpose-built ballast wagons were made at Lochgorm Works in 1867/8. In 1873 eighteen old I&NR wagons were hired to the Sutherland & Caithness Railway for ballasting purposes at a rate of 5/- (25p) per week each. Diagram 11 of the 1901 book shows a dumb buffered low sided wagon, which presumably the early versions were, but all construction from 1893 had sprung buffers. In connection with revised methods of track maintenance, a dozen ballast wagons were added to stock in 1892/3 and in 1901/2 twenty more were built in the workshops at a cost of

| 8-ton Ballast Wagons | | | | | |
|---|---|---|---|---|---|
| Diagram | | Nos. | Type | Size L x W/wb (ft-in) | Drg No |
| HR 1901 | LMS N Div | | | | |
| 11 | | 1177-1188, 2148-2157 | I | 15-6 x 8-0/9-0 | |
| 23 | | 2525-2536 | J | 15-6 x 7-9/9-0 | |
| | 20 | LMS 297184/201/ 11 | | 15-6 x 7-7/9-0 | 2579 |

£65-10-0 each. Despite the two inch difference in width, presumably HR diagram 23 and LMS diagram 20

*One of the 8-ton 2-plank drop side and end ballast wagons built at Lochgorm in 1893 to diagram 11 exhibiting some Jones features, but a full width headstock, became LMS No. 297192 and was photographed at Inverness on 20 July 1952. Note the step hung off the sole-bar at the left hand end. (RE Wilson)*

*The remnants of Highland livery were apparent on this 8-ton 2-plank ballast wagon No. 2747 when spotted at Inverness on 14 June 1938. It is still fitted with Drummond's patent each side brake gear with the small lever at the left hand end, while the canvas flap is unlikely to prevent dust from entering the axle-box as intended. (DLG Hunter)*

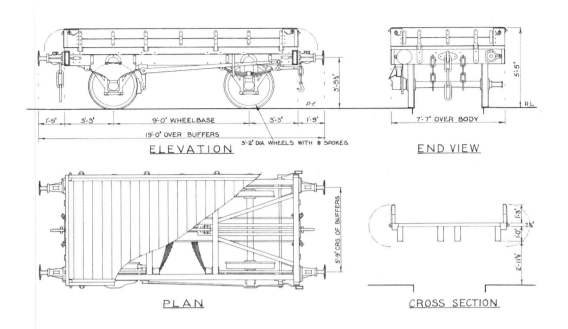

ELEVATION

END VIEW

PLAN

CROSS SECTION

*Figure 78 - Drummond 8-ton 2-plank ballast wagon to diagram 23. (Author)*

*At Inverness on 7 October 1952 former LMS No. 297217 also built in 1902 at Lochgorm showing the other side of a wagon once fitted with Drummond's patent each side brake gear. The 'N' on each corner indicates that, as a departmental wagon, it is not part of the Common User pool. (JL Stevenson)*

*A recently painted similar wagon at Inverness on 20 July 1952, by now re-numbered MD297205 and its patent brake gear altered to have an independent lever on each side. (RE Wilson*

represent the same type of vehicle.

At the time the quality of ballast was not regarded as particularly important and often consisted of gravel, mostly from glacial moraines, although ash would also be used. The former was usually obtained from borrow pits adjacent to the line. Those known include: Grandtully, Ralia (South of Newtonmore), Boat of Garten, Moy, Bunchew (two pits), Port na Chuillen (Kyle Line), Ardvannie (Edderton), Rogart, Marrel (Helmsdale), and Altnabreac (red sand from this pit).

## Rail-Mounted Cranes

Like most railways, the Highland and its constituents found a use for rail-mounted travelling cranes for a variety of purposes, including around the workshops, breakdown work, engineering activities along the line and for goods traffic at locations without suitable fixed cranage. The I&AJR was soon procuring, in 1859, a 6-wheel dumb-buffered hand crane with outside W irons and octagonal tapered wooden jib, later rated at 2½ tons. There was another 6-wheel dumb-buffered crane with outside axle-guards of probably greater capacity and fitted with a pair of shear legs, while a small 4-wheel dumb-buffered hand crane was out-shopped from Lochgorm in 1874.

Most examples were hand operated, but following an accident between Dunphail and Forres on 24 May 1886, a 15-ton steam breakdown crane was acquired from Cowans Sheldon of Carlisle. As a full drawing and details have recently been included in *Railway breakdown cranes*, Volume 1, published by Noodle Books in 2012, they will not be repeated here. A shed in which to keep the crane, when not in use, was promptly erected at Inverness at an estimated cost of £192. An all steel 10-ton 6-wheel hand crane from John Wilson of Liverpool was added as No. 2 in 1903/4 at a cost of £550.

***Above*** - *The I&AJR 6-wheel dumb-buffered hand crane built in 1859, nearly a century later out to grass at Fort George and by then rated at 2½-ton capacity. (I Peddie)*

***Right*** - *The grease lubricated axle-box and outside guard irons to the I&AJR crane. (I Peddie)*

*Opposite top -* Other timber jib hand cranes were acquired by the Highland as demonstrated by this view of a small 4-wheel dumb-buffered hand crane No. 1177, built by the company in 1874 and in due course used around the Needlefield Works. (DLG Hunter)

*Opposite bottom -* A 6-wheel crane tackles a contretemps at Struan around the turn of the 19/20th century by lifting a somewhat damaged 8-ton 4-plank mineral wagon to HR diagram 10. The shape of the maker's plate on the counter-weight box is consistent with Cowans Sheldon's. The two poles attached to the jib head and resting on top of the superstructure are shear legs which could be lowered to the ground and used to assist with particularly heavy lifts. (AG Ellis collection)

*This page -* Steel jibbed 10-ton Wilson 6-wheel hand crane HR No. 2 undertaking the erection of a footbridge at Conon on 25 June 1911. (Dale collection, courtesy Strathspey Railway Association)

| Match Wagons for Rail-Mounted Cranes | | | | |
|---|---|---|---|---|
| *HR 1901 diagram* | *Nos.* | *Type* | *Description* | *Size L x W/wb (ft-in)* |
| 28 | LMS 297232 | O | Crane wagon (6 wheels) | 19-6 x 8-0/13-0 |
| 32 | | | 10 ton crane wagon | 24-0 x 7-7/13-6 |

## Miscellaneous Service Vehicles

With the adoption of gas lighting of carriages in place of oil lamps, it was necessary to construct travelling gas holders to supply gas from the plant at Inverness to outlying recharging centres, such as Perth and Wick. For this purpose an example was obtained from Consolidated Engineering Co. for £175 in 1902. Nos. 1 and 2 were later to be found at Helmsdale and Bonar Bridge.

In 1903 the need for a shunter's truck at Perth was met by building one in the workshops. Numbered 66, it was allocated to diagram 30. It was 15ft 6in long by 7ft 4½in wide on a 9 foot wheel base. A hand brake standard was mounted in the middle and was surrounded by a single plank topped by a hand rail. A photograph of either type of the above has so far eluded the author.

*In 1907, as part of the Engineer's Department's efforts to improve the quality of track ballast, this wagon and plant was obtained. An oil engine driven stone crusher was mounted on one end of a bogie wagon, while accommodation for the operator and his tools etc. was at the other. (WG Chalmers collection)*

### Stone-Breaker Wagon

The recognition that a hard wearing angular stone was to be preferred for ballasting track led to the purchase in 1907 of a stone-breaking wagon. This consisted of a stone crusher driven by an oil engine, together with accommodation for the engineman, all mounted on a bogie wagon at a cost of £610. Presumably the intention was to take this to a suitable source of rock beside the line, quarry the stone, crushing and grading it before use on the track. In 1919 a siding for the stone-breaker at Inverness was proposed.

### Stores vans

The Highland must have had stores vans, because stores vans Nos. 4, 11, 12 were duplicated 1914, but no further information has come to hand.

### Fire engines

On 1 March 1865 Col. Fraser-Tytler and the Duke of Sutherland had an interview with Captain Shaw, head of the London Fire Brigade, to discuss the purchase of a fire engine for the company's use. Capt Shaw recommended hand engines in preference to those worked by steam, and offered to supply a pair of such in perfect order complete and ready for work for £240, which was duly accepted. Thereafter the stock returns list two until the turn of the century, but were these rail or road mounted, perhaps carried on a wagon?

### Mess & Tool Vans and Crane Wagons

As early as 1870 the need for a dedicated tool van to accompany the breakdown crane was identified and a goods wagon was converted at a cost of £120, thereby allowing the passenger luggage van purloined for the purpose to be returned to revenue earning traffic. Five years later to update the breakdown train, a new crane wagon was built and two old light vans converted into heavy vans for the sum of £800. To this last was added another 10 to 12-ton crane wagon for conveying chairs, spikes, fish bolts and keys with which to repair the track.

Tool vans with all the necessary tools, packing etc were in April 1907 located at: Wick, Kyle of Lochalsh, Inverness, Forres, Aviemore, Blair Atholl and Perth, while following a review in 1911, tool vans had been added at Helmsdale and Dingwall, together by June 1916 at Tain, at an estimated cost of £200.

In 1907 an old carriage was fitted up for sleeping accommodation and cooking for the convenience telegraph labourers when working out on the line. The construction in the workshops of a new purpose-built 6-wheel breakdown tool van was authorised in September 1908. This was an altogether more workmanlike vehicle specially fitted out with all the tools likely to be required for breakdown work. Initially it joined the breakdown train at Inverness, but by April 1948 had gravitated to Polmadie as LMS No. 297299, where it survived until at least February 1961.

*The Highland possessed two long lasting heavy duty 6-wheel wagons associated with the breakdown train at Inverness. One, in due course fitted with a jib rest, acted as a match truck to the 15-ton Cowans Sheldon steam crane, while the other was loaded with permanent way materials likely to be necessary in repairing the track following an incident. Built at Lochgorm in 1875, LMS No. 297232, marked LMS PWay Dept all in serif letters and numerals, was found at Inverness on 7 October 1952. It also shows the full length drop-side and lower foot board, together with long hand brake lever and self-contained buffers. The presence of a vacuum hose pipe and clasp brakes suggest the vehicle is fully brake fitted. (JL Stevenson)*

*In 1909 the Highland built for itself a fine new 6-wheel breakdown van neatly fitted out internally with hooks, racks and shelves to accommodate all the tools necessary for such work and provision made for a guard. By April 1948, this van had migrated to Polmadie as No. 297299, where it was photographed on 26 June 1955. (JL Stevenson)*

| | | | | | | | | | |
|---|---|---|---|---|---|---|---|---|---|
| **HR Goods Brake Vans** | | | | | | | | | |
| *Diagrams* | | | *Nos.* | | *Tare* | *Type* | *Description* | *Size L x W/wb* | *Drg* |
| *HR 1901* | *LMS N Div* | *HR* | *LMS* | | *wt* | | | *(ft-in)* | *No* |
| 24 | - | 1-19 | 294006 | | 7T 9c | A | | 18-0 x 7-3/11-0 | |
| 25 | - | 20-55 | | | 11T | B | 6 wheels | 24-0 x 8-0/15-6 | |
| | | | 294054/8, 297267/8 | | 15T | | Rebuilt Type B | | |
| 26 | 13 | 56-65 | | | 13T 13c | C | | 16-3 x 7-5½/9-0 | H82 |
| 30 | 18 | 66 | | | 11T 2c | | Shunters' brake wagon | 15-6 x 7-4½/ 9-0 | 2793 |
| *38* | 12 | 16, 21 | 294007/13/5/8 | | 20T | (D) | 6 wheels | 20-0 x 8-0/12-0 | 3200(1) |
| | | 71 | 294023/6/8/30/2/8 /69/71/2 | | | | Steel under-frame Type D | | 3200(2) |
| *39* | 14 | (23-27) | 294024 | | 20T | (E) | | 20-0 x 8-0/12-0 | 3727 |
| *40* | 27 | 81 | | | | | Open veranda | 16-4 x 7-5½/9-0 | 2045 |

## Goods Brake Vans

### Early Goods Brake Vans

Loose coupled goods trains have always necessitated a brake van at the rear to enable the guard to assist the enginemen in controlling the train on down hill gradients, by keeping the couplings taut and when needing to stop, or even more critically in the event of a broken coupling and the possibility of a run away. The severity of the gradient on the east side of the River Spey (1 in 60) led in August 1858 to the sanctioning of two additional brake vans specially for this location. Other brake vans were replaced, three new ones being built at Lochgorm Works in 1868. By the end of 1867 the need for sand boxes in brake vans was recognised and orders given for them to be fitted. At the same time six more brake vans were built in lieu of four ordinary close vans and two ordinary open wagons, in anticipation of the opening of the Skye line in 1870. Six additional goods brake vans were supplied by the Midland Wagon Co. at £328 each in time for the opening of the Sutherland & Caithness line in 1874. These were soon found to be insufficient and ten more were built in 1876 by Brown Marshall & Co.

Highland brake vans were allotted to individual guards with their names and home stations painted in white letters on a black board affixed low down at the left hand end of the sides. This naturally encouraged the guards to take particular care and keep them in good order and clean.

### 7½/10-ton 4-wheel Goods Brake Vans Type A

The 7½-ton goods brake vans Type A to diagram 24 were later weighted up to 10-tons. These and Type C vans were referred to as Klondykes, presumably because the gold rush in the Yukon was contemporary with their introduction. Sir Eric Hutchinson reports that both types were unpopular with the men as to keep effective lookout on sinuous lengths of line they had to move from one side to the other as the curve of the line

changed hand. Management disliked them because the limited space inside and narrow doors made them unsuitable for road van work.

The photographs of Type A vans late in life show them to have been vacuum brake fitted and often marshalled in mixed trains on branch lines, presumably after they had been displaced from regular goods trains when one would have expected them to have been unfitted. Late still they appear to have been re-sheeted with different width planks over-sailing the framing and dispensing with the half-round cover strips. Buffers were replaced by self-contained parallel housing type and tie bars added between the axle-guards of some vans. Although there were the usual end steps, there does not always appear to have been the normal associated half-round handrail stretching from side to side extended to just under the roof level, the lack of which will have made it extremely difficult to access the roof.

### 11/15-ton 6-wheeled Goods Brake Vans Type B

By October 1883 6-wheeled goods brake vans were definitely intended when the invitation to tender for six was authorised. A decade later a dozen more were provided by Brown Marshall at £277 each. By the time Drummond drew up the diagram book in 1901, the company's front line goods brake van stock was made up of thirty-six 24 foot long 6-wheel vans Type B Nos. 20 to 55 to diagram 25. With a central roof lookout, these were known as Big Vans Type B of 11 to 15-tons in tare weight, to diagram 25 were clad with horizontal boards. The vans' size and the two sets of double doors made them ideal for road van work, i.e. of dropping off and collecting parcels and other items too small to make up a wagon load.

Two vans had side lookouts at the centre of the van, instead of on the roof, and were noted as having worked on the Kyle line. A drawing exists for a similar van with the roof lookout at one end, but it is not known whether any such were built.

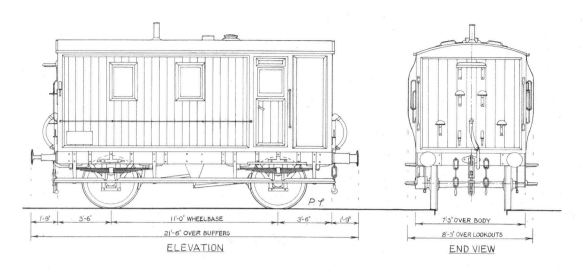

*Figure 79 - 7½-ton 4-wheel goods brake van to HR diagram 24. (Author)*

*A somewhat down at the heels Highland Railway goods brake van parked at the end of a spur, probably by then as a Loco Dept tool van. Note the missing top step board and the lack of semi-circular hand rail to grip when climbing onto the roof, although two grab handles are present at the end of the roof. (AG Ellis collection)*

*By 16 October 1939 when seen at Muir of Ord LMS No. 294006 had been weighted up to 10 tons, but had lost the cover strips to the edges of the match boarding. Although piped for the vacuum brake, it is unclear whether this brake operated on the van. (DLG Hunter)*

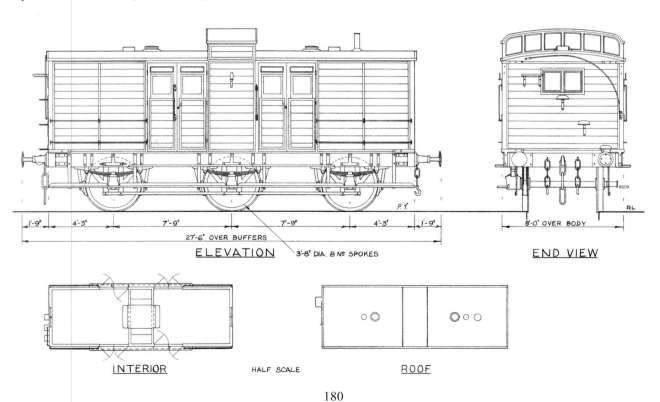

ELEVATION          3'-8" DIA. 8 N° SPOKES

END VIEW

INTERIOR          HALF SCALE          ROOF

*13-ton 4-wheel Goods Brake Vans Type C*

With the arrival of Drummond on the scene a reversion to 4-wheel goods brake vans was made at saving in cost, when ten were built by RY Pickering in 1898 for £197-10-0 each. These 13-ton Type C vans to diagram 26, were based on a Caledonian design dating back to 1883 with panelled body sides and ends with the enclosed verandas. Indeed one van with open verandas of pure CR design was built and allocated to LMS diagram 27 as No. 81. Later in life the panelling was replaced by vertical match boarding, while a note on the LMS diagram 13 suggests that at least one van was up-rated to 15 tons.

*Unimpressed by Jones 6-wheel brake vans, newly arrived Drummond tried to force meagre Caledonian practice of 4-wheel vans on Highland guards, with the result that they were not popular. In workshop grey No. 59 posed as built by RY Pickering in 1898. (RY Pickering, author's collection)*

***Above** - In finished condition Nos. 56 to 58 are ready for delivery. (RY Pickering, author's collection)*

***Opposite bottom** - Figure 80, Jones 11-ton 6-wheel goods brake van to HR diagram 25. (Author)*

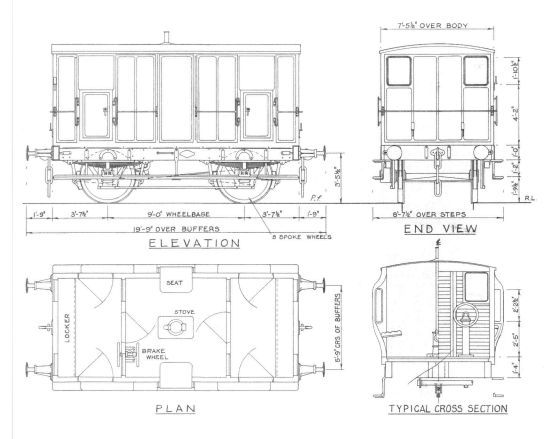

*Figure 81 - Drummond 13¾-ton 4-wheel goods brake van to diagram 26.  (Author)*

### 20-ton 6-wheel Big Vans

The fresh design of 6-wheel vans with a central roof lookout was approved in September 1908 at an estimated cost of £308 each.  These vans, also known as Big Vans, to LMS diagram 12 were increased in tare to 20-tons, but only 20 feet over headstocks.  This later type initiated by Drummond had vertical boarding and the lookout was curved down to the cantrail of the main roof.  Again their size and two sets of double doors made them useful for road van work, although they were more usually rostered for heavy long distance through trains.  Eight vans were constructed in the workshops in 1908/9, two in 1911, six more in 1913 by when the cost had crept up to £320.  To eliminate the risk of the guard striking his head as he ascended to his lookout position, new vans constructed and some early vans were altered with central roofs that ramped up to both sides of the lookout.

### Rebuilt 24 Foot Long Brake Vans

Towards the end of World War 1, the Highland Railway again found itself short of goods brake vans and unable to continue its modest programme of replacing life-expired vans by new construction of the  Type D, as it had done before the war.  On 13 November 1918 the

Board therefore authorised the rebuilding of five vans to diagram 25, where the extra length would have continued to prove very useful for road van work.  The intention had been to weight up all the other 6-wheel vans to 20 tons, but, perhaps due to limitations in the strength of the under-frame and running gear, this was limited to 15 tons.  In the event only five of the older vans were taken in hand and modernised, at a cost of £30 a van, to conform in appearance with the 1908 type.

The body cladding was renewed with vertical planking, in lieu of horizontal.  The roof lookouts were reshaped in profile and by the provision of ramped ends over the steps leading up to the raised platform within the van from where the guard kept watch.  The degree to which the running gear, couplings and buffers was changed varied depending on the condition of the original and the replacements available.  In some cases the solebars were strengthened by the addition of metal flitch plates, resulting in the removal of the crown and washer plates, but retention of the horse hook over the left hand wheel.

Usually the small drop-lights in the doors were retained but at least one had the larger size similar to the Type D.

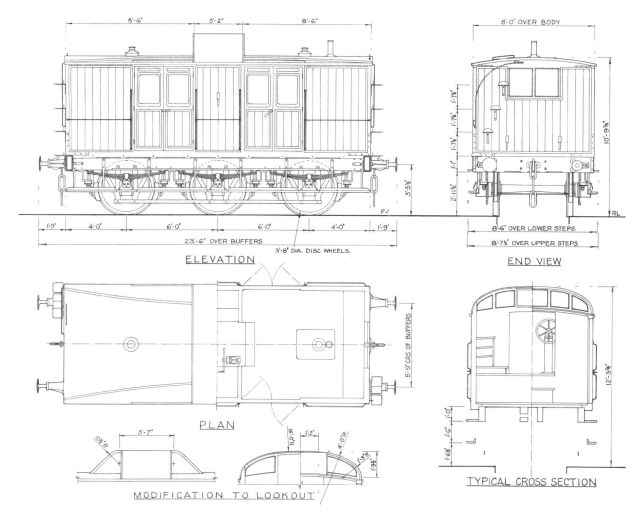

*Figure 82 - Drummond 20-ton 6-wheel goods brake van to LMS diagram 12. (Author)*

*Once dissuaded from his economy 4-wheel brake van, Drummond reviewed Jones 6-wheel version and produced a shorter type but weighted up to 20 tons, as exemplified by No. 21 fitted with spoked wheels. (HR collection)*

*The early examples followed Jones practice of a roof lookout accessed by steps from the van floor, but complaints were made that guards were catching their heads on the edge of the roof as they stepped up. To overcome this, central ramps were created in the roof and adopted for further construction. As No. 294007 in June 1937 shows, it took time, if ever, for this to be applied retrospectively. (RS Carpenter collection)*

*LMS No. 294014, however, in 1935 exhibits the ramped roof to the lookout and is fitted with disc wheels. (F Plant, HRS collection)*

*A view on the end of a 20-ton goods brake van on 4 April 1923, fitted up with an array of wooden fingers used to confirm the minimum gauge of line-side structures. Beyond to the left, partially obscured by a post carrying high-level signal wires, is the end of a HR covered carriage truck and to the right a Caledonian 5-plank end-door mineral wagon. (Dale collection, courtesy Strathspey Railway Association)*

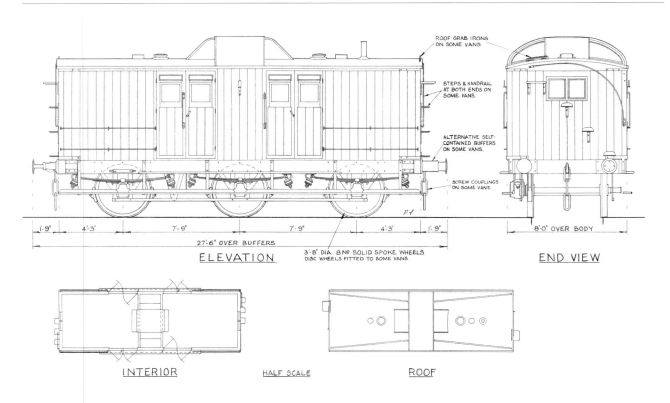

*Figure 83 - Rebuilt Jones 15-ton 6-wheel goods brake van originally to HR diagram 25.*

*A pair of rebuilt 24 foot long 15-ton Jones goods brake vans Nos.297268 and 297267, by then in departmental service acting as breakdown tool vans at Blair Atholl. (HRS collection)*

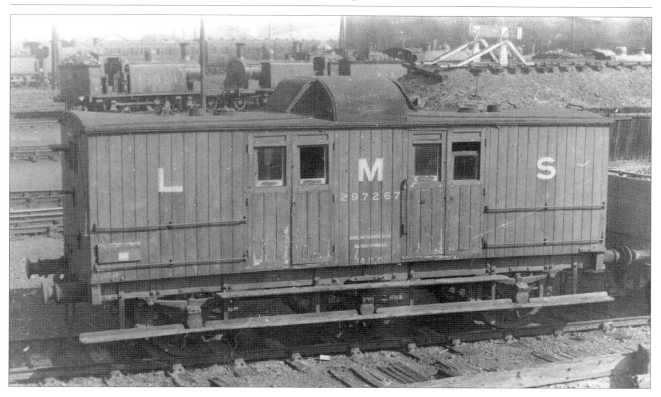

*LMS No. 297267 having moved to Perth. Note the small drop-lights, short springs, grease lubricated axle-boxes, 10 solid spoke wheels, 3-link couplings and self-contained buffers. (WO Steel collection, courtesy RJ Essery)*

*No. 294054 still in revenue earning duties sometime after 1936 when the smaller style of lettering and bauxite paint were applied. In contrast, it has flitched solebars, internally sprung buffers, screw couplings, 3-hole disc wheels, oil axle-boxes and longer axle springs. (WO Steel collection, courtesy RJ Essery)*

*20-ton 6-wheel Big Vans on Steel Under-frames*

Whilst all vans until 1918 had been mounted on timber under-frames, when quotations were sought for ten more towards the end of World War 1, a change was made to frames fabricated from steel structural sections, together with bottled shaped buffers, and a comparison made between five with grease and five with Armstrong oil axle-boxes. This order was fulfilled in 1918 by RY Pickering at a price of £995 each. Up until this point all vans when had been fitted with spoked wheels, but by LMS days not infrequently these were changed for disc wheels.

**Left** - *The final production of 20-ton 6-wheel brake vans had steel under-frames. No. 71 was built by RY Pickering in 1918. (RY Pickering, courtesy HMRS)*

**Bottom** - *LMS No. 294069 near the coaling plant at Inverness in August 1938. Note the bottle shaped buffer housing and disc wheels. (DLG Hunter)*

*Another steel under-framed 20-ton goods bake van No. 294023 labelled* **HIGHLAND SECTION PERTH**. *(WO Steel collection, courtesy RJ Essery)*

*20-ton 4-wheel Goods Brake Vans*

The final design of goods brake van for the Highland to LMS diagram 14 was a 4-wheel 20-ton van on a steel under-frame with disc wheels, bottle shaped buffers and vertical boarding to the bodywork and side lookouts. It is uncertain whether these ever appeared in Highland livery. In due course they were piped for vacuum brake.

**Passengers travelling in a Goods Brake van**

In some places, such as northern Scotland especially before the almost universal ownership of cars, the railway was often the only means of communication over even quite short distances and upon which the like of doctors in general practice might depend to reach patients in urgent need of their care. Nonetheless, in such remote regions, passenger services were necessarily infrequent and advantage had to be taken of any additional possibilities.

One finds, therefore, that the Highland Appendices to the Working Timetable contained an instruction for the conditions under which passengers were allowed to travel in the brake van of goods trains, when there was no convenient passenger train service. To do so, they were expected to make application to travel by a goods train by undertaking to accept all risks and dangers of conveyance, and that the Company would not be liable for any loss or injury occurring to him, however caused, by signing the special conditions printed on the back of tickets to be used for the purpose. In addition the passenger had to pay the ordinary first class fare and subject to the train being timed to stop at the stations from and to which the passenger desired to travel.

This arrangement had arisen following a request from a Dr Irvine of Pitlochy on 18 April 1865 who sought permission to travel in the guard's van of goods trains when his professional duties required him to do so. Understanding the practice of travelling in guard's van by goods train was already carried on to a considerable extent, the Board resolved that the station masters should have discretionary power to allow passengers to travel in this way in cases of emergency on their signing ticket taking all risks themselves. This became particularly useful on the overnight goods train from Wick to Helmsdale, where the passenger could make a connection with the early morning train to Inverness. The appendices do not appear to restrict the routes, other than north of Stanley Jct. Nonetheless, and indeed as some of the tickets illustrated show, the arrangement continued into the LMS and early BR period for another decade or so, by which time freight trains in the region were becoming rather few. It is known that a similar arrangement applied on the Great North of Scotland, although in this case a separate indemnity in the form of a small card had to be signed by the intending passenger and that was still being used up to 1969.

One imagines many readers can only wish they too had found out about this delightful arrangement in time to have taken advantage of it before it was too late.

*References:*

Highland Railway, *Appendices to the working timetable*, 15 April, 1 June 1916 and 1 May 1920 ufn.
LMS, *Sectional appendix to the working timetables, Northern Division*, March 1937, ERO 46485.
Vallance HA, *The Highland Railway*, 2nd Edition, David & Charles, 1963.

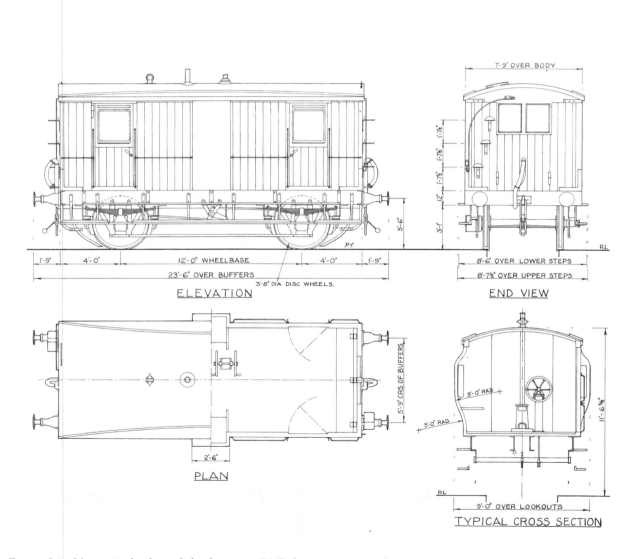

*Figure 84 - 20-ton 4-wheel goods brake van to LMS diagram 14. (Author)*

*The final design of goods brake van maintained the 20-ton tare weight and on a steel under-frame, but reverted to being 4-wheel. LMS No. 294024 shows that an all enclosed body made it suitable for conveying the guard and any small packages in comfortable conditions no matter the weather outside. (Author's collection)*

*Compared with the previous view, No. 294025 has bottle shaped buffers rather than parallel type. Despite the vacuum pipe connection, the van is fitted with 3-link couplings. (LGRP, HRS Collection)*

*Admittedly the railways had been nationalised by 18 August 1956, but this LMS ticket has been made out to Nethy Bridge on the former LNER North Scottish Area. (Glyn Waite collection)*

*An LMS passenger ticket by goods train for the 6.0am train from The Mound to Golspie on 22 August 1956. (Glyn Waite collection)*

The London Midland & Scottish Railway Company do not profess to carry Passengers by their Goods Trains & no Passengers will be conveyed thereby except at their own special request, & on this express condition, that such Passengers undertake all risks & dangers of conveyance, & that the Railway Company shall not be liable for any risks whatever, or for any loss or injury occurring to the Passengers, however caused. No Passenger Carriage will be attached, & those travelling by Goods Train must ride in the Guards Van.
I agree to the above terms.

..............Clapper..............Passenger.

*On the reverse side was the wording of the indemnity to be signed by the intending passenger, in this case a D Capper. (Glyn Waite collection)*

*In 1923 4-6-0 Clan class No. 53* Clan Stewart *heads north with the 11.50am train from Perth for Inverness, having originated at Glasgow (Buchanan Street) at 10.0am, and with through coaches from Edinburgh (Waverley). Immediately behind the engine is a pair of Drummond Locker/Lavatory Composites, followed by a Caledonian 65 foot long 12-wheel corridor Brake Third; possibly a Highland corridor; a Pullman car and further coaches. (HL Salmon author's collection)*

# Appendices

## 1. HIGHLAND RAILWAY CARRIAGE DIAGRAMS

### List of Carriage & Non-Passenger Coaching Stock

| 1901 | 1908 | 1923/ N Div | Nos. | Whls | Description | Lochgorm Drg No |
|---|---|---|---|---|---|---|
| 1 | 1 | 1 | 1-6 | 6 | Coupe ended 1st, Type A | 1017 |
| 2 | 2 | 2 | 7-10, 12-23 | 6 | Coupe ended lav 1st, Type B | |
| 3 | 3 | - | 11 | 6 | 1st saloon, Type C | |
| 4 | | - | 24-39, 41-55 | 4 | Rib sided coupe ended 1st, Type D | |
| 5 | | - | 40 | 4 | Rib sided 1st saloon, Type E | |
| 6 | 6 | - | 56 | 6 | 1st class saloon, Type F | |
| 7 | 7 | 3 | 58 | 6 | Lav 1st, Type G | 2247 |
| - | - | 4 | 48 | 8 | Coupe ended locker lav 1st | 2503? |
| 8 | 8 | 5 | 59 | 8 | Director's saloon, Type H | 2527, 2531 |
| 9 | | 8 | 1-6, 29, 41-46 | 6 | Locker compo, Type A | 1181 |
| - | - | 9 | 41, 45-46 | 6 | Composite converted from diagram 9 | |
| 10 | 13 | 10 | 7-19 (81-82) | 4 | Rib sided compo, Type B | |
| 11 | 16 | 13 | 20-22 | 8 | Brake compo, Type C | 2406 |
| 12 | 17 | 14 | 23-24 | 8 | Locker compo, Type D | |
| 13 | | 15 | 25-28, 30 | 6 | Compo, Type E | |
| 14 | | 16 | 31-32 | 6 | Coupe ended compo, Type F | |
| 15 | | 17 | 33-40 | 8 | Coupe ended compo, Type G | 2503 |
| 16 | 21 | 18 | 47-48 | 8 | Semi-corridor lav compo, Type H | 1909 |
| 17 | | 19/44 | 49-54, 57-80 | 8 | Locker lav compo, Type J | 2076, 2117 |
| 18 | | 20 | 55-56 | 8 | Lav compo, Type K | 2234 |
| | | 21 | 83-85, 90-91 | 6 | Compo | |
| 19 | | 26 | 1-22, 29-52 | 6 | 3rd, Type A | 1092 |
| 20 | 30 | 27 | 23-28 | 4 | 3rd, Type B | |
| 21 | 31 | 28/13 | 53-58 | 6 | 3rd saloon, Type C | 1645 |
| 22 | 32 | 29 | 59-70, 74-75, 81-82, 171-174, 187-194 | 6 | 3rd, Type D | 1835, 3225 |
| 23 | | 30 | 74, 79-97, 136-155, 175-186 | 6 | Rib sided 3rd, Type E | |
| 24 | | | 75-78 | 4 | 3rd, Type F (20'-1") | |
| 25 | | 31 | 98-117 | 4 | 3rd, Type G | 755 |
| 26 | 36 | 32 | 118 | 8 | 3rd, Type H | |
| 27 | 37 | 33 | 119-125 | 6 | 3rd, Type J | |
| 28 | 38 | 34 | 126-135 | 8 | Lav 3rd, Type K | 1232 |
| 29 | 33 | 37/79 | 71-73, 156-170 | 8 | Lav 3rd, Type L | 2475, 2486 |
| 30 | 43 | 39 | 1-12 | 8 | Brake 3rd, Type A | |
| 31 | | 40 | 13-14 | 8 | Brake lav 3rd, Type B | 2169 |
| | | 42 | 18 | 4 | Brake 3rd | |
| 32 | | 44 | 1-10, 24-26, 28 | 4 | Pass brake van, Type A | |
| 33 | 50 | | 11-12 | 4 | Pass brake van, Type B | |
| 34 | | 45/125 | 13-21, 27, 31-34, 46-57 | 6 | Pass brake van, Type C | |

| 1901 | 1908 | 1923/ N Div | Nos. | Whls | Description | Lochgorm Drg No |
|---|---|---|---|---|---|---|
| 35 | | 47 | 29, 36-38 | 6 | Pass brake van, Type D | |
| 36 | 54 | 48 | 30 | 6 | Pass brake van, Type E | 841 |
| 37 | | 49 | 39-45 | 6 | Pass brake van, Type F | |
| 38 | 52 | 46/126 | 22-23, 35, 58-62 | 6 | Pass brake van, Type G | 2266 |
| 39 | 59 | 52 | 1-2 | 4 | PO van, Type A | 1152 |
| 40 | 60 | | 4 | 4 | PO van, Type B | |
| 41 | 61 | | 5-6, 10 | 8 | PO van, Type C | |
| 42 | 62 | 54 | 7-9 | 6 | PO van, Type D | |
| 43 | | | 11-12 | 6 | PO van, Type E | |
| 44 | 63 | 55A | 13-14 | 8 | PO van, Type F | 2485? |
| 45 | 64 | 55B | 3 | 8 | PO parcel van, Type G | 2485? |
| 46 | | 57 | 1-25 | 4 | Horsebox, Type A | 914, 915 |
| 47 | | 58 | 1-14 | 4 | Open Carriage truck, Type A | 891 |
| 48 | | | 15-20 | 4 | Covered carriage truck | |
| 49 | | 59 | | 4 | Covered carriage truck 24'-0" | 2732 |
| | | 60* | | 4 | Covered carriage truck 24'-0" | 3259 |
| | | 61* | | 4 | Covered carriage & fish truck 24'-0" | 3328 |
| 50 | | 56 | 1-6, 14, 20, 26-31 | 4 | Horsebox 19'-8" | 2649 |
| 51 | | | 69-80 | 8 | Lav Composite | |
| 52 | | 7/32 | 1-5, 7 | 8 | Locker corridor compo | 3447 |
| 53 | 14 | 11 | 8-9 | 8 | Compo sleeping car/ 3$^{rd}$ | 3000 |
| - | - | 38/96 | | 8 | Brake corr 3$^{rd}$ converted from above | 306?, 3066 |
| 54 | - | 12/28 | 10-13, 17, 22, 24-26 | 8 | Corridor compo (2 door) | 3068? |
| 55 | - | 6/29 | 7, 16-17, 23-24, 33, 81-82 | 8 | Corridor compo (4 door) | 3326, 3327 |
| 56 | - | 24/36 | 14-15 | 8 | Locker lav compo | 3248 |
| 57 | - | 25/54 | 18-19 | 8 | Brake corridor compo | 3299/3300 |
| 58 | - | 22/45 | 86-87 | 6 | Locker compo | 3136 |
| 59 | - | 23/46 | 88-89 | 6 | Compo | 3137 |
| 60 | 40 | 36/65 | 101-108 | 8 | Corridor 3$^{rd}$ (3 door) | 3194, 3195 |
| 61 | - | 36/65 | 109-112 | 8 | Corridor 3$^{rd}$ (4 door) | 3194? |
| 62 | 39 | 35 | 195-196 | 8 | 3$^{rd}$ saloon | 3016 |
| 63 | - | 41/112 | 15-16 | 8 | Brake lav 3$^{rd}$ | 3064 |
| 64 | - | 50/127 | 69-77 | 8 | Passenger brake van | 2785A &B |
| 65 | - | 51/128 | 78-79, 81-83 | 8 | Corridor pass brake van | 3046, 32?? |
| 66 | - | 55/130 | 5-6, 10 | 8 | PO van | 2485 |
| 67 | | | 57 | 6 | 1$^{st}$ saloon | |
| 68 | - | - | | 6 | Passenger brake van | |
| - | - | 62* | | 4 | Meat van 10'-0" wb | 2918 |
| - | - | 63* | 2849-68 | 4 | Meat van 11'-0" wb | 3295 |
| - | - | 64* | | 4 | Open fish truck | 2654 |
| | | | 11 | 6 | PO van | |

Notes:
1.  The 1901 carriage diagram book ran to 48 diagrams. Those subsequent numbers in *italics* were used by DLG Hunter in his book for later designs which he introduced later to avoid confusion.
2.  Although the contents of the 1908 book are known, a copy has not come to hand.
3.  The two part numbers in the 1923 list are also to be found in the Northern Division book. The first part was the original 1923 number, to which the second part was added when carried into the new book. Those numbers followed by an asterisk * are only in the N Div book.

# 2. HIGHLAND RAILWAY WAGON DIAGRAMS

## List of Wagon Diagrams.

| 1901 | LMS N Div | Nos | Cap'ty | Type | Description | Size L x W /wb (ft-in) | Lochgorm Drg No |
|------|-----------|-----|--------|------|-------------|------------------------|------------------|
| 1 | | 1-20, 27-83, 126-283, 1322-75, 1497-1546 | 8T | A | Goods wagon | 15-6 x 8-0/9-0 | |
| 2 | | 21-26, 94-103 | 8T | M | Swivel timber wagon | 11-0 x 8-0/6-0 | |
| 3 | | 84-93, 296-315, 817-832, 1093-1122, 12-1321, 2288-2307 | 8T | U | Cattle wagon | 16-0 x 8-0/9-0 | 1226? |
| 4 | | 284-295, 781-786, 1138-51, 1747-87 | 8T | Q | Covered Goods van (Old) | 16-0 x 8-0/9-0 | |
| 5 | | 316-343, 2308-2319, *2537-2636* | 10T | H | Loco' coal wagon | 15-6 x 7-9/9-0 | |
| 6 | | 344-644-684, 1152-1176, 2158-2287, 2367-2514, 2737-8 | 8T | C | Open box wagon | 15-6 x 7-7/9-0 | |
| 7 | | 680-768, 843-942 | 7T | L | Timber wagon | 15-6 x 6-10/9-0 | |
| 8 | | 769-780 | 8T | S | Luggage van | 16-0 x 8-0/9-0 | |
| 9 | | 787-816 | 8T | X | Sheep van | 15-6 x 8-0/9-0 | |
| 10 | 4 | 943-992, 2637-2736 | 8T | G | 4pl mineral wagon | 15-0 x 7-7/9-0 | 1832 |
| 11 | | 1177-1188, 2148-2157 LMS 297184/92 | 8T | I | Ballast wagon | 15-6 x 8-0/9-0 | |
| 12 | | 1847-2146 | 4T | K | Fish wagon | 18-0 x 8-0/11-0 | |
| 13 | | 1747-1787 | 8T | R | Covered goods van (Old) | 16-0 x 7-7/9-0 | |
| 14 | | 833-841 | 8T | D | Open box wagon | 15-0 x 8-0/9-0 | |
| 15 | 5 | 993-1092, 1184-1221 | 8T | E | Open box wagon | 15-0 x 7-7/9-0 | 1834 PD 15/2/1897 |
| 16 | 7 | 1222-1291 | 8T | F | Open box wagon | 15-6 x 7-7/9-0 | 3053 PD |
| 17 | | 1477-1496, 1788-1797, 2340-4 | 8T | ? | Sheep van | 16-0 x 8-0/9-0 | |
| 18 | | 1798-1846 | 8T | V | Cattle wagon | 15-8 x 7-7/9-0 | |
| 19 | | 1376-1476, 1547-1746 | 8T | B | Goods wagon | 15-6 x 8-0/9-0 | |
| 20 | | 2147 | 7T | N | Engine wagon (6 wheel) | 18-0 x 8-0/13-0 | |
| 21 | | 2320-2339 | 11T | T | Meat van | 17-6 x 8-0/11-0 | |
| 22 | 15 | 2365-2366 | | W | Valuable cattle wagon | 23-6 x 8-6/13-0 | 2440 PD |
| 23 | 20 | 2525-2536, LMS 297201/5/11/7 | 8T | J | Ballast wagon | 15-6 x 7-7/9-0 | 2579 PD |
| 24 | | 1-19 | 7T 9c | A | Goods brake van | 18-0 x 7-3/11-0 | |
| 25 | | 20-55 | 11T | B | Goods brake van (6 whls) | 24-0 x 8-0/15-6 | |
| 26 | 13 | 56-65 | 13T 13c | C | Goods brake van | 16-3 x 7-5½/9-0 | H82 PD |
| 27 | | | | P | Tar wagon (6 wheels) | 16-0 x ?/11-0 | |
| 28 | | LMS 297232 | | O | Crane wagon (6 wheels) | 19-6 x 8-0/13-0 | |

| 1901 | LMS N Div | Nos | Cap'ty | Type | Description | Size L x W /wb (ft-in) | Lochgorm Drg No |
|---|---|---|---|---|---|---|---|
| | | | | | **List of Wagon Diagrams. Cont.** | | |
| 29 | 11 | 1123-1137 | 8T | S | Covered goods van (new) cupboard doors | 16-3 x 7-6/9-0 | 2313 PD |
| 30 | 18 | 66 | 11T 2c | | Shunters brake wagon | 15-6 x 7-4½/9-0 | 2793 PD |
| 31 | 22 | 1-6 | 13T 15c | | Road van (6 wheels) | 35-8 x 8-0/23-0 | 2776 PD |
| 32 | | | | | 10 ton crane wagon | 24-0 x 7-7/13-6 | |
| 33 | 1 | 1497, 1507/22/75/87, 1634/57/8/60/89, 1703/31/42, 2161/9/90, 2760-93 | 16T | | 6pl coal wagon | 18-4 x 7-8/10-0 | 3185 |
| *34* | | 2869-3018 | 12T | | Coal wagon (end door) | 15-6 x 7-6/9-0 | |
| *35* | 25 | 908 | 7T | | Twin swivel timber wagon | 15-6 x 7-7/9-0 | 3458 |
| *36* | 26 | LMS 297053 | 8T | | Swivel single bolster wagon | 15-6 x 7-7/9-0 | 3563 CC 9/1/19 |
| *37* | 24 | 21-26, 94-103 | 8T | | Swivel single bolster wagon | 11-0 x 8-0/9-0 | 2605 PD |
| *38* | 12 | | 20T | | Goods brake van (6 wheels) | 20-0 x 8-0/12-0 | 3200 |
| *39* | 14 | 23-27? LMS 294024 | 20T | | Goods brake van | 20-0 x 8-0/12-0 | 3727 |
| *40* | 27 | 81 | | | Goods brake van (open veranda) | 16-4 x 7-5½/9-0 | 2045 |
| | 2 | LMS 296759 | 15T | | 6pl coal wagon | 17-0 x 7-8/10-0 | 2715 PD |
| | 3 | LMS 296738/60/95, 296804/23/5/32/51/5/62/73 | 12T | | 6pl coal wagon (1914/5) | 15-11 x 7-4/9-0 | |
| | 6 | | 12T | | 6pl mineral wagon | 16-6 x 7-10/9-0 | |
| | 8 | | | | Covered goods van | 20-0 x 7-6/13-0 | 3322 |
| | 9 | | | | Covered goods van cupboard doors VB & WP | 18-0 x 7-6/11-0 | 3103 |
| | 10 | 1158-77 | 10T | | Covered goods van sliding doors | 18-0 x 7-6/11-0 | 3307 PD 9/8/11 |
| | 16 | 85 | | | Cattle wagon | 15-9 x 8-0/9-0 | 2275 PD |
| | 17 | LMS 294515 | 8T | | Sheep van (iron bars) | 15-9 x 8-0/9-0 | 2297 PD |
| | 19 | | 10T | | Timber wagon | 15-6 x 6-10½/9-0 | 2773 |
| | 21 | | | | 6 wh road van 2 sliding doors | 35-8 x 8-8/23-0 | 3306 PD |
| | 23 | | 15T | | 6 wh rail & timber wagon | 25-1 x 6-11/19-0 | 2699/ 2700 PD |
| | (17?) | LMS 294528/55? | 8T | | Sheep van (planked) | | |

Note: The 1901 diagram book ran to 33 diagrams. Those subsequent numbers in *italics* were used by DLG Hunter in his book for designs introduced later to avoid confusion.

# THE HIGHLAND RAILWAY SOCIETY

The Highland Railway Society caters for all those interested in the varied aspects of the railway, including its predecessors and its successors to the present day.

An illustrated quarterly journal is distributed to members and contains a wide variety of articles and information. Members' queries are a regular feature and details of new books, videos and models of interest are reported. The Society's publications include a series of books commemorating the 150th anniversaries of the opening of various sections of the system.

Meetings are held in both Scotland and England. An annual gathering is held each September and includes a full day of talks, films, etc., as well as an opportunity to meet fellow members.

The Society has library, photographic and drawing collections which are available to members. Copies of drawings are available for purchase. Modellers are well catered for. Complete kits are produced in limited runs. Specially commissioned modelling components such as axle boxes, buffers and springs are available, plus a comprehensive set of transfers to enable any Highland loco to be named.

Membership details can be found on its website at www.hrsoc.org.uk.

# BIBLIOGRAPHY and REFERENCES

Highland Railway Journal

Locomotive Magazine

Railway Magazine

Strathspey Express

Transport & Railroad Gazette

*Report on accident at Pitlochry on 21 October 1865*, Board of Trade, 1865.

Chacksfield JE, *The Drummond brothers - a Scottish duo*, The Oakwood Press, 2005.

Charles G, *The Duke of Sutherland's saloons & locomotives*, The Railway Magazine, Jan 1950, pp9-10, 18-19.

*Circular to Railway Companies with reference to continuous brakes*, Board of Trade, 1877, TNA ref: RAIL1053/193.

Fenwick, K, *Great North of Scotland Railway Carriages,* Lightmoor Press, 2009.

*First-class carriage for the Highland Railway*, Railway Engineer, Vol IX, No. 7 (July 1888).

Geddes H & Bellass E, *Highland Railway liveries*, Pendragon & HMRS, 1995.

Highland Railway, *Appendices to the working timetable*, 15 April, 1 June 1916 and 1 May 1920 ufn.

The Highland Railway and its constituents and sucessors 1855-1955, Stephenson locomotive Society, 1955.

Kidner RW, *Carriage stock of minor standard gauge railways*, The Oakwood Press, 1978.

Lacey RE & G Dow, Midland Railway carriages, Vol 1, Wild Swan, 1984.

LMS, *Sectional appendix to the working timetables, Northern Division*, March 1937, ERO 46485.

Long C, *'Less weighty and cumbersome': The story of the Plan 130 sleeping cars*, The Golden Way, The Journal of the Pullman Society, Nos. 84-87 (2010) or Great Northern News, Nos. 174-176.

Radford JB, The American Pullman cars, Ian Allan, 1984.

Tatlow P, *Highland Miscellany*, Oxford Publishing Co, 1985.

Tatlow P, *Passengers travelling by freight train*, LMS Journal No 19, Wild Swan Publications, p74-76

Tatlow P, *Railway breakdown cranes, Vol 1*, Noodle Books, 2012.

Wilson HS, *A history of the travelling Post Offices of Great Britain and Ireland*, Railway Philatelic Group.

Vallance HA, *The Highland Railway*, 2nd Edition, David & Charles, 1963.

White R & Tatlow P, *Private traders' wagons & coal traffic on the Highland lines up to 1939*, HMRS Journal Vol 14, No. 8 (Oct-Dec 1992), pp242-251.

Wray T, *Charles Fay and James Newall mechanical brakes*, Backtrack, March 2010, pp 186-188.

# ACKNOWLEGEMENTS

A work of this nature and duration is not accomplished without the willing assistance and support of a large number of people and organisations. A wide range of sources for material on Highland Railway carriages and wagons are often individually of small worth, but nonetheless collectively assist building up of the overall picture. Records at West Register House of the Scottish Record Office, now renamed and relocated the Scottish National Archives at General Register House in Edinburgh, together with the National Archives at Kew and the Library of the National Railway Museum at York, were consulted and assistance kindly provided by their members of staff.

British Railway officials at all levels have kindly assisted wherever they could, showing great friendliness and pleasure that one should be taking an interest in their work. Help came from the Public Relations & Publicity Officer of the Scottish Region in Glasgow. Likewise similar facilities have been afforded on heritage railways, including the Bo'ness & Kinneil, and the Strathspey Railway.

Reference has been made to books and periodicals in many public libraries, such as the Science Museum in Kensington, Birmingham City Library, Motherwell Public Library, University of Aberdeen, University of Glasgow, and a few private libraries.

Whether a member or not, several railway societies have been of great assistance in responding to my enquiries over the years. Among these are: the GNSR Association, Highland Railway Society, Historical Model Railway Society, LMS Society, Pullman Society and Stephenson Locomotive Society. Correspondence has been entered into and meetings arranged with various fellow enthusiasts and railwaymen of which perhaps: Smokie Bourne, Duncan Burton, Richard Casserley, Richard Chown, George Ellis, Bob Essery, Keith Fenwick, Howard Geddes, Charles Long, Ed McKenna, Sandy McLean, J Pitman, John Roake, Bill and Ian Steel, Mrs Watkins, Martin Welch, Duncan Wheeler, Richard White, RE Wilson and Alistair Wright, deserve special mention. My thanks to them all, thus enabling me to offer this work and the accompanying drawings.

# Highland Railway Carriages & Wagons - Index

| | | | |
|---|---|---|---|
| Abbots Ripton accident | 22 | Brown Marshall, Birmingham | 14, 27, 38, 50, 98, 145, 178 |
| Acknowledgements | 198 | Brush Electrical, Loughborough | 14, 84 |
| Allan, Alexander | 6, 27, 33 | Buffers | 143 |
| Animal Diseases Act 1875 | 163 | Building styles | 14-16 |
| Armagh accident | 22 | Buchanan & Co, Motherwell | 14, 156 |
| Ashbury, John, Manchester | 14, 165 | Buddicom, William | 6 |
| Axle-boxes | 17 | Caledonian Rly | 7, 16-17, 22, 24, 59, 116, 125 |
| Axle-guards | 15 | Cambrian Rlys | 55 |
| Automatic vacuum brakes | 15, 22-23 | Capital account | 16 |
| Ballast wagons | 171-173 | Carrbridge accident | 49 |
| Banff & Morayshire Agricultural Co Ltd | 162 | Carriage & non-passenger coaching stock diagrams | 16, 193-194 |
| Barclay, William | 6 | Carriage & wagon builders | 14 |
| Beamish Museum, County Durham | 58 | Carriage trucks | 129-132 |
| Biography & references | 197 | Carriage washing shed | 11 |
| Birmingham Rly C&W | 14, 49 | Cattle wagons | 163-165 |
| Board of Agriculture Regulations | 163, 170 | 'Chariot ends' | 16, 44 |
| Board of Trade (BOT) | 18, 19, 22-23, 108, 143-144 | Clark & Webb's chain brake | 22 |
| Bogies | 15, 18-20, 48-49 | Cleminson Patent under-frame | 38-41 |
| Bolster wagons | 159-161 | Common user agreement | 143 |
| Bo'ness, SRPS Museum | 58, 62 | Communication, passenger | 23 |
| Brakes | 15, 19-23, 143 | Contagious Diseases (Animals) Act 1879 | 163 |
| Bray Waddington, Leeds | 14, 145 | Corridors | 16, 38, 82-97 |
| Bread vans | 108 | Coupé ends | 16, 33 |
| British Railways (BR) | 17, 58 | 'Cove roof' | 16, 59, 82, 111 |

| | |
|---|---|
| Covered carriage trucks | 131-132 |
| Covered goods vans | 148-150 |
| Cowans Sheldon, Carlisle | 11, 173 |
| Cowlairs Works | 6, 7 |
| Crane wagon | 176 |
| Cumming, Christopher | 7 |
| Deeside Rly | 27 |
| Diagrams | 16, 143, 193-196 |
| Dingwall & Skye Rly | 6 |
| Dining cars | 82 |
| Director's saloon | 72-73 |
| Disc wheels | 17 |
| Diseases of Animals (Disinfection) Order 1926 | 163 |
| Disposal of withdrawn carriages | 35 |
| Distinguishing features | 14-16, 141-143 |
| Dog boxes | 100, 103 |
| Door latches | 24, 44 |
| Double-deck sheep vans | 165-170 |
| Dougall, Andrew | 27 |
| Drawings | 5, 14, 143 |
| Drummond, Dugald | 7 |
| Drummond, Peter | 6, 7, 10, 16-19 |
| Drummond, P, 6-wheel coaches | 59-64 |
| Drummond, P, bogie low arc roof coaches | 65-72 |
| Drummond, P, corridor stock | 82-97 |
| Drummond, P, later non-corridor coaches | 77-82 |
| Drummond, P, passenger brake vans | 106-113 |
| Drummond, P, patent each side brake | 128, 134, 144 |
| Drummond, P, sleeping cars | 73-76 |
| Duke of Sutherland & rolling stock | 54-58, 147 |
| Duke of Sutherland's Rly | 29, 31 |
| Dunachton accident | 39 |
| Duplicate (number) list | 16 |
| Easter Ross Farmers' Club | 163 |
| East Lancashire Rly | 22 |
| Eastleigh Works | 7 |
| Edinburgh & Glasgow Rly | 6 |
| Electric lighting | 23-24, 87, 111 |
| Engine wagon | 162 |
| Faulds, Robert & Co, Glasgow | 14, 163 |
| Fire precautions | 108, 176 |
| Flakes, fitting of | 145, 170 |
| Foot boards | 15-16, 18 |
| Foot warmers | 24 |
| Forrest & Barr, Glasgow | 7 |
| Fort Steel (Canada), Provincial Museum | 58 |
| Fox bogie | 19-20 |
| Fraser-Tytler, Col | 6 |
| Galton, Capt, Rly Insp | 22 |
| Gangway connections | 16, 38, 82, 84 |
| Gas holders | 24, 175 |
| Gas lighting of carriages | 24 |
| General arrangement drawings | 5 |
| Glasgow & South Western Rly (G&SWR) | 7, 16 |
| Goods brake vans | 178-191 |
| Grease, axle | 11, 18 |
| Great Northern Rly (GNR) | 22, 51 |
| Great North of Scotland Rly (GNSR) | 11, 22, 24-25, 27, 72, 84, 143 |
| Great Western Rly (GWR) | 55 |
| Inverness & Aberdeen Jct Rly (I&AJR) | 9, 25, 27-31, 143 |
| Inverness & Nairn Rly (I&NR) | 6, 9, 27-28 |
| Inverness & Perth Jct Rly (I&PJR) | 25, 28 |
| Iracier axle-boxes | 16, 18, 82, 111 |
| Hamilton Ellis, Cuthbert | 5, 16, 38, 44, 52 |
| Handles, commode | 15 |
| Harrison TE | 23 |
| Heating of carriages | 24, 51 |
| Hendrie, John & David | 9 |
| Highland Railway Society | 4, 197 |
| Horseboxes | 126-128 |
| Hull & Barnsley Rly | 18 |
| Hunter, David LG | 5, 16 |
| Hurst Nelson, Motherwell | 14, 70, 73, 87, 90, 92, 153 |
| Hutchinson, Sir Eric | 5, 159, 178 |
| Jones, David | 6, 15, 18-19 |
| Jones coaches | 33-52 |
| Jones 37ft 9in Post Office mail vans | 116-118 |
| Jones 6-wheel Cleminson coaches | 38-40 |
| Jones 6-wheel coaches | 41-47 |
| Jones 6-wheel passenger brake vans | 103-105 |
| Jones bogie coaches | 48-52 |
| Jones sleeping cars | 35, 38 |
| Joseph Wright, Birmingham | 14, 28 |
| Kilmarnock Works | 7, 11 |
| Klondyke goods brake vans | 178 |
| Kynoch, G & G | 162 |
| Lavatories | 25, 39, 44, 49 |
| Lighting of carriages | 23-24 |
| Lime wash | 163 |
| Liveries | 25, 144 |
| Lochgorm Works | 6-13 |
| London & North Eastern Rly (LNER) | 108, 110 |
| London & North Western Rly (LNWR) | 55, 116 |
| London & South Western Rly (LSWR) | 39 |
| London, Brighton & South Coast Rly (LBSC) | 6, 7, 39 |
| London, Chatham & Dover Rly (LD&CR) | 39 |
| London, Midland & Scottish Rly (LMS) | 11, 16, 25, 144 |
| Lookout, guards' | 15-16 |
| Luggage rails | 15 |
| Luggage vans | 125-126 |
| Mansell wheels | 17 |
| Marks, F, Pullman employee | 52 |
| Meat vans | 133-136 |
| Mess & tool vans | 176 |
| Metropolitan Carriage & Wagon, Birmingham | 14, 28, 31, 35, 126, 131 |
| Midland Carriage & Wagon Co, Saltley | 14, 116, 148, 163, 166, 178 |
| Midland Great Western Rly | 7 |
| Midland Rly (MR) | 25, 51-52, 82 |
| Miscellaneous vehicles | 175-177 |
| Mitchell, Joseph | 6 |

| | |
|---|---|
| Morayshire Chemical Works | 162 |
| Nationalisation (of railways) | 17 |
| National Railway Museum, York | 58 |
| Needlefield Works | 8-13 |
| Nelson, Hurst, Motherwell | 14, 70, 73, 87, 90, 92, 153 |
| Newall, J, brake | 19, 22 |
| Newark brake trials | 22 |
| Nine Elms Works, London | 7 |
| Non-passenger coaching stock | 17, 98-139 |
| Non-revenue earning | 170-177 |
| Norman & Co, Glasgow | 7 |
| North British Rly (NBR) | 7, 22, 24, 84, 125 |
| North Eastern Rly (NER) | 7, 23, 84 |
| North of Scotland Chemical Works | 162 |
| North Staffordshire Rly (NSR) | 72 |
| North Sunderland Rly | 35 |
| Numbering | 16, 144 |
| Oil lamps | 23 |
| Oil lubrication of axles | 18 |
| Oldbury Rly C&W Co. | 14, 44 |
| Open carriage trucks | 129-130 |
| Open fish trucks | 136-139 |
| Open wagons | 144-148 |
| Panelled coach sides | 15-16 |
| Passenger alarm apparatus | 23 |
| Passenger brake vans converted from PO vans | 113-115 |
| Passenger comfort | 24 |
| Passengers travelling in goods brake vans | 189-192 |
| Patent Axle Box Foundry Co Ltd | 18 |
| Pickering, RY, Wishaw | 14, 59, 61, 67, 68, 77, 87-88, 92, 108, 111, 135, 156, 181, 188 |
| Pickersgill, William | 7 |
| Pigs, conveyance of | 168 |
| Pintsch's gas lighting | 24 |
| Pooley, W & Sons | 80 |
| Post Office mail vans | 113-124 |
| Post Office vans - early vans | 113, 115-116 |
| Post Office vans - Jones 37ft 9in vans | 116-118 |
| Post Office vans - later vans | 118-124 |
| Pre-Jones coaches | 27-31 |
| Preservation of heritage vehicles | 37, 44, 52, 58, 62, 101 |
| Pullman Car Co. | 35, 38, 51-54, 73, 84 |
| Rail-mounted cranes | 173-175 |
| Railway Carriage Co, Oldbury. | 14, 157, 165 |
| Ramsbottom, John | 6 |
| References & biography | 197 |
| Regulation of Railways Act | 22-23, 25 |
| Restoration of heritage vehicles | 37, 44, 52, 58, 62, 101 |
| Revenue account | 16 |
| Ribbed-sides | 15 |
| Rib-sided passenger brake vans | 98-101 |
| Road vans | 106, 141, 178 |
| Robert Stephenson & Co, Newcastle | 6 |
| Romney, Hythe & Dymchurch Rly | 58 |
| Running boards | 16 |
| St Rollox Works, Glasgow | 7, 8, 11 |
| Scottish Agricultural Industries | 162 |
| Scottish Central Rly (SCR) | 6, 25, 27, 31, 33-35 |
| Scottish Railway Preservation Society (SRPS) | 58, 62 |
| Scottish Wagon Co, Edinburgh | 151 |
| Second class, withdrawal of | 25, 48 |
| Sheep vans | 165-170 |
| Sheets, wagon | 144 |
| Shunter's truck | 175 |
| Side chains | 18 |
| Sleeping cars | 11, 16, 24, 35, 38, 51, 73-76 |
| Smith, Fredrick G | 7, 16, 120 |
| Specially constructed vehicles | 162 |
| Springs | 19 |
| Steel disc wheels | 18 |
| Step boards | 15-16, 18 |
| Steps, end | 15 |
| Stone & Co, Deptford | 23 |
| Stone breaker wagon | 176 |
| Strathspey Rly | 37, 44 |
| Stroudley William | 6 |
| Sutherland & Caithness lines | 6, 33, 171, 178 |
| Timm's springs | 19 |
| Tool & mess vans | 176 |
| Traders' tank wagons | 162 |
| Travelling gas holders | 175 |
| Trevithick, Francis | 6 |
| Urie, David C | 7 |
| Urie, Robert W | 7 |
| Vacuum brake | 15, 22-23 |
| Valuable cattle vans | 127-129 |
| Ventilators | 15 |
| Vertical match boarding | 16 |
| Wagon builders | 14 |
| Wagon diagrams | 143, 195-196 |
| Wagon sheets | 144 |
| Watson, W, mill-right of Errol | 14, 126, 145, 157 |
| Westinghouse brake | 22 |
| Wheels | 18 |
| Wheel springs | 19 |
| Wilson, Gavin | 5 |
| Wilson, John | 173 |
| White wash | 163 |
| Wolverton Works | 55-56, 58 |
| Wright, J & Sons | 14, 98 |
| Yolland, Lt Col, Rly Insp | 22 |

# HURST, NELS

**Builders of Railway Carriages, Wagons, E**

OF EVERY

## Makers of Wheels & Axles, Railway Plant

# THE GLASGOW ROLLING STOCK &

### And at CHATSWORTH WAGO

**MANCHESTER OFFICE:**

Northern Assurance Buildings, Albert Square.